Red Man Reservations

Red Man Reservations

CLARK WISSLER

Curator-in-Chief, Department of Anthropology
American Museum of Natural History

Introduction by RALPH K. ANDRIST

Collier Books, New York, New York
Collier-Macmillan Ltd., London

The Macmillan Company
866 Third Avenue, New York, N.Y. 10022
Collier-Macmillan Canada Ltd., Toronto, Ontario

First Collier Books Edition 1971

Red Man Reservations was originally published in
hardcover by Sheridan House as *Indian Cavalcade
or Life on the Old-Time Indian Reservations* and is
reprinted by arrangement.

Library of Congress Catalog Card Number: 70–163229

Printed in the United States of America

Contents

Introduction

RALPH K. ANDRIST

CLARK WISSLER WRITES of reservation Indians and Indian reservations as they were at the turn of the century. It was not a happy time for red men. The last
wars had been fought and the last in a long series of
defeats suffered. The buffalo were gone; even most of
their bleached bones had been gathered by homesteaders and shipped east to be turned into fertilizer and
carbon for refining sugar and whatever else old buffalo
bones were used for. The Indians existed in a sort of
limbo; most of them were on land the white man did
not covet—at least not excessively; there was nothing
much left for them to hunt; and men who a generation
earlier would have been proud warriors of strong nations were reduced to sitting in the sun and letting the
dust sift through their fingers.

Three and a half centuries ago the American Indian
had roamed, fought, and hunted without let or hin-
drance over all the expanse, from Atlantic to Pacific,
that later became the first forty-eight United States.
Then the white man came with his gentle and civilizing
influence, and each year the Indian found himself with
less and less, until he held only meager scraps of a

domain that had once seemed endless. There are today 250, more or less, of these Indian holdings—reservations—remaining to the descendants of the original inhabitants. They range in size from the huge but largely arid and sterile Navaho reservation in the Southwest down to scores that measure no more than a few acres in extent. Back at the turn of the century, when author Clark Wissler was meeting the people about whom he writes in his book, there were a somewhat greater number of reservations than there are now, and a good many of those that have survived contain much less Indian land now than they did then.

Wissler's tales, he tells us, rise from visits to ten reservations. He is purposely vague about where those reservations were, and he avoids tribal names, but he leaves a trail of clues. The peoples he visited were the tribes who had once roamed the Great Plains as horseback, buffalo-hunting, tepee-dwelling nomads. It is quite evident that Wissler spent considerable time in the Dakotas with the people of the great Sioux nation. He very likely visited the handsome Crow Indians and probably the Cheyennes in eastern Montana. And in one chapter where he tells of trout streams, of mountains in the distance, and of crossing the international border from the reservation into Canada, he could have been in only one place, with the Blackfeet, whose reservation lies against the Rockies and abuts the Canadian border in Montana.

Many of Wissler's stories and anecdotes are almost period pieces now. Almost, but not quite, because he was a fairer, more detached observer of the scene than most of his contemporaries. He saw Indians as human beings, in a time when far too many people still looked on them as little better than vermin. He recognized that they had been mistreated in many ways. But Wissler was a product of his time: he was indoctrinated to think of the Indian as an obstacle in the way of white settlement, and he believed that the best place for the red man was on an isolated reservation.

The story of Indian removal and Indian reservations is a long and complex one, too long to relate in a page or two, but it deserves a bit more detail than the scanty few sentences Wissler gives to it. Although Wissler did not get around to publishing his book until the late 1930s, his observations were made, his notes taken, and his philosophy pretty well formed at the beginning of this century. At that time the idea persisted that God, in his infinite wisdom, had created this land and filled it with a wealth of resources solely for the use of the white man at such time as he should appear on the scene. And when he did make his appearance, it followed, as the night the day, that the improvident Indian, who had not the acumen to slash off the forests, erode the land, or foul the streams, would have to step out of the way of a superior civilization.

The process started early. The Jamestown settlers arrived in 1607, the Pilgrims in 1620. Both bands got friendly receptions from the natives—in fact, across the country red men almost always greeted whites amicably on their first encounter—and the Indians were happy to let the first colonists have the plots of land they asked for. It did not take long for the natives to realize that there was no limit to their new neighbors' lust for land. Uprising in Virginia came in 1622, in New England in 1637. The godly Puritans were by far the more bloodthirsty in suppressing their Indians.

From then on the Indian was in almost constant retreat before the stream of pioneers heading westward, whose demand for more land never ceased. Land was obtained from the Indian tribes by treaty, sometimes peacefully, sometimes with the help of war. The process came to be pretty standardized: a tribe would be induced to give up its lands and to move farther west

on the payment of a small price and the solemn promise that it would be secure in its new home forever
after. Forever was usually a short time; soon the west-
ering settlers would be moving in, squatting on the
tribe's new lands, and demanding government protection from the threatening savages. Then another treaty,
another removal farther west. Usually the removals
were accomplished without resistance; after having
been uprooted a couple of times most tribes had little
fight left in them.

The commissioners charged with making the treaties
—which were always negotiated as between the United
States and another sovereign power—became quite
skilled at their craft. Gifts and a feast were provided;
there was much panoply and speechmaking. In most
cases the commissioners and the Indians were not even
talking about the same thing, because the Indian had
no concept of land as something that could be bought,
sold, or given away. In time, as their chiefs came to
realize that the marks they made on a piece of paper
had serious consequences, they refused to sign treaties;
a chief of one southern tribe was put to death for
agreeing to a treaty. The commissioners met these difficulties with bribes and threats, and dealt with minor
chieftains when the real leaders were obdurate. On a
good many occasions liquor was the midwife that
brought an otherwise difficult treaty into being. Such
business took a strong stomach or a complete lack of
conscience. Lewis Cass, governor of Michigan Territory and skilled at dealing with Indians, was so filled
with remorse after one treaty-making session that he
swore that only direct orders from Washington could
force him to repeat such a performance.

So swiftly did the tide of white settlement flow that
by the early 1800s there were few empty spaces east of
the Mississippi into which to push unwanted Indians.
But west of the Mississippi lay an enormous expanse of

grassland. Its eastern edge was covered with tall-grass prairies on which lived tribes that farmed as well as hunted and lived at least a semi-sedentary village life. Farther west, where the climate was more arid, the grass was shorter, and there roamed the true nomads, the tepee-dwelling, buffalo-hunting tribes, virile people with their own chivalry of war and honor: the Cheyenne and Arapaho, Sioux and Crow, the Comanche and Kiowa, and the Blackfeet. Over these grasslands grazed millions of buffalo, an endless supply of food for the Indians.

It struck certain wise men in Washington that the remaining Indians in the East should be sent into those grasslands to live under the open sky. That would end the problem forever; no one would ever again want their land, for as every settler knew, soil that would not grow trees would not grow crops. The Western plains were not called the Great American Desert without good reason. Certain arrangements had to be made; the farming Indians on the prairie had to be made to move to make way for the newcomers, but it was accomplished. President Andrew Jackson, a thoroughgoing frontiersman in his disregard of Indian rights, pushed the removal of the remaining Eastern tribes to the new Indian Country. Most went without resisting, though some fought to stay and many felt anguish at leaving ancestral homes. Too, thousands died on the way because removals were bungled by corrupt contractors.

Nevertheless, by about 1840 almost all Eastern Indians were established in the Permanent Indian Country (a few avoided removal in one way or another), and though, as former forest dwellers some of them may have felt uneasy under such an immensity of sky, at least they had the assurance of the Great Father in Washington that as long as grass grows and waters flow, all the great sea of grass as far as the Rocky

Mountains would belong to the Indian. Or would it? Within ten years the commissioners had shown up again with their gifts and all the panoply of treaty making, and were threatening and cajoling another tribe into giving up a piece of the Permanent Indian Country (settlers were learning that grassland could make mighty fertile farms). The Oregon Trail crossed the Plains, miners beat a road to Pikes Peak and drove away the buffalo, the railroads started building. The great buffalo-hunting tribes fought back valiantly; the defeat of George Armstrong Custer is one of the legends of the West. There were other bright victories, but the defeats were far more numerous, and before 1880, when some of the old men Wissler met were still in strong middle age, the fighting on the Plains was over and the last bands of Indians driven onto reservations. Their way of life was disappearing anyhow; throughout the 1870s and into the 1880s hide hunters were busily exterminating the buffalo; in 1883 the last small herds of bison were wiped out. With them went the basis of the way of life of the nomadic tribes.

For the free-ranging Plains Indians, reservation life was tantamount to being shut up in a pen—and usually the pen kept growing smaller. Take the story of the Sioux as a prime example. The original reservation marked out for the Western Sioux covered all of South Dakota west of the Missouri River, and the tribe also had hunting rights extending into Montana and Wyoming. Then gold was discovered in the Black Hills. When the Indians refused to sell that part of their reservation—it was holy ground to them—the Army found a pretext to make war. The Sioux inevitably lost, though not before spectacularly ending the career of glory-hunting Colonel George Armstrong Custer, and they were forced to cede a third of their reservation and their hunting rights in Wyoming and Montana.

Within a few years settlers in the Black Hills region

were grumbling about the difficulty of getting to eastern Dakota with that Sioux reservation in the way. So in 1889 the Government's treaty makers conned the Sioux into ceding a corridor a full sixty miles wide through the heart of their reservation, and to show their versatility, they also got the Sioux to give up the westernmost fifty miles of the reservation. What was left was divided into five reservations, and as such they show on the map today.

However, if you think that all the land within those five remaining reservations belongs to the Sioux, you show little faith in the ingenuity of the white man in finding ways of separating the Indian from his birthright. It had long been held that only the blessing of private property would civilize the Indian. If he owned his own little plot of ground instead of possessing a reservation in common with his tribe, the argument ran, he would become acquisitive, frugal, hard-working, and Bible-reading—in short, a reasonable facsimile of a white man. From time to time various tribes had been persuaded to allot their lands—usually about 160 acres to a person—and sell the rest. The procedure, called severalty, had the blessing both of friends of the Indian who were convinced that his only salvation lay in becoming "civilized," and of those whose most benign impulse was to separate the red man from more of his land.

The process became national policy in 1887 with the passage of the Dawes Severalty Act, which allotted 160 acres to Indian heads of families (less to others), while debarring them, for their protection, from selling their allotments for a period of years. It opened the rest of the reservation for sale to whites. Huge amounts of land were lost by the tribes. Few Indians could farm their 160-acre allotments because, for one thing, few knew much about farming, and for another, most of the land was ill-suited for small-scale farming. A

Kiowa chief acidly observed that if the President was so eager to have the Indians raise corn, he should send them land that would grow corn. Sharp operators leased allotments from Indians, had themselves appointed guardians for minor children or incompetent children, in short, used all manner of chicanery to get land. That severalty was designed more for the benefit of whites than Indians can be seen in the fact that it was not pushed on the arid reservations of the Southwest, whose acres did not interest white speculators.

The pace of allotment slowed down after a few years when the cream had been taken off but did not end completely until 1934, when the policy of severalty was repudiated and replaced in Washington by one of encouraging tribal ownership. It was too late to undo most of the damage; between 1887 and 1934 Indians were separated from some 86,000,000 of their 138,000,-000 acres of land—and it was all done quietly, without wars or shooting or stirring anyone up except a few do-gooders. Most of what remained to the red man was arid, sandy, or rocky, land white men did not want.

Among the greatest sufferers from severalty were the Sioux, the same whose reservation had been whittled down so much. Great parts of their reservation that was left over after the allotments had been made were sold to ranchers; many Indians leased their own allotments to whites. So, when Clark Wissler tries to impress by writing that the reservations he visited were together equal in size to all of New England and New York combined, accept his figures gingerly. The reservations may have been large, but only a small part of them actually belonged to the Indians.

The pressure from settlers and speculators to rob the Indian of his land has been one of the two rocks on which Indian policy in the United States has foundered. The other has been the corruption within the system. From its beginning the Indian Service has been a hotbed of graft and flagrant wrongdoing. With some notable exceptions, it attracted men more interested in making a fast dollar than in serving their wards. The Indian agents or "Majors" to whom Wissler introduces us are a mixed lot, but in general the wise and good ones did not fit in with the system and did not stay long. One of his agents grazed cattle on the reservation and used the names of dead Indians to hide his activities, but this was a small and circumspect operation compared to some ambitious and blatant swindles. As typical as any was the case of an agent on an Apache reservation who spent almost all his time on a private mining venture, and used food and materials from the agency warehouse to support it. When an inspector came to investigate, the agent sold the inspector a mine, and the inspector, in turn, got the son of the Commissioner of Indian Affairs to take part in his mining operation. With such agents, it is not surprising the interests of the Indian got only cursory attention.

Wissler's portraits are of Indians at a time when their spirits and prospects were at a low ebb. Ill-fed, suffering from tuberculosis and other diseases, confined to reservations without purpose or hope, at the beginning of the century the Indian's numbers were declining at a rate that seemed destined to make him truly the Vanishing American. Today that picture has changed. His numbers are increasing, and at a rate faster than the general population. Young men and women have rediscovered a pride in being Indian and are reviving ancient tribal customs that the whites tried so hard to extirpate.

There is also a new attitude toward the reservation itself. Not long ago I listened to three or four young Sioux explain to a small group that the common notion among whites that a reservation was a sort of prison for Indians was completely erroneous. Not so, they said earnestly. These were lands reserved to the Indians, the pieces they have left of all they once owned. A century ago the United States Army more than once rode out to drive the great-grandfathers of those same young men back onto the reservation. And, make no mistake about it, those Sioux warriors of long ago did look on it as a kind of prison.

New Canaan, Connecticut
1971

Foreword

THIS IS A book without a purpose. It is neither history, nor sociology, nor any other kind of -ology, merely personal recollections of old time Indian reservations. The situations depicted belong to the past, for Indians of the present generation live under wholly different conditions, so I feel free to set down something of what was seen and heard while loitering around the Indian agencies and camps of the time. Doubtless I misunderstood much that was seen and have but faulty memory of what was heard, yet I enjoyed every day to the full.

The personalities flitting in and out of these pages are dead—many long dead. No worthwhile purpose would be served in identifying them in name, time and place, so their true names have been omitted, a few of the characters being composites, which will the better reflect my impressions of life on these old Indian reservations. My chief interest was in the aged men and women past the half century mark, men who rode down the last buffalo and were the last to tread in the war path; women who skinned many buffalo, dressed their heavy hides, reared and clothed their families in the open country.

This should explain why it is that none of the people mentioned here survive. Naturally, the old of today were the young of that time so I have felt free to write frankly, since the living are in no way responsible for what happened in my time. I mention this because some harsh words may be set down in these pages, if any given situation seems to merit such comments at the time, but if so, the excuse is that no one, after a close look at life anywhere, can escape the urge to make harsh statements, and if there should be a reader who resents them as unjust, I shall be sorry, because the chances are that life in the Indian country was neither better nor worse than in the average American town of the time. As someone has said, the best thing about the good old days is that they are a long way behind us.

These visits to Indian reservations began with the dawn of the present century and ended in 1905, but the atmosphere depicted is typical of the preceding 90's. In all, ten reservations were visited, some of them several times. The territory covered was considerable, since the total area of these ten reservations was approximately equal to the states of Maine, New Hampshire, Vermont, Massachusetts, Rhode Island, Connecticut and New York. The number of Indians was estimated as 17,000, or about one Indian to each six square miles. Within these reservations there were no fences and few real roads, merely open country, as it had been for ages. But change was the order of the day, the Old West was all but gone.

No one need have been upon a reservation long to see that the Indian way of living was on its way out and another kind of life was moving in. The older Indians knew their sun was even then below the horizon and that the twilight of oblivion was deepening. On the other hand the white men round about saw in their sky the glow of a glorious dawn, their visions were of fenced farms, radiating railways and rising cities. So if the Indian personalities you meet seem restrained and melancholy, remember that twilight enveloped them and that there was to be no dawn. Yet, do not assume that they were suffering from inferiority complexes, for they accepted their fate stoically, believing that they were better men than the whites surrounding them, that their way of life was superior, and that with its passing, the world would be a far less desirable place to live in. On holidays they stripped off the garb the white man imposed upon them, painted their bodies, mounted their ponies, and rode forth as the last of the grand cavalcade just passing into oblivion.

Red Man Reservations

1

On the Reservation Trail

THERE WERE no automobiles in the days of which I write and naturally few real roads. If one went anywhere he took to the saddle or rode in a wagon. However, the elite traveled in strong buggies drawn by two good horses, and on rare occasions by four, because in bogs and mud-banked streams, a horse could with difficulty drag himself through, so the extra pull of the buggy must not exceed the margin which sometimes was so close that four horses would be needed to cover it. Yet I suspect that, here as elsewhere, style ruled and to turn out with a one-horse buggy was unthinkable; even the Indians used at least two horses to a wagon.

Most of the railroads stopped at the Missouri, and though a few continental lines stretched away to the Pacific, the traveller to the Indian country depended upon the horse. Mail for the reservations would come from the nearest railroad town by stage, usually a light covered wagon in which an occasional passenger could find a seat among mail bags, cartons and packages. Here and there the old time stage coach survived, clattering along with four to six horses. From one to four days was required to reach an Indian reservation and naturally on such long drives, if the only passenger, one talked with the driver; somewhat like the stage driver of old, he was the link between the thinly settled communities and the railroad towns, and so with the world at large. His arrival at an agency was always an event, for he knew the latest news. All of this may seem strange in this day of morning and evening papers, not to mention the radio in continuous action. With these out of the picture it is easy to understand why the driver of the twice-a-week stage was popular. As individuals, these drivers were never brilliant and rarely prosperous, but dignified and punctual as befitted a person who carried the United States mail.

I mention these homely matters because they were conspicuous in life on an Indian reservation. Could one have stepped from the train to an agency for the first time, the sight might have been depressing enough, but after a long trip with the mail driver, one felt like cheering when the agency came into view. I remember one long dreary drag through mud and chill, when having exhausted all means of entertainment, I lapsed into complete silence, while the driver dozed in his seat. Seemingly, hour followed hour, when suddenly topping a gentle swell in the ground, we were thrilled to see a few low straggling buildings in the distance. With a jerk of the whip, the driver said, "There," as the horses quickened their pace. Before us lay a valley in which a stream was suspected because of a waving line of green trees, probably willows and aspen. The agency buildings were one story, some with dull red roofs, and I noted two stumpy spires suggesting churches. A windmill or two rose above the sky line as landmarks, the whole presenting a bleak outpost appearance.

I noted that the low buildings were gathered somewhat irregularly around a rectangular space which later I found was called the Plaza, but into which the trotting horses carried the stage, halting in front of the general store, in which was the post office. The driver having suggested that I walk to the hotel while the mail was being unloaded, I crossed the open square, empty except for two or three wagons and several Indian ponies, while sitting upon the ground were some Indian women and children, waiting patiently for the return of their men folks. The hotel was a small house with a long narrow room through the center which served as office and barber shop; on one side was a dining room, on the other two bedrooms. However, the landlord said these were for transients and since I intended to settle down for awhile, he would put me in the attic. This proved to be comfortable enough with a window that could be opened and which in any event gave a wide view of the square and so of life on the reservation.

The landlord was born in Kentucky, but having heard that a young man should go west and grow up with the country, worked his way out driving oxen, took up a claim and developed a farm, but now having a son old enough to carry on, he had followed the custom of leaving the farm for the town, if this agency could be called a town. The barber was an Indian, but had acquired the characteristics of the trade in one respect, for he talked as he worked, but when not working, he slept in the barber chair so soundly that if you wished a shave, you must first awaken him, then implant in his sluggish brain the idea that he was to arise so that you as customer could take the seat. Sometimes this was a slow process.

The dining room at this hotel was typical, the plainest of furniture and service, three long tables, one for Indians, the others for whites. The rules of this agency required that Indians be furnished meals for a quarter, whereas white people paid twice that amount, one of the rare instances where the Indian had the advantage. However, the landlord got even by requiring that the Indians eat from an oilcloth covered table, without napkins, and with cheap table service. Even so, it was luxury to what many of them experienced at home. The food was about the same as for the whites, though the Indian got a large bowl of soup into which he put all the crackers the liquid would tolerate. I heard none of these Indians complain about this discrimination, on the contrary they expressed a preference for the procedure as the one best suited to their tastes, and since they did not speak English there were no conversation clashes. Of course, it was only now and then that an Indian could afford to eat here, it being for them the last word in luxury.

The white boarders, unmarried employees and traders, together with transients and visitors, some twenty to thirty persons in all, for the most part males, formed a kind of clearing house for information and gossip. A regular attendant at this board kept abreast of reservation affairs, heard abstracts of news from the world without, picked up choice anecdotes and an occasional bit of humor. During my stay, several interesting characters were in daily attendance. There was a young clerk, new to the service, lately from Milwaukee, who seized every opportunity to impress upon us the superiority of life in his native city, until finally some one was moved to inquire why he ever left the place. A sputtering German from St. Louis claiming to be an artist, was ready to pass opinions on any subject whatsoever. Having once visited the Hopi Indians and observed the snake dance, he regarded the rest of us as contemptible green-horns. Another interesting character was a veteran trader, born in Scotland, served in the U. S. Army, was discharged at Ft. Laramie, took up the Indian trade, got himself an Indian wife and was now the grandfather of numerous mixed-blood children. Finally there was a gray haired doctor, whom everybody liked, but who was fussy about his seat at the table; if a stranger should take his place by mistake, no matter how many other empty chairs there might be, the doctor would turn on his heel and leave the hotel without eating. So the waitress was always worried trying to guard the doctor's seat between trips to the kitchen.

Another venture into the Indian country began one day in May. The train rolling westward across the plains ran into a snowstorm, which became thicker and thicker. Long after darkness set in, we reached my scheduled stop and the accommodating porter put me off into the snow, saying the station was forward. As the train vanished, I stumbled along the track in the blinding storm toward the dim light at the station where was stationed a lone telegraph operator. When I asked if there was a hotel, he said the landlord had been to the train with a lantern, but seeing no one alight from the coaches, had gone back and would soon lock up. So I stumbled on in the direction he pointed and surprised the hotel man who could not recall ever having met a passenger who rode the pull-mans in the rear. I got a room, such as it was.

The blizzard raged and raged beyond all reason— everybody around was certain no such weather had ever been known, but that is what one hears everywhere.

The Indian country was some distance away and because of the snow the stage did not run. So I was snow bound in May. There was no town, merely a few houses, a store and a large saloon. The bar-keeper looked like a prize fighter and a gunman combined, and was said to be proficient in either occupation. A few men took their meals at the hotel, one of whom always placed a large revolver beside his plate. On inquiry I learned that he expected a call from an enemy, the brother of a man he had killed. When I asked what the diners were expected to do when the shooting began, the answer was throw themselves upon the floor. I secretly rehearsed this procedure, but fortunately there was no shooting during my stay.

One day I asked this alert gunman why he stayed in a place where his life was in constant danger, and thereby put myself in contempt. As he saw it, only cowards would run away, his self-respect required that he remain as a perpetual challenge to his enemies. Maybe he was right, but it all seemed so unnecessary, so futile, this spending one's life waiting with finger on the trigger, for an enemy whose appearance was after all problematical. I have often wondered how it came out in the end, if he lived out his natural life, and if when he lay down to rise no more, did his friends see to it that his gun was in the coffin?

Before I got away from the town it filled up with cowboys, given a few days off for their quarterly drunk, but this was not very exciting because all knives and guns were checked at the store and locked in a safe. Anyhow the boys were soon too drunk to hurt each other. One of them did try to ride his horse into the saloon for a drink, but he was so drunk and the horse so docile, that the sight was neither heroic nor picturesque. To tell the truth, I was bored, since the actual did not measure up to the story books.

One day while sitting by the stove in the hotel, the door opened, an energetic figure in a large coat began stamping off the snow and, this operation completed, entered. In a pleasant deep voice the stranger said it was a "—— —— rotten storm," to which I heartily agreed. However, I was surprised to observe, when the stranger threw off the great coat, that a woman and not a man stood before me. Around her waist was a heavy belt, with cartridges and a six-shooter, which she unbuckled and hung over the back of a chair.

I tried to look indifferent as the conversation began. My impression was that here was a woman of ability, masculine in manner, accustomed to issuing orders,

seeing them carried out, and able to take care of herself in a man's world. No names were exchanged, but I
recalled certain stories about a Mother Hinds who held
sway in a nearby frontier town, famous for its lawlessness. Finally, I ventured to inquire if she had come all
the way from the town and being assured that she had,
I felt certain of the identification.

According to the folklore about this lady, I expected
her to bear the marks of dissipation and vice, but quite
to the contrary. Even her occasional profanity was far
from unusual on the frontier and was handled so skillfully that one could not help enjoying it. After a brief
visit, she went her way.

Soon a priest entered to absorb a store of heat from
the stove; he too had ridden a long way. Somewhat
mischievously, I told of my recent guest, and the satisfaction of having met her face to face while in this
country. To all this the priest made no reply, so I
inquired if he knew the lady. His reply was emphatic,
"What, that ungodly woman? God forbid." He then
hurried away as if to escape from the presence of one
who seemed to be pleased over such a chance meeting.
On my part, I wished the good Father had come a little
sooner. However, I was willing to call it a day.

Eventually the weather cleared. A typical old-time
stage coach still ran from the railroad, past the agency
into some mining country beyond. I had to wait several
days after the coach resumed operations, the reason
being that all seats were booked for the time, but at
last everything was ready for the start. The trader at
the district agency I was to visit had ordered a bag of
silver coin brought down and I, a stranger in the country, was asked to carry it. It was a heavy bag and its
contents obvious. Six fresh horses twitched nervously
as the baggage was put aboard, but at a word from the
driver, they were off. Two strange men had joined us,
strange because I had not seen them before. They were

friendly enough, having the appearance of ranch managers. Later in the day they became more familiar, making sly remarks about my heavy baggage. Finally, one suggested to the other that they hold me up, when a certain small canyon was reached. I was not alarmed by this pleasantry.

Late in the day the coach stopped, the two men dragged their bed rolls out upon the ground, took from them repeating rifles, filled their magazines with shells, buckled on belts with six-shooters. I noted the driver did the same. Not a word was spoken. Finally, I asked the meaning of all this. The answer was that they anticipated a hold-up down the road. I expressed the hope that they did not suspicion me, for I was soon to stop at the agency. Their reply was to the effect that they knew all about me and the money bag, that if I were quick on the trigger they were sorry to lose me, but otherwise it was just as well for the safety of my treasure.

We soon arrived at the store in the agency, where the precious bag was delivered to the trader, and after discharging the mail, the stage rolled away, everybody armed as in the movies. Was there a hold-up? No, not then, but on the next trip, when the driver was alone, the bandits appeared. However, there was neither mail nor money aboard, so the driver was allowed to proceed. Later I heard that on my trip down I had unknowingly ridden with a heavy consignment of cash guarded by two United States marshals. Further, this explained how it came about that I was asked to sponsor the bag of coins.

There was no hotel at this small agency, so the trader offered me a bunk in the attic of the store. The next morning I was awakened by the buzzing of the flies, and in the increasing light saw in the other end of the attic many hanging coyote and wolf skins, still green, as the trappers say. This was a somewhat disquieting sight and I shifted my bed roll to a pile of lumber outside, which was too high to be reached by horse, steer or dog. One morning, shortly after, I was awakened in the gray dawn by a deep grumbling, roaring sound, the bawling of cattle. Presently the herd came into view, in close formation. It was a mass of horns in moving shapes, the largest herd I ever saw. Two cowboys were riding ahead as decoys; impressive, tall, graceful figures, such as one could see anywhere in the cow country. On the flanks outriders herded all stragglers back into line. It was soon evident that my lumber pile was directly in the line of march and would be engulfed. Imagine yourself standing on a small platform, looking into the faces of the front line of steers advancing without hesitation as if to overwhelm you, and then being surrounded on all sides by a moving mass of cattle, your feet on a level with their backs, but knee-deep in horns. The view in the rear was less inspiring because of the lazy stragglers and an unpicturesque cook-wagon accompanying the roundup; but even these soon vanished over the adjoining swell, leaving the agency to its usual routine, a few Indians coming in to trade, an occasional stage stopping just long enough to put off the mail and, at rare intervals, a lonely traveler.

Perhaps the reader may wonder, why a reservation, and, what was it that urged the writer to visit and revisit these out-of-the-way-places? The answer may lie in the pages that follow. Once while walking in the far-off city of Sydney, Australia, I was startled by two boys dashing unexpectedly from an alley, one with a few feathers in his hat band, a toy hatchet in one hand, a wooden knife in the other, yelling at the heels of a second boy. It was, however, no strange sight to me; a make-believe scalping was being staged. It is curious how the Indians of history and story have captured the imagination of the world's children. In our own country, I note how this fascination grows with the generations, instead of diminishing; nor is it difficult to find an explanation if we seek for one.

Few seem to realize that the Indian is perpetuated in memory as the most original and conspicuous feature of our romantic history; the building of the Great West, which meant successive adventures in the great forests west of the Appalachian summits, the immediate valley of the Mississippi, the arid plains and the Southwest and finally the California-Oregon country. Our forefathers faced these hurdles one after the other, many of them going down fighting. Yet it is commonly overlooked that the real Indian wars were fought east of the Mississippi. In Washington's time several armies were sacrificed before Wayne achieved victory and in his case two years of preparation were necessary on a scale comparable to a foreign war before victory was attainable. The renowned Pontiac carried on manfully for a long time, nor are the Indian wars of the South to be ignored. Finally, one need but visit the old battle ground of Tippecanoe, Indiana, noting the marks of conflict surviving more than a century to realize that a fight occurred at that place as compared to which many farther western Indian engagements appear as mere skirmishes.

West of the Mississippi in the lands of the Sioux, the Comanche and the Apache were later some picturesque conflicts, but for the most part games of hide and seek between mobile horse riding Indians and slow moving troops. The usual complaints of the soldiers were that the Indians ran away before a real fight could be staged.

Finally, on the Pacific coast the struggle seldom rose to the military level, as in parts of California where the killing of Indians was a sport to enliven Sundays and holidays. We mention these matters of history because these conflicts were immediately antecedent to the settling of Indians on reservations, for following each real war, the defeated Indian tribe was dispossessed of most of its habitat and settled upon a selected plot, usually the area least coveted by the conquerors. So even reservations followed the frontier westward, and it was this long contest, beginning in the east with a life and death struggle and diminishing in intensity as the frontier advanced, that gave the Indian first place in the traditions of our people.

On the other hand there is no denying that even conquered Indians were troublesome. It had long been their mode to gather food when they saw it and it was too much to expect them to pass a farm empty-handed or to be 100 per cent efficient in distinguishing between game and domestic animals. So a certain amount of isolation was necessary to protect the Indian, hence the reservation, and its capital, the agency.

2

The Major

On a reservation the most talked-about person was "The Major." The Indian Bureau addressed him as Agent, but locally he was Major. This had at least one virtue, for though agents came and went with surprising frequency, the Major went on forever. So far as my observations go most of the incumbents of that office liked the title; they seemed to become receptive when the word was pronounced with the dignity appropriate to a great functionary, but we should not begrudge them this beneficence, because there was little honest reward for their services. Time and agitation on the part of Indian sympathizers have brought the standing of these officials to such a pass that we are in danger of overlooking their former power and glory.

In the days of which I write, a reservation was land under direct control from Washington and all the laws passed by territorial and state governments were null and void inside the reservation line. The Indians soon found this out and not infrequently enticed ambitious peace officers to pursue them, with about the same result as when a dog chases cats among trees, for once the Indians crossed the line, an irate peace officer could do nothing but swear. True he could complain to the Major, but in such a case that august personage usually sympathized with his Red children. Anyhow, the Major was supreme within his domain, responsible to Washington only, so why should he condescend to recognize the local government? And he was an autocrat, if ever there was one—a dictator we might call him now.

True there were resolutions by Congress and orders from the Indian Office, but these were usually general, whereas he was in supreme command of an Indian population, which deluged him with its troubles and its wants.

So far as my observations go the Indian joyfully acquiesced in the implied wish of the Great Father to share his burdens and at all times hung around the Major's door, seizing every opportunity to lay a batch of troubles upon his desk. I heard that once upon a time in the morning the Major found a dead infant upon his doorstep and made the mistake of giving it a dignified burial in a coffin. Soon other bodies appeared in front of his house, harsh measures being required to dodge further assumption of such responsibilities. This may not have happened, but is in keeping with the spirit of the time and place.

Often when calling at the Major's office I waited my turn with an Indian complaining about the non-return of a borrowed gun, a dusky woman to see what could be done about her run-away daughter, a hen-pecked brave whose wife would not stay in of nights, etc. It requires little imagination to understand that among the hundreds of rules from Washington, few would fit such an array of human clashes, so the Major was forced to act upon hunches, at once and arbitrarily. Like the father of a big family, it was up to him to meet the situation promptly and not to be too judicial about it either. To a people among whom the scalping

knife and the tomahawk were still handled affectionately, no leader deserved respect unless his punish-
ments were harsh. The people back home might be
scandalized and think how the poor Indian must abhor
such cruelty, but I seriously doubt if they understood
the Indian they wished to champion. All of which
means that Indian agents often did what would not
look nice in print.

When a white visitor stepped over the reservation
line he proceeded at once to the office of the Major. If
neither an Indian nor an official of the United States,
he would be under suspicion until he could clear himself. Even after years of visiting in the Indian country,
I could not approach the Major without some misgivings, for he might not like my looks, might not take my
credentials at their face values, nor sympathize with
my objectives. If he chose to say no, there was no
alternative to immediate departure. Yet these fears
were probably groundless so far as I was concerned,
since I looked like a harmless academic nut, a class
politely designated locally as "bug hunters" with the
emphasis upon the first word. This does not mean that
I was never under suspicion, as later events will demonstrate, but in due time I would be looked upon as
too visionary to be dangerous. One gruff Major I en-
countered was frank enough to say that no one should
expect him to believe that an intelligent, healthy man
would spend his time going about to hear a few lazy
old Indians tell lies. However, he gave his consent that
I might stay around awhile, at least, until he found
out my real game.

I am not blaming agents for all this, because I am
convinced that a duly suspicious Major was an efficient
one. One day two strange men arrived announcing that
they were painters, stopping in merely to see if the
trader might not like a sign, or a government clerk's
wife care to have her kitchen furniture brightened up a

bit. They brought their paints and oils with them, in ordinary looking jugs and cans. The Major heard their story and grudgingly gave them 48 hours to canvass around to see if there were any such jobs. Then while the painters were on their rounds, he went to look the jugs over, sniffing at them sufficiently to discover a bootlegging outfit. Result: the whole supply confiscated and the painters evicted.

An average sized agency called for a large staff. First there were two or more clerks, one of whom could act as Major in an emergency. An issue clerk, carpenter, blacksmith, wheelwright, butcher and farmer were sure to be on hand. Then a doctor, sometimes a veterinary, and a few school teachers. And we should not forget the stableman and his Indian helpers, who kept the Government horses and who could repair harness after a fashion. Of course, there were the traders and their clerks, a barber and occasionally an itinerant tailor. Two or more missionaries presided in as many little frame churches and finally there would be a kind of hotel where a visitor could spend the night. The number of white families might easily reach twenty. All of these were ruled over by the Major, together with a thousand or more Indians. Unusually large reservations had subagencies to further complicate the situation. After all a reservation need not have been a lonely place, but living there was much like a long voyage in a ship, the officers, the crew, a few first cabin passengers, some second cabin and a large steerage list; they could not keep out of each other's sight, and when white folks left the reservation, they secretly hoped never to see each other again. The Major always seemed a little forlorn. Like a dictator, he kept aloof; I cannot recall ever getting acquainted with one of these agents. As for a really informal conversation, that was unthinkable. I used to feel sorry for them; I could smoke a pipe with the doctor, listen to the barber's stories, joke with the trader, but nothing like that with the Major.

The troubles of the Major were not always with the Indians or with his staff, but often originated in Washington. Well meaning officials, thousands of miles away, many of whom had never set foot on a reservation, did not hesitate to issue edicts. Once, so I heard, an order came that since Indians were prone to waste their time listening to drumming, and further, were in danger of relapsing into pagan ways, true reform could best be inaugurated by stopping all such drumming. I admit that when the Indians were camped around there was an interminable din, even through the night; it was not conducive to refreshing sleep, but it was Indian and so I rather liked it. Nor did the white residents complain; in fact, they would feel lonesome when the drums were silent.

The Major knew such an order could not be enforced without disorganizing everything, but he called in the leading Indian chiefs and read the new order from the Great Father. They listened and sat in silence for a time. Then one pulled his blanket tighter and began to speak. He felt that the Great Father was not at fault, but that his stupid adherents hid from him the true state of affairs. He had noted that white men were fond of drums, that when soldiers were around the drum was heard and even at a burial. He could not conceive that the Great Father should be so unmindful of his children, but in order that he might know their hearts, prayed that a letter be written to him, telling him how much the drum meant to the Indians, but that should the Great Father in accordance with his infinite wisdom, decide that all drums be put away forever and require the white people to do so, then his Red children will not hold back, but they too will sound the drum no more.

Most Majors liked their jobs and so made a show of enforcing all such foolish rules by telling the Indians what the Great Father said, and then stopping their ears and covering their eyes. For example, a curious

kind of religion had for long been an eyesore to the
Indian Office. It usually went under the name peyote.
Full accounts of the procedure in this form of worship
are to be had in the appropriate literature, so it may
suffice to say that passages from the Bible may be read
by the cult leader, dressed in white to impersonate
Christ. The congregation is fed peyote, part of a narcotic plant, which causes many to see visions and
makes them especially susceptible to suggestion. The
leader of the cult seeks to make them shun liquor and
laziness, many cures being reported. Of course, the
Christian churches were dead against it and it violated
the narcotic laws, so long ago strict orders were issued
to all agents to stop the practice and prohibit meetings
of this cult. Still it went on as ever. Once when I made
a formal call at the office, I casually asked if there was
any peyote around and was promptly set right by the
Major declaring that there was no peyote for the good
reason that it would not be tolerated. That same evening while passing the Major's residence, I heard from
across the little valley in which the agency buildings
nestled, the familiar notes of a peyote song and the
sound of the accompanying rattle. There are many
kinds of Indian songs, but each ceremony usually has
songs of a distinct type, which can be recognized once
you become familiar with them. I saw the Major
calmly smoking his pipe, apparently listening intently
to this weird but moving music. To make sure of it, the
next day, when calling at the doctor's office, I asked
his Indian interpreter if it would be possible to hear
some peyote songs. The Indian said he thought it could
be arranged, that in fact, he had attended a rehearsal
nearby last night.

Perhaps it was a wise Major who isolated himself
from too much information.

Once an acquaintance of mine boarded a street car
in Boston and asked if he could stand on the platform

to smoke. The conductor replied that, if the question had not been asked, he could, but that now the rules must be enforced.

Washington and the public expected Indian agents to take the initiative in leading their wards along the white man's road, but failed to realize the resisting capacity of the Red Man, or even to expect that he would resist. Massachusetts Avenue whites might be horrified at some of the things Indians did, never dreaming that those same Indians would have been scandalized over Mrs. A.'s formal house party. Such social blindness has been the plague of the Indian Service for more than a century. Perhaps no department of the government at Washington has been subject to so many sentimental drives as have been made against that of Indian Affairs. It seems that after the Civil War, abolition sentiment shifted from the slave, theoretically no longer existent, to the oppressed Indians, and many rising authors had visions of a second Uncle Tom's Cabin. I am not contending that all this humanitarian effort was misplaced, and grant that the unfortunate lot of the Indian was made a little more bearable thereby. On the other hand, the constant yielding of the Government to these frequent drives, prevented the maintenance of anything like a consistent policy in adjusting Indian life to civilization.

Religious and educational enthusiasts could often cause more confusion and tragedy than the most ignorant agent; probably because their objectives were one hundred per cent good and their understanding of local conditions zero minus. No doubt we shall go on bungling Indian affairs for the simple reason that the problems presented are of no particular economic and social importance to the nation at large.

On the other hand, the Major at his desk, surrounded by his Indians, faced real, human problems. Even at his worst, he was often moved to improve the

happiness and contentment of his Indians, but when he
did see a solution and set out to lead his people toward
it, a reprimand from Washington might be his only
reward. Thus we heard that in the 80's it was decided
to move the buildings on a certain reservation. These
buildings were all of logs, so the plan was to tear them
down and transport the logs to the new site, setting the
houses up again in the same order. Fortunately, the
Major was given money to pay for this labor. He was a
practical man, called the chiefs together and offered
food and real wages if the Indians would do the job
promptly. The chiefs entered into the idea enthusiasti-
cally, anything to break the dead monotony of reservation life. And it was an enjoyable time, a great camp
was pitched, the camp soldiers set up their tipi and
prepared to see that the orders of the chiefs were carried out. The women, the great workers of aboriginal
days, took hold with a will; they hauled logs upon
horse travois and even put the dogs to work again as in
the past. Well, the buildings were moved in short order,
everybody was happy, even the Major. The Indians
were sorry when it was all over; they would have liked
nothing better than to throw their old time tribal
strength upon some new public works project. However, nothing like this was to happen again, for when
the Major's report got to Washington, hands went up
in the air: "Women and girls employed at hard labor
by the Government—horrible! Stop it!"

Some years later, after cities had grown up here and
there, with farms where once were cattle ranges, one
agent took seriously the Washington idea that every
Indian should be a farmer. Looking over his reservation he saw a small valley with a stream large enough
to irrigate acres and acres of land. Here to his way of
thinking was the grand opportunity. So he talked the
matter over with the chiefs, who were ready to follow
any promising lead, but in their opinion, they must

have a leader who knew how to carry on in the new enterprise. So they decided that if the Major would head it up, they would follow. The plan worked beautifully, under the Major's personal supervision, a crop was put in, duly it matured, was harvested, and marketed. The Indians were happy with their checks and their new credit at the store. Children had warm winter clothes and there was a sack of flour in every cabin. When the news got to Washington, a halt was called. The idea was a good one, they said, and the Indian should be encouraged to farm, but the Major must keep hands off—individualism, every man for himself, was to be the guiding slogan. When spring came, the chiefs called in to know if it was not time to begin planting, but the Major read them his instructions. The Great Father's words were final, each Indian was ordered to go out by himself, to plant his seed, and when the crop was ready, haul it some 200 miles to market. Needless to say, that was the end of the experiment. Of course, there was a hint that the Major got a rake-off, but nothing was proven. The real objection was more fundamental than that and American life being what it was then, the decision to forbid all such schemes was probably wise.

Of course, these are extreme cases, but I heard of many more, enough to exhaust the reader's patience. Nor was it always the Major who came to grief. Once a young divinity student was sent to a little deserted church on a reservation. Being young and zealous, he began to look the situation squarely in the eye. He saw a people devout enough in their own way, but shy of the church. Tired of preaching without a congregation, he called a council of the old pagan priests and medicinemen, explaining to them that he and they were laboring toward the same objectives, the elevation and betterment of their fellowmen. He invited them to look upon the little church as a religious headquarters, pro-

posing that they bring their sacred bundles to hang
upon the walls and that each of them, including himself, conduct services. It worked well, the little plain
building soon came to be a true sanctuary and the
congregation grew until outdoor meetings were necessary.

Then one fine day a traveling bishop came on an
inspection tour; to say that he was shocked, is to put
the matter mildly. For him no pagan trappings must
pass the threshold of a Christian church. The young
enthusiast was dismissed as a heretic and the Indians
were more convinced than ever that neither the church
nor the Government would permit one to befriend
them.

This incident is cited to forestall the idea that the
wickedness and incompetence of the average Indian
agent can be set down as the prime cause of the constant confusion in Indian policy. In our opinion, at no
time, nor even now, has anyone the wisdom and understanding to give the country a first-class Indian administration. Social muddling through is the best to be
expected, even with our own problems in Washington.

Every President from Washington down, has shown
dissatisfaction with the personnel of the Indian Service.
Grant, having faith in the discipline and honesty of
army officers, proposed that they be assigned to agencies. The politicians were aghast, recognizing in this a
body blow to graft and privilege, so got a bill through
Congress prohibiting the use of army men in civilian
posts. Defeated here, the old General tried another
method. Having noticed that history claimed the
Quakers of Pennsylvania as the true friends of the
Indian, he decided that adherents to that religion might
do even better than soldiers and forthwith began to fill
vacancies with Quakers. The politicians did not like
this very well either, but since the Quakers were a well

organized body, had votes and a fair share of the country's wealth, there was little they could do about it. So a new kind of Major came on the scene; now instead of resounding to terse words, not usually printable, the walls of the dingy agency offices echoed soft "thee's and thou's." From all we could learn the Indians liked the change, the traders and local grafters did not; but like every other such reform, it passed with the next administration turnover. The Indians expected such changes and greeted each new scheme as merely another empty gesture from Washington.

I suppose that most of my readers have by this time wondered if there ever was a good agent, especially since for a century or more, both official and social Washington have made him the scape-goat. Yes, there have been courageous, honest and lovable men in that office; also there have been rascals and innocent incompetents; that could be truthfully said of any post in the public service. Here and there in these pages will be noted examples of laudable behavior on the part of agents. On every reservation visited I heard Indian traditions of one or more great agents, though I doubt if any of these were rated high in Washington. The agent who took a realistic sensible view of the situation and called a spade by its right name, stood a good chance for a place in tribal tradition, but for this very reason would arouse the ire of the idealists in the East. It is a pity such points of view must always clash. Every realistically minded agent saw himself the imposed head of a tribe of Indians, fenced into a reserve like predatory animals, more for the protection of the white people without, than for the well being of the Indians within. His duty was to keep these Indians from alarming settlers by wandering abroad, and to feed, clothe, and house them upon an inadequate budget. He found himself in the position of the rightful chief of the tribe, the Government seeking to destroy all native leadership.

Yet we have seen that when an agent tried to lead, Washington forbade. Thus a kind of vacuum was created where leadership ought to be. If one reads the published reports of Indian agents, he will note that some agents sought to please their superiors by boasting of their efforts to crush every native leader. I recall one such, as:

"I have endeavored to destroy the tribal relations as much as possible, and also to destroy the influence of certain chiefs. I have allowed relatives to band together and would appoint one of the number a chief or headman and suggest to him to take his people off to some good locality and make permanent houses. Of course, every band formed this way weakens the influence of some chief in proportion as it takes individuals from his band. Bands that at one time numbered over a hundred people, have been reduced in this way to less than twenty. I have had many houses made in this way by Indians who never worked before. The advantage to the man appointed by me was that he became more prominent and controlled the funds derived from the sale of beef hides."

Well, all we have to say is that this Major should have been ashamed of himself.

In contrast to this, take note of what another agent did. When visiting the Blackfoot Reservation in Montana, I heard laudable accounts of an agent named Wood, in fact he was almost a mythological character. Both from the Indians and the records at Washington, we get an inkling of his genius. As he saw it, the Indians on his reserve were floundering for want of intimate social leadership. It was plain to him that no agent resident from three to five years could exercise such functions, but that the solution lay in the rehabilitation of native leaders. The rules and regulations sent out from Washington said nothing about this, but he launched out boldly, called the head men into council, not for a mere talk, but for days of deliberation. To quote, "On coming here I found the Indians disorganized and spiritless; the different bands unfriendly, some hostile to each other and without any head-chiefs. They appeared to have no purpose in life except to hunt and procure robes and peltries for the traders."

He comments further that this condition had been going from bad to worse for twelve years and had been brought about chiefly by whiskey traders who urged the younger men to disregard their chiefs, the old moral values and to pay no attention to the agent's orders. It was plain that the whole tribe was moving faster and faster toward extinction. This unusually wise agent made careful inquiry as to the former political and social organization of the tribe and wrote out a brief account of how their ancient institutions functioned. To set up a regime as far as possible in harmony with the original tribal government was the solution as he conceived it. So he called the head men into council and laid before them a plan to formulate a scheme of government, a kind of unwritten constitution. The conferences were long and sometimes stormy, but in the end a scheme of tribal control was evolved. The details of this unusual conference have passed into oblivion, but fortunately were, for the most part, verbal and in Indian—no one in Washington could understand that, and so in no position to object. The main function of this long council was to select leaders and develop in them a sense of responsibility. Under this agent's wise guidance a triumvirate was set up—three top-notch Indians to enforce the rules and lead the people. The agent made it clear that he stood behind these leaders.

Did this grand scheme work? It did, and so well that though Washington soon sent this priceless agent on his way, his successors were forced to accept the situation, though sometimes against their wills, because of the morale and the solidarity of the tribe. There were

tragic years ahead for this tribe, but those three wonderful chiefs never flinched, nor did the loyalty of their
followers weaken, to the end that their tribe is today
one of the most famous.

Major Wood deserves a place in history.

A newly appointed Major must have found his job
baffling. I never had a chance to look in upon such a
scene for all of the agents I saw had been in office long
enough to acquire the mask that usually passes for
superior intelligence. Yet once I met up with a Major
somewhat new to his job. Arriving early one morning
at an agency well known to me, I called first upon my
friend, the trader. He was delighted to see me, of
course, but at once I felt that all was not well. In
response to my rising anxiety, he took me aside, and
the confidential information he imparted began with
the key to the situation: "there is a new Major in the
office." One complication lay in that he had been a
Captain in the regular army and expected to be so
addressed, and woe to anyone who addressed him in
the traditional manner of the reservation. Yes, Captain
Bump was in charge and there was the secret of the
difficulty. How he got into this job, no one seemed to
know, but it was soon apparent that he was a stranger
to political precepts, and as to the ways of business he
was totally indifferent. Always it had been the way of
agents to take the trader's word as to an Indian's debts
and wink at the seizing of his cattle and horses, but
Captain Bump had never heard of it. Stranger still, he
refused to urge the Indians to pay their debts and
would not approve the taking of their cattle. Further,
he insisted that the account books be opened for his
inspection. Of course, when he issued an order, he
expected obedience. Such woeful tales did I hear that I
made my necessary first call with many misgivings.
However, I was received courteously and truly felt that

for the first time I sat face to face with an agent who knew what he wanted to do. He brought his fist down upon his desk with a bang, saying, "You are just the man I have been looking for. Tell me what and who these Indians are."

He told how he had written to Washington for light, but to no purpose. "How did anyone suppose that he could do a good job without knowing something of the history and customs of the tribe under his care." Neither before nor since have I met an agent who even expressed a desire to know any of these things.

Of course, the rugged honesty of Captain Bump soon got him out of the Indian Service, but the Indians were not complaining, nor were they surprised at his passing. Regarding the good intentions of the Indian Service the cynicism of the Indians was boundless.

3

When Big Cats Were Around

AT THE OUTSET I was woefully ignorant of the order of life on an Indian reservation, and soon inadvertently put my feet into an entangling web of circumstances which for a time proved embarrassing, to say the least. Yet if life is one round of disillusionment, as many pessimists insist, then all my days in and around Indian agencies were strictly normal. So far as I knew at the time, my first visit to an agency was according to instructions. I hired a driver with a two-horse buggy to carry me some fifty miles from the nearest railroad station to the agency. I took a room at the little frame hotel and then inquired the way to the Major's office to present my credentials, but found he had gone to the railroad by another route. However, the clerk looked at my letters of introduction, seeing no reason why the Major should object to my stopping for awhile. Accordingly, I dismissed my driver and called upon the agency doctor, then the trader, and finally the school superintendent. Being all but a stranger to this kind of life, everything was interesting, even down to the most commonplace details. I now realize how naturally this attitude could be misinterpreted. Perhaps my curiosity resembled a cat's.

On the second day, I was startled by an Indian with an interpreter asking, "Are you a Big Cat?"

Not knowing just what was meant and believing myself a human being, the answer was, "No."

The Indian turned abruptly on his heel and strode away. When I asked the interpreter to explain, he grinned and went his way. Somewhat mystified, I sought the agency doctor, learning that a Cat was a detective, or a secret agent, and that a Big Cat was one detailed from Washington on a special assignment, to check up on the doings of the Major and the traders. Well, I was not a Big Cat, but the cat was out of the bag, so to speak. I was under suspicion, and no doubt closely watched. At first, this was amusing, but soon it began to interfere with my freedom of movement. Conversation with agency employees was constrained, they showing a disposition to answer in monosyllables only.

However, I found many things to occupy my time for the agency seemed astir over the "white man's big Sunday," the Fourth of July. Every holiday impressed the Indian of my day as just a bigger Sunday; the best thing he could see in a Sunday was that no one worked, or urged him to work, hence to his mind it was about the only time the white man acted sensible, but the distinctions the white man drew between Sunday and July Fourth were lost on his pagan mind. What he did grasp was that it was more important than other Sundays, because whereas the Major frowned upon shooting off guns on ordinary Sundays, upon this big Sunday the more shooting the better. Several times I tried to find out just what the glorious Fourth meant to Indians, but without much success. However, I was soon to experience my first Fourth upon a reservation.

The few white people around spent most of their spare time talking excitedly about it. There was nothing strange in this because all came from the larger centers where one feels that he is part of a living society; whereas here they were lost amid open spaces and Indian tipis. The most trying phase of their existence was to stand up against the feeling that they were gradually and surely losing touch with their own kind. On every side I saw efforts, sometimes almost tearful, to magnify fragments of institutions, commonplace enough at home—no one I ever met spoke of the reservation as home. The position of the wife and mother was often tragic. I heard of two women who tried to keep their hold upon life by lonely tea parties in which they set chairs for friends back home. I remember one little girl with deep blue eyes, recently come to the reservation, who begged me to send her a letter, a picture or something from the outside, saying, "Oh! it is so lonely here." So one may understand how it was that the white people around the agency seized upon the Fourth of July with a strangle hold; here at least was the ghost of their national life, and by firing off guns and waving a flag they could feel they were in step with the invisible folks back home.

The Indians began to gather around the agency on the 2nd of July, forming a large camp, the tipis were arranged in a large circle with an opening toward the east. It would have been more picturesque if the Indians had left their wagons at home for it is one thing to see the fine symmetry of a tipi silhouetted against the background of a landscape, and quite a different thing to see it through a wagon wheel. I amused myself noting the misfits of the old and the new, a few young women wearing grotesque calico sun-bonnets, an occasional old man in long leggings and moccasins, but hanging loosely from his shoulders a ready-made, dirty, white-man's shirt. I could not help wondering how he would look in a night shirt, no doubt he would have been proud of one. Occasionally a metal washtub was leaning against a tipi and once I saw a woman sitting on the ground washing clothes in one of them, using a wash board. Indians usually sat on the ground, for tipis were not designed by chair-using peoples, the living space in such a dwelling being well below a clearance of four feet. Like in a modern automobile, you stooped low and backed up to sit down. Of course a tipi is high in the center, but one cannot stand in the fire.

When night came the great camp grew primitively pictureque because the kindly shadows obscured the unsightly wagons and other evidences of the machine age, while the tipis were revealed by the light of the fires within. When a woman bent over a kettle in her cooking, her greatly enlarged silhouette would show a dark shadow upon the canvas of the tipi. I sat through a part of the night enjoying the novel scene. It was by no means a quiet camp; many horses were grazing outside the circle, occasionally one snorted, and those wearing hobbles thumped along like men with crutches. The ground upon which I sat seemed to pick up even distant faint sounds when it had a chance in the rare intervals of silence. Every now and then one of the two to three hundred dogs sneaking around would point his nose toward the heavens and howl, whereupon whole packs would become vocal. However, this racket would be promptly suppressed by a few old women scolding while beating on the ground with large sticks of firewood. I suppose this at once reminded the dogs of frequent beatings with similar clubs, anyhow I marveled at the effectiveness of the method.

After the night had fully settled down I heard the low mellow beat of an Indian drum, then another and another, until every part of the camp was in action. Every now and then there was singing, men and women together. This continued far into the night. It was the first real Indian singing I had heard and it was a revelation. I now realized that this music was designed for singers sitting on the lap of Mother Earth, to be heard by listeners around the adjoining camp fires. Substituting a wooden floor and plastered walls for this virgin sounding board is a slander upon Indian genius.

The next day was the Fourth. There was no shooting but a good deal of bustle, boys, men, and a few young women riding about on horses. Here and there a few men were gambling in a curious game played with a rolling ring and long slender sticks, but the bets were in silver coin. I was told that in the old days when gambling was gambling, men sometimes staked their wives and lost. However, as usual the women of the camp were in action, carrying water, chopping firewood or scurrying along as if working by the white man's clock. Two women passed me with a washboiler full of steaming hot water; this appearing unusual I followed. Soon the boiler was set on a fire in the open, around which a number of women were gathered; then to my surprise a woman dropped a fat puppy from her blanket, beat it to death with a stick of firewood, singed the hair off and dropped the lifeless body into the washboiler; seeing several other puppies about to meet the same fate, I hurried on. Later there were a few horse races, some of the riders were children, some adults. Prizes were given, but a good deal of coin changed hands on the side. Of course, gambling was forbidden by the Major, but since he discreetly stayed away, he knew nothing about it. No doubt in his annual report to Washington, he wrote that all gambling had been stopped.

As I strolled about the camp, every now and then an Indian would grin at me and make curious gestures. These were always the same; the right hand, closed and thumb resting on the second joint of the index finger, was raised until the tip of the nose rested upon the end of the thumb. My first guess was that these Indians were thumbing their noses at me, but by and by it dawned upon me that in the sign-language this meant, "Big Cat." Even little boys sometimes made these gestures and then scampered away. Finally I began to practice this sign talk which greatly added to their merriment.

There was a good deal of love making as in every Indian camp. A number of young dandies strutted about in fine store clothes, supplemented by beaded hat bands, garters, belts, and sometimes a heavily beaded waistcoat. A handsome blanket, usually with a gorgeous beaded band across its middle, was an indispensable part of the courting equipment.

The girls were good dressers too, if their parents could afford it; but any girl who kept herself clean and neat stood an equal chance with the gaily dressed. Courting, like most other affairs in an Indian camp, was in the open, the couple, standing quiet and erect, bundled themselves in a blanket. It was no uncommon sight to see a dozen of these stationary blanketed couples around the edges of the camp.

At this particular time and place it had become fashionable to carry parasols, and to see a girl galloping around on horseback, a flashy parasol bobbing up and down over her head, was a sight not to be seen anywhere else.

In the afternoon there was a parade around the camp, the horses gaily decorated, covered with beaded trappings, while many of the men and boys wore the artistic headdress every white person in these days expects an Indian to wear. Many of the old men were stripped to breech cloth and moccasins, riding barebacked, displaying all their old war regalia and not a few carrying imitation scalps on the ends of poles. In the bright sunlight, this was a scene never to be forgotten. The most impressive affair of this kind was the following year in a camp of almost five thousand souls,

when some eight hundred mounted Indians, resplendent in paint and beaded trappings, paraded through the
camp. The greatest wild west show ever staged, was
nothing in comparison to that.

Later in the day one of the white men explained that
I, and all the other white men in the camp, were to
assemble in the yard at the Major's office to participate
in a sham battle. Soon we were on our way and upon
arrival found the Major with all his employees, mar-
shalled inside the picket fence around his office, and
armed with shot guns and liberally supplied with blank
shells. I was offered a gun, but preferred to use a
camera. Presently, a few Indians were seen peeping
over a hill, imitating the call of a coyote, that being the
way scouts signalled in the old days. In a few minutes
someone shouted, "Here they come." It was a picturesque charge of mounted warriors, riding directly at
us, but when near, wheeling suddenly to subject our
front to a brisk fire. There was shooting enough to
satisfy any Fourth of July enthusiast. Time after time
they charged at us and once one of the warriors made
the cat sign as he passed me. From time to time Indians dropped from their horses to sprawl or sit upon
the ground as if wounded, until many were thus
counted out. Suddenly, as the horsemen were returning
to another charge, the make-believe casualties sprang
to their feet, dashed to the picket fence in front of us,
and reinforced by the dismounting warriors, seized the
Major, carrying him some distance as a prisoner. Upon
his agreeing to pay a steer as ransom, he was released.
This ended the celebration.

The next day was unusually quiet, all the Indians
having moved back to their usual summer camping
places. I was sitting on the little wooden porch in front
of the hotel making notes on the events of the past few
days, when a white man rode up, asking if this was a
place where a stranger could stop for the night. There

was nothing unusual about him. His black horse gave
evidence of docility but efficiency, and was obviously
weary from hard riding. The rider was of moderate
stature, wore blue overalls, a blue-gray shirt and a
rather nondescript felt hat. Around his neck was a
large bandana. Rolled up behind his saddle was a yellow slicker. He wore a simple belt, but no arms. No
waistcoat or other garment was in sight. One of the
pockets of his shirt bulged slightly and under the flap
one could see the edge of a note book. From one hip
pocket protruded a large, long slab of chewing tobacco.
He looked like a New Englander or an Englishman,
and spoke with an accent which might belong to either.
His greeting was friendly and at once we plunged into
an animated conversation. It was soon apparent that he
was a man of some experience and culture, and had
been in most of the large cities of the country. He
volunteered the information that he was employed by a
distant horse ranch, his mission here being to look for
strayed horses. He seemed to like the looks of this
agency and proposed to make this his headquarters for
a time, riding the country round about looking for
horses.

There seemed no reason to doubt his statements, for
he rode away each morning to return at night, or the
next day. When questioned as to what kind of a day he
had, he would sometimes say that he found a horse or
two, at other times nothing. However, I noticed that no
horses accompanied him when he rode back at night,
and when he explained that he left them on the range
to be rounded up later, I began to suspect that he was
looking for horse thieves rather than horses.

He gave his name as Carr. One evening he offered
me some advice, the trend of which was that everybody
was certain that my object here was to get something
on the Major. He suggested that if I worked things
right, I could get the use of government teams, clerks,

interpreters, etc., because the Major was scared. In response for more light on the situation, he expressed surprise at my ignorance. Briefly, some 8,000 head of steers had been shipped up from Texas to graze on the reservation until fat enough to market in Chicago. They were owned by a few outsiders and the Major, but in order to make the business appear legal, a fictitious bill of sale had been drawn in the name of Indians now dead. Naturally, Indians could run their own cattle on the reservation, but no white man could pasture his cattle on the Indian's grass. In other words, here was a case of fraud. Free pasture for 8,000 steers was a bonanza. Anyone should do well at that game.

Now I understood. No wonder the Major was jumpy. When I learned that the landlord of the hotel was in with the Major, many mysteries were explained. Certain signs in my room thus meant that my papers and baggage had been scanned and it came to me why, when Mr. Carr was engaged in conversation with me, the landlord found it convenient to repair the gate, mow the grass or engage in such other work as would bring him within ear-shot. Many other puzzling matters were cleared up, as why I was unable to get a horse to go out upon the reservation; whenever I broached the subject, the available horses were said to be lame or strayed. Mr. Carr explained that this fear of me was not entirely due to a guilty conscience on the part of employees, but largely a result of my lack of discretion. Thus, the first day when my driver was dismissed, he inquired as to when he should return for me and my answer had been, "When it comes time for me to leave here, I shall find a way to get out." Other equally naive remarks made the situation worse instead of better.

After thinking things over, I concluded that this was no place for me; that some other reservation would be preferable. Further, I began to suspect Mr.

Carr, because the doctor informed me that Carr told the Major and everyone around that their suspicions of me were well founded, that I was a Big Cat. So I prepared to depart. I told the landlord that I had hoped to see a real herd of cattle, but that there was no time for it. Of course, he said that the reservation was no place to see many cattle. To the Major I was frank to bluntness, telling him that my purpose here was to study Indians, but that because he suspected me of being a Big Cat, he had made it impossible for me to accomplish my objectives and that I was leaving in disgust. He was apologetic, protesting ignorance on all these matters, but obviously pleased that I was going. However, I could not resist the temptation to suggest that he had made a mistake, for a Big Cat now had all the information he needed, but that none of it came from me. He had been watching the wrong party.

Mr. Carr apologized when I took him to task for using me as a blind, but justified his action on the ground of public service; he seemed to think I should be glad to help out in a good cause. Well, maybe. Anyway, I was learning more about Indian reservations.

When visiting reservations after this I was slow with chance remarks, but even so, here and there I was under suspicion. There were just grounds for suspecting strangers because every now and then a casual visitor proved to be a Little Cat, and on rare occasions, a Big Cat. The latter term was applied to Chief Inspectors; and there was always tension when one of these was on the ground. After I began to feel at home on reservations and was tolerated as a probable disinterested observer, a warning might be whispered in my ears that a Cat was about.

The traders were even more uneasy than the Major because many of their methods would not look so good to an outsider. Further, their big profits made the

salary of the Major look like a school boy's allowance.
As one Major put it, in contrast to the income of the
trader, his salary was little better than a glass eye at a
key hole. In such a situation, it was an exceptional
Major who was not in one way or another enjoying a
rake-off. The trader felt safer if the Major was in on
something; but then both would tremble at the knees if
anyone said, "Big Cat."

I recall how jumpy the agency officials were on one
occasion because a stranger came to the store, posed as
a salesman looking up new business, ran a practiced
eye over the shelves and extracted what information he
could as to retail prices. A few hours afterward the
usual warning came from the Major's office that an
inspector was on the ground; of course, there was
consternation. Even my advice was sought, in the hope
that if worse came to worst, I might know somebody
of importance in Washington. I often read about how
apprehensive people are under dictatorships, where
every other person may be an informer; that may or
may not be true, but among the white officials and
traders on a reservation every one seemed under suspicion. On the other hand, the Indians did not worry;
they seemed to enjoy nothing more than having a "Big
Cat" around. Over and over again they would ask me if
I belonged to that class.

Red tape is a curious thing, everybody denounces it
until appointed to office, whereupon his first act is to
spin a lot more of it just like a spider in a new home.
Indian agencies in our time were enmeshed in it, not
only in strands stretching out from Washington, but in
the counter windings set up by the Major himself. As
an example of government red tape I cite the rule that
an object once bought or received could not disappear
until an auditing inspector gave permission.

If a broom wore out, it could not be thrown away,
nor could a broken axe-handle be discarded, for the

stated reason that each must be counted at least once again. If the audit sheet said 50 brooms, the same 50 brooms must be seen at the next audit. I suppose there was reason to this. For one thing, it may have increased employment by requiring more clerks, but on the other hand, it did not prevent fraud. I heard of a Major turning over the new brooms to the trader in return for an equal number of derelicts, which goes to show that one can usually creep through the finest looking net of red tape. Everywhere I heard of such tricks in substitution, as trading good oats and hay for mouldy, worthless stuff, substituting a lot of trash for good rations intended for the Indians, etc. Many of these tales seemed too crude to be true, but doubtless such things did happen upon many reservations. At times, the very air seemed stuffy with graft.

Not infrequently, horses and cattle wandered off to be secretly killed by Indians or white thieves or mayhap die natural deaths in out of the way places. Strange to say, the rules did not permit an animal to be lost, he must be either alive or dead. So when an animal had not been seen for a long time, the Major would ask two disinterested white men to swear that to the best of their belief said animal died a natural death. Fortunately, the document did not require that you see the animal dead, merely that you had reason to believe it died. I occasionally accommodated the Major by accepting the evidence offered as reasonable, and so swore. Some gossip once came my way that after a certain bad winter, sworn statements were filed to show that some 1200 head of government cattle had frozen to death, whereas the truth of the matter was they were driven off the reservation to join a private herd.

One story I enjoyed was about a government bull—a picturesque friendly beast who grew old and grizzly. As the years passed, he came to be looked upon as little short of an agency mascot. He had lived so long that each time the auditing inspector came around he would ask if the old fellow was still alive; but at last he was missing. No one had seen him for a long time. For years he had been a steady loiterer about the corrals and the hay stacks, but now because of his unusual age, everyone was certain he had died. There was no difficulty in getting the necessary signatures this time. Eventually, the inspector came to check up the property lists, and when handed the affidavits on the bull, he laid them down and remarked with feeling upon the passing of this famous old veteran, but in the midst of the eulogy a deep bass challenge was heard. Even the inspector recognized that sound, long familiar to all residents of the reservation. Looking out toward the plaza, they saw the bull facing the Major's quarters as if to say, "Here I am!" As the Major tore up the now useless papers, the inspector remarked dryly that the bull was just in time, a minute later, he would have been officially dead.

That bull was still alive upon my last visit to the reservation and I have often speculated as to how long he did hold out. During my stay, he cracked down on an ugly bull-dog, recently brought into this land of Indian curs. One day the dog saw the bull standing quietly in front of the Major's office and perhaps the sight set off an hereditary urge in his family tree. Anyway he went after this traditional enemy of his race. At first the bull ignored him; he had fought off far bigger game in his day as his scarred body testified. Finally with a leap, the dog caught a fold of the skin on the bull's lower jaw and held on as such a dog can. The bull seemed surprised, and finding that a mere toss did not shake off the dog, put his entire strength into the next effort. It was now the turn of the dog to be surprised, his hold slipped when his neck was cracked like a whip and his body went whirling through the air to fall some distance away with a dull thud. For a time the dog lay still, then he limped away, as the bull resumed his favorite post.

The reader may wish to know if the Indians were disturbed by the rascality in the reservation system. At first they knew too little of white methods to realize just how they were being defrauded; what they did know was that treaty promises were rarely kept and that much of the food offered them was revolting. Yet in my day, they seemed to have an uncanny understanding of the game. Not infrequently they sent letters to Washington, but nothing came of it. Eventually the pessimism of the Indians was so pervading, their lack of confidence in all statements so pronounced, that they expected the worst and did nothing.

Yet it would be unfair to the Indian Service and to the many good agents of that day to close this chapter here. There was no other place for the Indian to go. The frontier was all but gone, white people were taking up the land everywhere, the reservation gave the Indian a haven. He was, in a sense, a prisoner in a concentration camp, but his scalp was safe. He enjoyed free medical service, and free schooling. At times he was hungry, his food poorly chosen, but few starved to death after 1890. Naturally, the Indian was far from happy. I suspect that if all promises had been kept, all officials had been honest and intelligent, there would still have been sorrow and gloom because the foot of the conqueror pressed down upon the neck of the Indian.

4

Ration Tickets and the Beef Issue

THE OLD WIFE of a celebrated Indian chief to whom I
was once introduced, shook her fist and said—"You
belong to the wicked race that took away our buffalo."
The conversation had turned to the question of rations
and the beef issue. She cast aside the dignity and poise
befitting her position, and spoke with a sharp tongue:
"Sickness is now on every hand. Children are dying.
Strong men are going to their graves before their time.
All this happens because of the bad food the white
man gives us."

Her speech might have been moving had she not
rolled up her sleeve to show her "emaciated arm."
Some days earlier I had watched her chopping wood
with a white man's axe, giving it the full swing from
the shoulder seen only in a professional. So I addressed
her as "Grandmother" and tried to convey the idea that
even on white man's food she was a better wood-
chopper than most white men. She was pleased with
this flattery, but bared her arm once more and declared
that it was a sorry sight compared with what it was
when she had all the buffalo meat she could eat. With
that, she picked up her dirty sack and set off to get her
share of the detested beef, now ready for issue.

From the time when the Indians of the Old West were first segregated on reservations the food problem was always one of the most troublesome for the Government agents. It was their job not only to keep some semblance of order among a war-like, dispossessed population, but to provide food for a nation of red men who for centuries had made their living by hunting and who had built up around the chase a set of traditions so deeply engrained that they had become almost instinctive.

A system of allotted rations was developed which grew directly out of the various compensative treaties by which the white man sought to placate the Indian for the robbery of his more prolific hunting lands.

To the old time reservation Indian, the agency roll and the ration ticket were synonymous, and on issue days they meant food. Little beaded skin pockets were made to protect these tickets, and such may occasionally be seen in museum cases. The practice of issuing goods and food began in Treaty days, for the Kings of England and France recognized the reality of the several tiny Indian nations, sent to them messages of good will, as one King to another, and though the procedure might sometimes be a farce, there was a serious side to it in that these Christian rulers eased their conscience by admitting that the Indian had rights of possession, which were not to be denied without compensation. So a treaty would be drawn up in which the Great Mothers or the Great Fathers, as the case might be, promised that if the Indian would keep his feet off certain lands and his hands off the white-man's scalp, he might enjoy certain other clearly defined lands upon which to hunt forever, free from white intrusion. Finally, the Indian was to receive the value of certain sums of money in specified goods.

For example, we may cite a treaty made at Laramie, Wyoming. Here in 1851 representatives of many Indian tribes were gathered to negotiate such a document. Some of the items in that treaty were as follows:

The hunting territories for each of the several tribes were marked out on a map.

Each tribe was to recognize the United States as dominant.

Each was to remain within the bounds to its specified territory. In other words, to stay at home.

They were not to cross into Canada nor have anything to do with the British.

They were not to fight among themselves.

In the way of compensation for these and many other obligations each tribe was to receive certain benefits. For example, the Blackfoot of Montana were to have delivered to them each year, for ten years, $35,000 worth of goods and $15,000 more was to be spent by the Government on schools and agriculture. Considering all the trouble these Indians had previously made, this was cheap enough. There was a joker, of course, in specifying goods in dollars; fine pickings here for the politician with a pull. Transportation up the Missouri River was primitive and uncertain. What was even more to the point, many Indians along the river looked upon a cargo boat as a specially designed target for rifle practice, a procedure which often reminded the Captain of the boat that he had left something behind in St. Louis, necessitating his immediate return. Whatever the circumstances, it was not an uncommon occurrence for a consignment of treaty goods to disappear somewhere along the river, nor need we be surprised if Indians waiting through the summer occasionally expressed their impatience in terms of powder and ball. To them a treaty was a treaty no more, if broken. However, the Government agents would urge the Indians to be patient, assuring them the fault was not with the Great Father whose heart bled for them, and eventually some of the goods would arrive at a designated point on the river bank.

From a reputed eye-witness I heard the story of one such issue of treaty goods. There was a quantity of stale army biscuit and wormy salt pork; this they rejected at sight; anyway buffalo were still near at hand. There were coffee and rice. The latter they had never seen; the former was rarely urged upon them by the traders. Some of the Indian women took the green coffee beans, put them into a kettle and boiled and boiled; each time they tasted the mess it was worse than before. So, at last, they abandoned the coffee in disgust.

There were several hundred rolls of calico. They knew what this was, but the trader had sold them only a few yards in a piece. Never had they come into possession of such an unending fabric. A few mischievous youngsters found it was funny to jerk at the loose ends, watching the cloth unroll, especially when one ran with it. Many rolls were unwound in this way. Finally, one inventive fellow tied the loose end to the tail of a horse, gave the animal a kick in the ribs, whence, seeing the strange shape in his rear, the horse stampeded. This was the beginning, and soon several hundred frightened Indian ponies were dashing here and there on the plains with long, gaily colored streamers behind. All the camp, young and old, screamed themselves hoarse at this ludicrous sight.

But let us return now to the experience of the Blackfoot who were to receive $35,000 in goods each year. One of the early consignments contained a few thousand fish hooks. Perhaps that does not move you, but this tribe would not eat fish, the mention of it was enough to turn their stomachs; they felt about it just as you would if you were asked to eat caterpillars. What could these people do with all those fish hooks!

A few years later we find these Indians petitioning

the Great Father in Washington to cut out the fish hooks, the coffee, rice, hard tack, and other useless stuff, and to give them more powder and ball, blankets, shirts and flour. It is to be hoped their complaint was heeded. Incidentally, we note that the Great Father was further reminded that though they had been promised schools, nothing came of it.

It was in such bargains by treaty that the pattern was set for the subsequent ration and annuity systems. The unfortunate feature of the procedure was that all these treaties, like many others, were "scraps of paper." Before the Indian had time to adjust himself to one contract, another would be made, curtailing his hunting lands or removing him to new locations until at last, hemmed in by white homesteaders and cattle ranches, he was cooped up on reservations and forced to stay at home. It was the monotony of staying at home that broke the hearts of those natural gypsies.

The great reservations were between the Mississippi and the Rocky Mountains, the land of the cowboy and the Indian of Wild West fame. For the most part, these Indians ate buffalo meat and little else. Even our doctors now admit that one can live in health on a diet of meat alone if all parts of the animal are consumed. But the coming of the reservations was coincident with the passing of the buffalo, and of buffalo hunting.

The popular notion of my day seemed to be that Indians lived on dog flesh. Some tribes did eat puppies on special occasions but other tribes held such food in abhorrence. Merely to take note of the gangs of adult and aged dogs slinking around an Indian camp might refute the idea that they were important food animals. So although some Indian tribes could not sympathize with the white man's aversion to dog, many of them would agree that the very idea of such food was nauseating; they would starve rather than eat one. And if the Plains Indian loved his dog, he adored his horse. So it is not strange that he never ate horse except in cases of dire need. Even in my time the mention of horse meat never met with approval.

When the Government undertook to feed these Indians, they first offered them army rations, hard tack and salt pork, but the stomachs of these fresh meat lovers revolted at such a mess. Illness and gloom stalked through the camps. Then live cattle were brought for the beef issue, and with them one of the most picturesque features of old reservation life was inaugurated.

At regular intervals cowboys with chaps, high-heeled boots and oversized spurs, eased bunches of steers toward the reservation, where after being duly inspected and counted, they were to be held by night-riders for issue on the following day. The reader who has never camped near such a night-herd has missed something that defies description. I experienced something like it once at a small agency.

The animals were held in close formation through the night, and their grumbling bellowing was continuous though rising and falling in rhythmical waves with every now and then a rushing roar as one hears on a beach during a windy day. For hours I lay in my camp bed marvelling at this unusual, weird sound, and visualizing the vague shapes of the night-riders keeping their cattle within bounds, prepared at any moment to cope with a stampede.

These cattle were to be taken over by the Indians, a few here, a few there, in an effort to set them up in the beef business, according to the theory that, though still wards of the Government, they should become self-supporting. It seems strange, at this distance, why the Government did not recognize the deep-set, spontaneous interest of the Indian in horses and set him to raising them. There probably was a complex of reasons. For one, the horse stood for the old life and so was to be frowned upon. Again, as noted, most Indians had an aversion to horse meat and since the whites did not eat horses either, scarcely could they be expected to encourage the Indians to raise them for food. On the other hand, the Indians were urged to raise cattle. In this, there was but moderate success. Somehow or other, even the western white man rarely warmed up to a cow as a pet and between him and the male of the bovine species, perpetual enmity was in evidence. This being the situation, we should not be too hard upon the Indian. To him cattle were but mongrel buffalo—white man's buffalo he often called them, and there were no traditions of domestic friendship between his ancestors and the buffalo. Anyway, the buffalo took care of himself, why not the ox? Of course, what was in the back of the white man's head was milk, butter and cheese. He took for granted that any person in his right mind would like milk. But the Indian revolted at the idea.

Nor does the Indian stand alone. The Chinese, surrounded for ages by milk-using peoples, refused to taste the stuff, saying that only savages and moral perverts would rob the calf of its proper food. Again in the cattle country surrounding the Indian, white sentiment was not what would be expected. For long, Montana was distinguished as the state exporting the most cattle and importing the most milk products. In those days one could start a shooting match by asking a cowboy if he ever milked.

One of the incidents of reservation days I treasure most happened when a roundup took place near our agency. One of the cowboys was brought in desperately ill. The agency doctor looked him over, then turned to the patient's companions and remarked that about the only thing to pull him through would be fresh milk. The cowboys looked sheepishly from one to another and asked where it was to be had. The rejoinder was, "Milk a cow."

"Won't canned milk do?" they asked.

"No," said the doctor, "he will die if you can't get him fresh milk."

The cowboys withdrew into a huddle and discussed, with emphasis on the latter syllable. Finally, they rode out toward the corral, rounded up a cow with a calf, and drove her into the enclosure. Of course, by this time she was in a fighting mood, but was roped in good cowboy style, thrown and tied. One cowboy took a tin cup, squatted beside the cow and seized a teat. Now, if you recall your first attempt at milking, you understand. You may know, also, that a cow must be in a friendly mood, otherwise, as the farmers say, "she will not let her milk down." Anyhow, after long labor and much profanity, about a spoonful of milk was in the cup. Then another cowboy took a turn, but with no better luck. Once around they accumulated three or four spoonfuls; then all stood up and swore most emphatically that not another drop would they milk, Jim could just die if he was so stubborn as all that. The terrified cow was released and with a snort or two, tail in air, "streaked for the blue."

I never saw Indians milk, but have heard that some of them did after they learned how in a school. Yet, when an Indian saw a steer or a cow his mouth began to water, his stomach was as completely conditioned in its reflexes as Pavlov's famous laboratory dog. But it was not because he recognized milk, butter and cheese; what he saw was a wealth of fresh meat. Even a few years ago I heard of an illustration. A sick baby being in need of milk, the doctor urged that a cow be bought. As of old the many relatives of the family rallied manfully to the call for help. Enough money was soon raised for a cow and a few Indian families set out for the outside farming country, where a purchase was made. But on the way back they were met by a messenger telling them the baby had died. So they made camp, conferred for a while, then butchered the poor cow and stayed on the spot until the last scrap was eaten. No wonder the most pessimistic people I ever knew were veteran employees in the Indian Service.

The old timers in the Indian Service could tell how cattle were issued in their day and it was as exciting as a buffalo hunt.

A large corral was built, a kind of primitive stock yard, from which the issue was made. There was a chute reminding one of the mechanism for loading steers into freight cars, but with the difference that the steer was shot out into the open instead of into a traffic prison. Above the chute rose a little house not unlike that of the switch tender in a railroad yard. This was the post of the issue clerk and the keeper of the ration roll. The clerk would call out a name and if an Indian responded and was identified, the one or more steers due his family group were driven into a little pen at the entrance to the chute. Then when all was ready the clerk made a mark in his book and shouted, "Release!" The gate to the chute swung wide and the panicky steers rushed into the open, where lay in wait a brigade of boys and men clutching repeating rifles and mounted on impatient ponies. True to fashion some were stripped to breech cloth and moccasins and smeared with war paint. The steers seeking freedom were greeted with a war-whoop and, more frightened than ever, tails in air, bolted toward the horizon. At their heels rode a yelling band of redskins. For several generations the Indians had ridden hard after buffalo and it was their fixed belief that meat was no good unless the animal had run miles at top speed. A range steer could run, he was built for the work, and when cornered he could fight, but the odds were all against him here, for when the leader of his pursuers thought his blood properly heated, the shooting began, and that was the end.

In due course came the butchering, the first job being to skin the animal. In the offing the women were waiting with packhorses; they soon arrived, for by tradition the meat belonged to them, so, of course, they must do most of the butchering and above all, carry the meat home. In the old days the man shot the animal down, refreshed himself by eating some of the liver or a kidney, then came home and told his women where they could find the carcass. And before you pass harsh judgment on the Indian's failure to do the heavy work, remember that the inexorable law of his people said that it was her meat.

Even an ultra modern abattoir is a poor place to go for exercising aesthetic impulses and if one yearns to know what our forefathers gazed upon in an Indian massacre, he should see butchering in the old way, faces, hands, and bodies smeared with red.

We are now looking in upon a time when a horse, war paint, and a rifle so revived the ancient patterns of Indian life that no white man was altogether safe. It was an easy step from the blood of a steer to something more serious, and we must not forget the repressed desires of the early reservation Indian for fresh scalps, for horse-stealing, for heroic deeds. So when the Indian let himself go at the beef issue, there was no knowing where he would rein-up again. Many old time employees admitted how they dreaded the beef issue.

Many stories were current about a certain hardheaded Major; even the Indians had traditions recounting his virtues and exploits. Once when he was in a tight place, surrounded by threatening Indians, demanding impossible things and threatening to seize the Government's property and make away with the whites, he calmly called their attention to the vast potential magic power of the whites and to bring it home to them, read appropriate passages from the Bible, how the Lord of Hosts would smite those who opposed His

will, etc., until the fear of the white man's God gripped
their souls. Certainly here was a hero in the Indian
Service, nor will you be surprised to learn that the
Major in question was a fighting Scotchman of the old
school.

Of course, one way to have shown the Indian a good
time would have been to turn the whole herd loose.
Something like this happened occasionally, as once in
Dakota when a violent thunderstorm at night stampeded the herd. It broke away toward the Black Hills
in fan-shaped formation so that all the cowboys could
do was to round up a handful. But the Indians went on
a grand hunt—and why not? The cattle were to be
theirs in the end. It was a gala time for the hunters. All
the old buffalo technique could be used in scouting for
the game and organizing the attack. And then, plenty
of fresh meat. It is true that many times the wrong
cattle were killed, for the hunters followed the slogan,
"Shoot first, ask questions afterward." A lot of trouble
was made for Government officials, but the Indians
experienced a temporary psychological rejuvenation.

The white man killed his beef in what he called the
civilized way, and even the most indifferent agents
were shocked over such savage customs as butchering in
the open. At last one of them wrote to Washington—

"Beef is still slaughtered for issue in the same bar-
barous and wasteful way as practiced in the days of
Abraham, and at the siege of Troy—shot, skinned and
dressed on the open prairie in the rudest way. . . . This
whole business should be reformed as speedily as may
be. Slaughterhouses should be built, with proper water
supply. Indians should be taught, and then hired to do
the butchering in an economical, cleanly way; and last,
but not least, the beef should be weighed out on the
scales, so that the weak and unprotected should be as
certain of their lawful allowance as the strong."

The last statement strikes us as funny, for Indians always share their food. To weigh it out would be about as useless as to insist upon filling a pond by pouring an equal amount of water upon each square yard.

Well, when even the agents began to talk against the beef issue, change was in the offing. Anyhow, on the reservation everything was so transient that the Indian was in perpetual bewilderment, for no sooner had he adjusted his economy to one code than another was substituted. And so it was with the spectacular beef issue. The efficiency experts at Washington were scornful of such ways of butchering, shocked at spreading the carcass upon a fresh clean bed of prairie grass. And so an order went forth (most every mail brought the agent new orders) directing that a slaughterhouse be erected. Of course, upon the heels of the order arrived a man recommended by his Congressman and duly appointed a butcher, as his credentials showed. Probably he had never killed a steer nor even seen it done, but what were the odds! The meat was for Indians. Anyway, a few Indians would be employed to do the real work, the butcher's job being to fill out some blanks, and pay-check orders.

So it was that the Great Father demanded that the Indian quit killing cattle and that the Major issue to them, over the butcher's block, clean, lean, meat. No doubt the reader is ready to applaud, but there was and is a joker in it all. Tuberculosis became rampant, children began to show all kinds of tooth trouble, etc., causing those in charge of reservations to send urgent calls for doctors and medicines to try to undo what was being done in the name of decency. Of course, we are still doing such things, shutting daylight from our bodies and at the same time paying high prices for medicines to compensate for the deficiency, insisting upon devitalizing foods but keeping the chemist and the druggist busy preparing vitamin compounds.

I visited some of these "reformed" butchering places, equipped with the improved sanitary methods. I found it best to hold my nose as I approached and shut my eyes to avoid seeing poor miserable old women quarreling over the parts rejected by the butchers, because Nature had taught them these were essential to health. This new way may have been efficient, but its sanitary aspects were nothing to brag about.

Under this new regime the ration tickets called for so many pounds of lean beef, ready for the pot; certain days were posted for beef issues, requiring the Indians to make long journeys in wagons or with packhorses.

In aboriginal times all Indians seem to have enjoyed gypsying around and the ration system offered a good substitute in the journeys to and from the agency. On many large reservations, each family claimed a log cabin, but was seldom found living there. They would set out a week or more before ration day to congregate in large camps around the agency. This was much more interesting than staying at home. After the beef was secured the surplus was dried, and this could best be done in camps here and there over the reserve. Some agents did not like this, as—

"The Indians [U. S. Indian Report, 1892, p. 454.] were accustomed once a month to take all their children and such belongings as they were able to take and move into the agency to receive their rations. They always started in time so that they could visit along the road coming in and were an equal length of time getting back to their homes. The results entailed were: Neglect of field and stock and the taking of the children from the schools; also, endangering of the health and lives of those who were at all weak physically. At an issue some time in January last, during the severe winter weather, a child was frozen to death on the mother's back. This, of course, is an extreme case, but the system entails great physical suffering on the part of the women, children, and the old and decrepit."

I do not take these remarks seriously for these Indians did like to go somewhere; moving camp was their joy. I never could understand why Indian agents objected to the Indians having a good time. Perhaps the answer is, that the white man got his rations by the sweat of his brow, the Indian by going on a picnic.

The theory back of rations was the same as behind relief in time of great depressions in white society: all rations were to be temporary, to ease off gradually, and thus put pressure upon the Indians to become self-supporting. There was often a hue and cry in polite society to do away with this so-called degrading charity, this creator of shirkers and dependents, until at last these reformers had their way. Rations were ordered abolished; starvation was looked upon as an effectual goad to force the Indians to superhuman efforts. Like all rules from Washington, these new orders were abrupt.

Rations stopped. Naturally it was a shock. The old and the sick could not work, so as a compromise a select list was made and rations issued to them. All this accomplished was to divide the individual rations into tiny feeds. Indians have always been liberal with food; not to divide with everyone in sight is unthinkable. So there should have been no surprise as to the outcome of limiting rations to the old people. Each of them lived with somebody and that somebody and all his many relations came in for a share. The result was tragic, for now everyone was hungry. Thus the starvation process of civilizing the Indian was put to work, but about all that came of it was greater poverty, malnutrition and gloom. Possibly among those directing our Indian policies were some hard realists who secretly hoped the Indian problem would be solved by death and disease, but if so, they were doomed to disappointment. For centuries the Indian had been hardened by adversity. He could go without food and drink an amazingly long time. On the other hand, when food was at hand there seemed no limit to his capacity. Perhaps this was his adjustment to the situation. Anyhow, the Indian did not starve to death and though his death rate rose, his birth rate remained high, if we can trust the statistics available. History tells us that temporary food shortages have always confronted mankind, and students of population tell us that, strange as it may sound, a depression seems to step up the birth rate whereas prosperity inhibits it. If this proves to be true, we suspect the long survival of the human race is due to such a compensating relation. Anyhow, everyone around the old reservations knew what an Indian could do with food.

Once, when traveling in the Indian country, we stopped for lunch, since nightfall should find us at the agency. Before our little fire was mature enough for cooking we spied an Indian coming our way. One of my guides once said an Indian could smell grub ten miles away and often it seemed there must be more truth than fiction in the saying. Anyhow, there were no Indians in sight when we made camp. He was an old man, with gray hair and a crooked leg which he assisted with a long staff, yet the speed with which he arrived was astonishing.

Soon he was seated near the fire and as we lunched we passed food to him, but the real exhibition of his technique came later. There remained a large package of crackers, about ½ pound of butter, a few slices of cheese, a bottle of pickles, a large can of salmon, two cans of tomatoes and a moderate amount of other leftovers. When we set this before him he hitched up his blanket and prepared for action. First he asked that all the cans be opened. This done, he fell to. Every now and then he would pause and attempt to say something which sounded like, "wash-tay." He being a Sioux, this probably meant "fine, good, etc." Though he had pre-

viously eaten as much as I had he consumed everything
put before him, and as we rode away, I saw our guest
industriously licking the tins that nothing be wasted.
No doubt his diet had been most meager for days, but
now luck having come his way, he could stand another
fast. He was especially fortunate in that no other Indian sniffed our smoke, for then he would have merely
shared in a moderate feast.

I have said that these Indians loved horses and revert
to it again because it cannot be over-emphasized. Some
of the mistakes the Government made could have been
avoided if this had been fully understood. Everyone
now knows that the prairie Indian lived with his
horses, in fact, he so loved horses in general that as
soon as he laid eyes upon one he wanted to steal it. His
folk-lore dinned into his soul the feeling that about the
only heroic deed was to get away with a stranger's
horse. The journals of fur traders bristle with denunci-
ations of the ingratitude of Indian guests, who though
wined and dined, did not hesitate on their way home to
steal the horses of their host. But how could the Indian
do otherwise, brought up on the idea that only a stupid
moron or a moral pervert would pass up an opportunity to run away with a horse. The annals of the Canadian Mounted Police—a grim record of Indian behavior—contain many enlightening incidents. Thus on a
Canadian reserve, a group of young adolescents,
moved by the heroic tales of their elders and feeling
that they had reached the age where it was up to them
to show they deserved a place in society, secretly
organized themselves into a war party and in due time
successfully raided a neighboring settlement. Trium-
phantly, they rode home yelling true to fashion, expecting to be lionized. In a way they were; most of their
elders admired them for doing what they themselves
dared not undertake, but the wiser heads knew that the
good old times had passed, so they reluctantly gave the

horses to their agent for return to their owners. To their simple minds that should have been the end of it, but they were to learn something new about the ways of the white man, for the police came, seized these children, and a court sentenced them to prison.

When reservations were first set up it was too much to expect that raiding for scalps and horses would cease immediately. Even in the old days, a war party was supposed to set off secretly; the reason for this is not clear, but perhaps explained by the fact that the Indian is rarely communicative about any of his serious intentions, not even to his family. So it need not be surprising that many such parties got away unknown to the agent. Yet every such situation drew the ire of those in power and in this case the agents organized spy systems. But this would have been ineffective if the telegraph had not come upon the scene. Hearing that a war party was out or about to set out, the agent would wire all the surrounding posts and settlements. This usually resulted in the annihilation of the party. On a reserve in Montana, I was shown where a raiding party of Cree made their last stand.

One afternoon, the Major received a wire that such a party was out and probably headed his way. At once the alarm was given and every adventurous Indian and squawman watched through the night. Eventually, the Cree raiding party was sighted and before they could seize horses, were surrounded. According to mode, they dug in on a knoll and fought it out. Eventually all were killed, duly scalped, despoiled of their arms and clothing and left to the buzzards as a warning to all future raiders. In my day fragments of their bones were still lying about and several stakes standing to mark where they fell. Perhaps the local historical society should put up a tablet to commemorate the ending of this chapter in human history, for this was the last attempt.

There is something peculiarly fitting in recalling ration day on these old-time reservations, because we now live in a situation that presents some analogies. When the Indians were placed upon reservations it was necessary to clothe and feed them. There was no escape from it, but once this policy was under way there seemed no humane way to turn back. So the Indian is still dependent upon Government aid in spite of all that has been done and undone to make him over into a white man.

It is not a pleasant subject, this story of governmental attempts to transform a nomad hunting people into a group of sedentary herders or farmers. But it shows once more how we go blundering about the world trying to improve the manners of other people only to make a mess of it. And the pity of it is that the damage can never be repaired. I cannot help but wish the good old days could come back for the Indian. Even the Office of Indian Affairs so yearns for the past that it has introduced living buffalo to some of the larger reservations, so that they can be ridden down in aboriginal style and the old time pemmican can be found in every tent. In imagination the Indian sees joyful meat eaters gathering around the evening campfire, muffled in warm buffalo robes. Yet it is a vain hope, for at best it will be but a counterfeit of the good old times when West was West and Indians were Indians. Popular sentiment is rapidly being won to the cause of Conservation and much laudable progress has been made toward the preservation of the birds and the beasts. But let us not forget that all over the world primitive man is being destroyed. The prevention of this deserves the best scientific thought of our time.

5

The Great Depression
in the Indian Country

ONCE WORD got out among the Indians of the reservation that I owned a buffalo skin—one that had come down from the olden time. First a venerable man paid me a visit, asked to see and feel of the skin. The reverence and humility with which he presented himself to it were impressive. Others came and returned, to kneel before this sacred object, to touch its deep fur and not infrequently, to pray. Even the sick were brought in to sit in its presence, all of which was so moving as to make one cease to feel happy in the selfish possession of this relic of the past, so I left it in care of the chief. Even at this hour, upon many reservations, similar relics of the buffalo are carefully guarded, and many devout Indians are bowing in prayer to "Our Father, the Buffalo."

All of which means that to the old-time Plains Indian the buffalo was life itself. In our day he placed a buffalo skull upon the altar when he appealed to his tribal gods for guidance. Even then these relics of the past were rare and a white man could earn their everlasting gratitude by presenting one to them. Recently the United States Government gave small herds of buffalo to the Dakota, Crow and Blackfoot Indians. The emotional response can well be imagined, the return of the buffalo even though to a wire-fenced range is a symbol of hope that the Indian may yet find a way out.

Some of my older readers will recall their elders stalking about in magnificent buffalo-skin overcoats, remember many a childhood sleigh ride when they were snugly placed between two adults, with chin resting upon the turned-over furry edge of a great buffalo skin lap-robe. The insatiable demand for such overcoats and robes urged the white hunters on to the extinction of the buffalo. The conservationists say this was a stupid tragedy, but it was inevitable, for the rise of farms and cattle ranches was incompatible with wild buffalo herds and would have demanded their extinction ultimately.

But to the Indians, the buffalo meant meat. Good meat, too, if we may believe them, and the enthusiastic praises of the many veteran plainsmen who ate little else from preference rather than necessity. The shock that our Western Indians experienced when the herds vanished, is an old story. But the suddenness of the loss was the appalling part of it. It is true that the end of the buffalo was foreseen by intelligent Indians and whites, but no one expected it to be so abrupt. We are told that even the white hunters, who the year before (1882) killed all the buffalo they could find, went confidently back to kill as many more. Where all these were to come from was not considered, the popular belief being that their number was inexhaustible. The aboriginal Indians entertained a belief that the Great God of the Buffalo kept reserve herds in an immense cave from which he would issue them in case of need. Perhaps the optimistic plainsman had somehow caught the spirit of the Indian's mythical background. The white men who formulated reservation policies and who drew up treaties for the Indians to sign knew the buffalo were doomed, but hoped to ease the Indian off to farming for a living as the herds declined. But even they failed to count on the suddenness of the event, and it upset all of their plans.

The following extracts from the annual reports of Indian agents covering the short space of four years present in their factual brevity a striking picture of the course of events. For example, the agent at Fort Peck, Montana, wrote:

1881—"The Indians had a fair hunt last fall and winter, a large hunting party remaining out in the buffalo country till early January when they returned with an abundance of dried meat and plenty of good buffalo robes which they sold to the traders at a good price. Good robes were sold to my knowledge for $12.

"Early in July, all the Indians who had horses went across the river 30 to 100 miles southwest, where they found buffalo in abundance. A large majority of the Indians remaining out during July and August, they claimed to have killed and dressed 4500 buffalos during this hunt. . . ."

1882—"During the past year, my Indians have had a great deal of trouble finding buffalo, on account of the white hunters and foreign Indians trespassing on their hunting grounds. My Indians secured but few robes last winter and nearly all the meat they lived on was taken from the carcasses of buffalo killed by white hunters, they wanting the robe only and making very little use of the meat. The traders paid very liberally for robes the entire winter.

"In the early part of last June I called the chiefs and head men together and told them that it was necessary that all should go to hunt buffalo; that our provisions would not reach for all. They went, but many went reluctantly. . . . Some returning report the buffalo scarce and scattering; that the grass . . . is burnt off, and that there is no feed for the buffalo on their reservation; that the white hunters occupy all of the country south of the Missouri River."

1883—"Heretofore this people was expected to hunt and provide for their own subsistence for at least two-thirds of the year, the government furnishing supplies for about one-third. While the buffalo roamed in large herds over these vast plains, it was an easy matter to subsist, and, according to the Indian way of living, they lived in luxury and there was no incentive for them to work; but now the game has practically disappeared, for between the Indians and the many white hunters the buffalo are a thing of the past in this Northwest. Neither the Department nor the Indians anticipated such a sudden disappearance of the game; therefore no adequate provision has been made for their subsistence during the present fiscal year."

That such a condition was widespread is indicated in the report of the agent at the Blackfoot reservation in Montana.

1884—"When I entered upon the duties of agent, I found the Indians in a deplorable condition. Their supplies had been limited and many of them were gradually dying of starvation. I visited a large number of their tents and cabins the second day after they had received their weekly rations. . . . All bore marks of suffering from lack of food but the little children seemed to have suffered most; they were so emaciated that it did not seem possible for them to live long; and many of them have since passed away. To feed these Indians, about 2300 in number, from April 1 to June 30 I had . . . only one and a half ounces bacon, three and a half ounces beef, and less than five ounces flour per day for each individual. I had no beans, rice, hominy, salt, nor any other articles of food except sugar, tea and coffee (of which I had only enough for the sick and infirm). . . . In the forepart of May I was reduced to such a strait that I was compelled to issue over 2000 pounds of bacon which had been condemned by a board of survey the past winter, but which I found not to be in as bad condition as had been supposed. In the latter part of June and forepart of July, so great was their destitution that the Indians stripped the bark from the saplings that grow along the creeks and ate the inner portion to appease their gnawing hunger. The buffalo on which these people formerly subsisted is now extinct and they will be compelled to rely upon the food furnished them by the government until they can be taught to support themselves by civilized pursuits."

These reports direct from the Indian country speak for themselves, but the pressure upon spirit and emotion was even greater than upon living economy and the suspicion is that many deaths after the passing of the buffalo were due to non-material factors. For confronting the Indian was a forbidding and uninspiring outlook. No longer could he look forward to the long hunting expeditions so dear to him, but what was worse all the worthy aspirations and ambitions sanctioned by his culture were thwarted. It was not merely unemployment he faced, the economic order of his tribe collapsed. This bore hardest upon the youth. Drinking, gambling and petty intrigue were now the only outlets to self-expression. Even with enough government food to keep body and soul together, the Indian was staring ahead into an unknown void.

This great economic and spiritual depression involved far more tribes than had been caught up in the toils of any other reservation calamity. The reason is not far to seek, for the great grass land, the main range of the buffalo, stretched from Texas to Saskatchewan up in Canada. Spread out a map if you will, showing the whole of North America and note how depleted the grand old continent would look if you should cut out all the surface between the Rocky Mountains on the west, the Mississippi River on the east, and from well down into western Texas up to Saskatchewan in Canada. In all this area the most accessible and satisfactory food supply was the buffalo, and as may be expected, the economy of the many tribes residing therein was primarily adjusted to the processing (to use a new word recently coined by the Democratic party) of the buffalo. In no other part of the Indian country of the United States was there such economic uniformity—

which is but another way of saying that the economy of the buffalo country was highly specialized. Hence, the sudden vanishing of the buffalo let the bottom out of everything. Under such circumstances, the Indian could see no escape ahead. There was little use in fighting the white man—he had always failed at that game. So all he could do was hope for the return of the good old days, the economic symbol of which became a buffalo skull.

The time was now ripe for a fanatical religious movement. Submerged racial groups have often sought a way out in an intensification of their religious folklore. Adversity has always challenged man. Sometimes he wins out. Sometimes he is overwhelmed. But psychologically, hard times prepare a people for change, making them receptive to any emotional appeal. This is seen to be true whether you go back into history to discover the roots of great religions or turn to modern Europe with its youth movements and militaristic fanaticism tantamount to religion.

Of course, there were optimists who saw a silver lining in the crisis among the Plains Indians. They hoped that the Indian, once bereft of his buffalo (which even to the white man symbolized the old way of Indian life), would come into the fold, so to speak, and be a more docile pupil of the schools and churches. That they were wrong cannot now be doubted. The history of all submerged people seems to fly in the face of this theory. Moreover, tangible proof to the contrary was available among the Iroquois of New York, surrounded by white people since the French and Indian War, and among the conservative villages of the Southwest where churches have stood for more than two centuries. Both these widely separated communities had their depressions but have remained pagan in thought and worship to this day. But let it not be supposed that the missionary attempts to educate these

Indians were wholly unsuccessful. Many times in the Indian country we heard thoughtless, contemptuous remarks flung at the efforts of missionaries and government schools. These critics forgot that many young Indians left school able to speak and write English, that in the large boarding schools, young people from many tribes were thrown together, that they had to learn English if they wanted to talk at all, that lasting friendships were thus formed which resulted in their writing letters after returning to their respective reservations. In short, that a groundwork of common ties and language was laid in these schools for the development of a widespread youth movement that could never have been possible without the unwitting aid of white teachers and missionaries. Tribes formerly hostile were now caught up in a network of friendships.

The religious "revolution" was coming and these educated youths were to be its main protagonists. It is interesting to note in this connection that youth has almost always been the vanguard of such uprisings whether in primitive cultures or in modern. It is a commonplace saying that irrational fanaticism is essential to every popular revolt, anyhow fanatics of a peculiarly Indian sort were soon to appear upon the scene. The Indian had for long been a believer in the superhuman. His own helplessness in the face of Nature was ever apparent to him, and just because so many situations in life mysteriously balked his individual efforts whereas others succeeded, he put his faith more and more in the good or ill wishes of the unseen. Such a power could not be tricked into helping him, but it could be humane. And if ever the buffalo Indian needed the help of the gods, it was at this hour. So the religious Ghost Dance craze, which is the white man's name for the movement, came into a perfect psychological setting.

As to how the thing actually started there are several

opinions, but for us it is enough to know that the real trouble began among the Dakota Indians where many were far from being reconciled to a future of gloom and servile defeat. There was still a powerful craving for buffalo meat, an inextinguishable longing for the beloved hunting expeditions in pursuit of the wild herds. Certain young men in particular revolted at the idea that the order of the world had changed, or that the gods of their fathers had deserted them for good. One or two of these ardent mystics received signs in their dreams which strengthened their faith that supernatural power was sympathetic to their cause. Then at just the right moment came the fanatic. Strange tales were heard of a great seer in the West who could, when in a trance, talk to the long dead and to the great unseen, handing down prophecies. Like the fabled wise men of old, these youths were drawn thither by they knew not what. The trances of this seer were impressive, he professed to see the buffalo again roaming the grassland and no white men in sight. When they returned home, the erstwhile pilgrims started agitating, many men and women soon found that by dancing and singing they too could go into trances and have visions of the past when the buffalo was king.

For generation after generation, all Indians had believed that the road to higher truth and power was to be sought in dreams and visions thus there was nothing essentially new in the Ghost Dance religion, it was the old belief cast in a new form and it seemed the one way out. Converts were made and vied with each other in having new visions. And as the frenzy grew, more and more emphasis in these visions was placed on the sweeping of the white race from the land. Naturally to get the buffalo back farms and ranches must be destroyed to make room for them.

The rapid spread of the Ghost Dance religion was largely because many of the younger Indians, educated in government boarding schools, had classmates among most of the buffalo Indians, and they not only had a feeling of friendship for each other but possessed a common knowledge of English, which even though the language of the hated white man, was of necessity used to plot against him. We say of necessity, because something more than twenty different languages were spoken by the buffalo hunting tribes. So in this time of acute unrest letters in English were passing back and forth from Montana to Texas, spreading the spirit of the new religion, and pleading for a revolt against white civilization. Really it was a changed world, the Indian preparing for revolt, using the fruits of his new education to marshal his strength in an effort to sweep the hated white race and its civilization back into the Atlantic Ocean. But since this underground language was English, secrecy was impossible. It was, in fact, a mixed-blood postmaster who first revealed the widespread agitation for revolt. He was unintentionally a kind of spy, learning of the revolt because some of the letters fell into the hands of uneducated Indians who asked him to interpret them. Then as things were coming to a head the Indian agent at Pine Ridge, South Dakota, in his annual report for 1890 called attention to a blunder of the Government which became a decisive motivating factor.

During the previous year, a government commission had signed an agreement with the Indians on his reservation by which they were to receive a liberal allowance of fresh beef. A majority of the Indians accepted this agreement in good faith and affixed their signatures to the documents. Later the agent was surprised to learn that the amount of beef promised had been reduced by one million pounds which meant that they would receive four instead of five million as called for in the agreement. All appeals to Washington were in vain, and accordingly the Indians not only lost all faith in the promises of the Government but, excited as they were, interpreted this action as the beginning of an attempt to starve them.

In the same report, the agent makes the following interesting comment:

"During the early spring (1890) a report reached these Indians that a great medicine man had appeared in the Wind River county in Wyoming, whose mission was to resurrect and rehabilitate all the departed heroes of the tribe and restore to these people in greater abundance than ever before known such herds of buffalo and other wild game as would make them entirely independent of aid from the whites, and that such confusion would be brought among their enemies that they would flee from the country leaving them in undisputed possession of the entire northwest for all time to come. Strange as it may seem, this story was believed by a large number of Indians and is this day. An Indian belonging to the Cheyenne River Agency who had lately visited the land where the new Christ is supposed to be sojourning temporarily came to this agency a few weeks since and before I learned of his presence, he had succeeded in exciting the Indians living upon Wounded Knee Creek to such a pitch that many of them swooned away during the performance of the ceremonies which attends the recital of the wondrous things soon to come to pass, and one of the men died from the effects of the excitement. On Friday, August 22d, about two thousand Indians gathered on White Clay Creek about 18 miles north of the agency to hold what they call a religious dance connected with the appearance of this wonderful being. Noticing the demoralizing effect of these meetings I instructed the police to order the gathering to disperse, but found the police were unable to do anything with them. I visited the locality where the Indians had assembled on Sunday, the 24th instant, accompanied by twenty of the police. The Indians probably heard of our coming for they had dispersed before we arrived at the grounds, several of the bucks, however, were standing around in the neighborhood of where the dance had been held. These men were stripped for fight, having removed their leggings and such other super-

fluous apparel as is usually worn by them and stood with
Winchesters in their hands and good storing of cartridges
belted around their waists prepared to do or die in defense
of the new faith. They were quieted after a time by being
made to understand that we had no desire to harm them
but had come to order the people to their homes, who,
it had been reported, were gathered here in violation of
orders. While nothing serious may result from this new
religion, as it is called by the Indians, I would greatly fear
the consequences should there be no restriction placed
upon it."

Naturally government agents were alarmed over the
savage enthusiasm and vague remarks as to the expected obliteration of the white race. Coming together
in large camps the converts spent most of the time
dancing and listening to the preachings of their leaders.
Presently no secret was made of the part the Indian
was to play, he was to be the chief avenger and the
powers above were to see to it that the bullets of the
whites were harmless. Certain thin cloth shirts were
made and painted with mystic emblems, the leaders
asserting that these would be bullet-proof on that great
occasion. Agitators were sent to all the reservations,
north and south, even to the hereditary enemies of the
Dakotas. There was skepticism and suspicion, but here
and there converts were made. Most of the buffalo
Indians were intrigued by the idea of a comeback—to
that at least, all were sympathetic.

These activities coupled with the discovery of the underground letter writing soon made many agents uneasy.
Calls for troops piled up in Washington, newspapers
over the West were vocal as to the danger of a new
Indian war, demanding that quick action be taken to
stop this fanatic movement. The agents on marginal
reservations pleaded with their Indians to have nothing
to do with the movement, since a war could but end in
their own destruction. Things went from bad to worse,

troops were concentrated at strategic points and General Nelson A. Miles placed in command. According to his plan, the authority of the agents was to be supported everywhere, they were to remain at their posts, regardless, and to their honor they did, give them credit for that. It was soon guessed that the first break would come at Pine Ridge Reservation, the center of the movement, and a prompt concentration of troops was made to prevent these Indians from leaving the reservation. And such was the show of strength that the Ghost Dancers could do little harm at home.

As in the fights with General Wayne at Fallen Timbers, with Harrison at Tippecanoe, etc., the Indians now faced an army well equipped and what is more, provided with new machinery in the way of rapid-fire light artillery. Their case was hopeless from the start. Further, the main body of their own people held back. For one thing, the new religion had left them cold, especially the old and experienced. Lacking faith in these new teachings because not sure they were genuine, they preferred to play safe. The final outcome everyone knows; some blood was shed, but the Indians were soon disarmed and forgiven. Yet the religious movement did not really die, but continued for many years as a form of worship and an outlet to the emotions of a limited number. The most fanatical of the hostile group at Pine Ridge drew apart, kept away from the agency and still form the most conservative community in the region.

A visit to the reservation a few years later, found none of the participants willing to talk about the affair. Though forgiven, they were still marked men, but on two subjects they were vocal. One of these was the greatness of General Miles. They looked upon him as everything a soldier should be, some declaring him the only worthwhile white man they heard about. Those who cherished personal contact with him were even more vocal in his praise. One of the favorite examples of his manhood was in substance, that in the Wounded Knee fight, an Indian took an army rifle from a soldier. After the final surrender, when all arms were being given up, this Indian insisted upon seeing General Miles in person, to whom he presented the rifle with a statement of how he took it in a life or death struggle in which he killed the soldier. General Miles returned him the rifle, remarking that war is war, that the victor came by it honorably, but now there was peace, etc., upon which they shook hands. The incident may not have happened, but the Indians believed it did and it was in keeping with their high regard for the man.

The second subject of which they seemed never to tire was the colored cavalry. Somehow they had neither seen nor heard of colored troops, but one day a regiment of colored cavalry rode into the agency. The day was hot so the troopers took off their shirts and began sponging down their mounts. At that moment word came that the hostile Indians had ambushed a patrol in an arroyo a few miles out. The regiment were ordered out instantly. The Indians met with a surprise when these black fellows rushed down upon them nude to the belt, riding horses barebacked, yelling like madmen as they charged. It must have been the unexpected, unconventional, noisy way of fighting that impressed these Indians. It was soon apparent that these troopers were in a fair way to become heroes in a myth—"black buffalos" they were called, probably because their hair was woolly and their skins black. Of course, the Indians had seen negroes before, it was their unexpected and unconventional behavior as soldiers that made them famous.

Grass soon grew upon the graves of those who fell victims to the suppression of the Ghost Dance uprising, and as the years passed few Indians seemed to think of these dead and their cause. But one thing remained ineffaceable in their memory. They could not forget the buffalo.

6

The Trading Post

A TRADING POST was conspicuous in every agency.
There might be a single general store or two or three in
close formation fronting upon a kind of plaza. Here
Indians and whites came and went, news was spread,
and joys and sorrows were experienced.

The gala time for the trader was government pay
day when Uncle Sam gave out the per capita annuity
checks—one for each Indian regardless of age and sex.
Indians employed by the agency in freighting in supplies, cutting wood, building fences and repairing roads
would receive checks at the same time. Several days in
advance all the Indian families began to move toward
the agency, camping on the way, ganging up into
wagon trains and cavalcades, trailed by loose horses
and packs of evil looking dogs. Soon the agency would
be surrounded by several hundred tipis, many parked
wagons and troops of hobbled horses. A good deal of
courting, gambling and beating of ceremonial drums
characterized such a camp. Among the white people at
the agency there was bustle and serious preparation.
The trader and his clerks were busy unpacking goods,
because before the end of pay day all the checks would
be handed over the counter.

So far as the Indian was concerned it was a holiday, a time when he looked his best. The most outstanding feature of male costume was a large high-crowned, broad-brimmed black hat, known as the Indian hat. Everyone wore such a hat, even though the remainder of his costume might be aboriginal Indian. So if all other signs failed you always knew an Indian by his hat. Who started this style, and why, I do not know, but the Indian holds to it stubbornly. Often a small boy had one of these enormous hats clapped on his head, giving him a droll, if not mournful appearance. And when the Indian male took to store clothes they were black. The ways of man have always defied understanding, for why should a proud Indian, accustomed to glorious face painting, fine beadwork and colorful feathers, adopt a severe monotonous black costume? There are those who see in this the attempt of the reservation Indian to express the gloom in his soul, his reaction to a colorless and hopeless future, but this sounds like a white man's rationalization. No white person could look at a lot of Indians gathered around a trading store without wondering whose funeral was about to take place. In no other way could he account for such quiet stiffness, subdued speech and decorum draped in black.

One lonely trader longed for a monkey and a parrot. This idea I encouraged until he sent out a mail order for two such pets. Fortunately, both the monkey and the parrot arrived just before the next pay day. The trader had laid in a large supply of peanuts which he sold to the Indians at a high price that they might feed his own monkey. Coming by the store in the evening I saw the monkey and the parrot each sitting dejectedly at the tops of their respective cages, while below a mass of peanuts covered everything. I tried to get the attention of the monkey; at last he turned a bleary eye upon me, then dropped down to the peanuts and with both hands began to cast them out, but there seeming no end to them, he presently resumed his perch and closed his eyes. As to the parrot, he merely ruffled up his feathers and preserved the silence and indifference of an Indian. Never have I seen so dejected a pair of pets. One of my Indian friends remarked that the monkey was interesting enough, but that the talking-bird was another white man's lie, for though he spoke to the bird ever so often in good plain Indian, the bird did nothing but scream like a crazy woman. Some days later this Indian was urged to give the parrot another chance, upon which the talking-bird used such profane English that the Indian admitted it talked like the agency blacksmith whose superb profanity amazed even the Indians.

The typical reservation store of my day was a low rambling structure, its floor level high enough so that the platform in front would be level with a wagon box, for the Indian often came to market with a two-horse wagon, and living not infrequently one to two days' journey distant, he bought in quantity. The trader usually began his career with a small one-room building to which he added as business grew, and what with extensions and side sheds his store came to cover an impressive floor space. At the rear were detached sheds and buildings for additional storage and still farther removed, a barn and a corral for his live stock. Under these roofs was gathered a motley array of goods, ranging from patent medicines to wagons. There were fine broadcloth, highly colored blankets, calicoes, ribbons, men's clothing, etc. Staple groceries were prominent, but there were a few things found in no other stores; for example, the large Indian hat we mentioned above, an assortment of bone ornaments and curious shell disks.

It was always interesting to loaf around one of these stores because Indians of all classes and ages came there. More likely than not when an Indian man came to trade, he brought his wife, children, and all the other women his household happened to shelter; it was a family event. They looked at the shelves piled with goods and into the two or three old-fashioned show cases, engaged in subdued and often whispered conversations, and if the children became vocal with wonder over something, they were immediately suppressed by a vigorous "sh-sh-sh" from the women. The man usually did the buying, not so much because that fitted into Indian custom, as because from the first white traders looked upon the man of the family as the one to pay the bills. They could not conceive of a man permitting his wife to carry the pocketbook. The other factor to be considered is that according to Indian custom, it was highly improper for a woman to enter the house of a strange man unaccompanied. Yet however this may be, the Indian male revealed the finer side of his nature when he came to trade. He would spend his last dollar of credit for something to please his wife, even though she were better off without it.

Once moved by sympathy over the obvious poverty of an Indian household, I gave them ten dollars for some poorly executed beadwork. Later I saw the family gather around the counter at the store. Some flour and tea were bought; then the man selected several bags of expensive candy for the junior members of the party. With some five dollars left, he spied a man's panama hat, which cost just that, placed it upon his wife's head, who marched off proudly. A few days later the hat was missing and when I inquired about it, learned that the family pup had worried it in a mud hole and that was the end of it. Further, no one seemed to mind; it was a good joke, though upon whom no one seemed to know, most likely upon me, the original donor of the cash.

Once I saw an old dignified man wrapped in a blanket around the middle of which was a magnificent broad beaded band. I wanted that band and bid for it up to $25.00, but all to no purpose. A few hours later I was astonished to see the same band hanging up in the store, and upon inquiry, learned that the old Indian had brought it in to exchange for $4.00 in groceries. I offered the trader $4.00 for it; he wanted $8.00, so we compromised by splitting the difference. Nor was this an unusual experience, for when the Indian wants to sell, price makes little difference; if he is not ready to sell, offers are useless.

The Indian soon found the store an ideal place for loafing. Young men and boys loitered around outside the door, rarely speaking a word, but staring stolidly. Their elders loafed inside. Most any day a row of middle-aged Indian men could be seen sitting on the floor of the store, their backs to the wooden counter, a large pipe passing back and forth as they listened to a monologue by one of their number. Here not only were the old times lived over again, but criticisms leveled at the Government, at white-ways, and at the shortcomings of their own people. As all the world over, the younger generation came in for denunciation because of their leanings toward ultramodern customs. Yet humor and mischief frequently prevailed.

I recall how one day, as such a row of old-timers was silently passing the pipe, they saw through the open door a well-known Indian tying his horse, preparatory to entering. Immediately one of them said in an unusually loud voice, "I say, the Old Man is dead."

This referred to a vile and disreputable mythological character, whose antics were known to every member of that tribe.

"No, you are wrong," said the Indian sitting beside him. "He is not only alive, but lives on this reservation."

"Where does he live?"

"On Goose Creek," the residence of the man tying his horse outside.

"How do you know that the man who lives on Goose Creek is the Old Man?"

Of course, the man outside heard all of this and just as he entered, came the answer.

"Because when women are around he acts just like Old Man; he must be the same person."

The new-comer showed no signs of embarrassment, the Indian ideal in such situations, took his seat, nothing more being said about the question at issue. This is a good example of Indian joking.

When the Indian received money he made haste to spend it. He acted as if he was afraid of losing it. It was a common sight to see a family on the way to the store five minutes after receiving a dollar and driving the horses hard. All the Indian seemed to know about money was that if he handed it to the trader he would receive some goods. How much he received he believed dependent upon the good will of the trader. To him it was like an exchange of gifts, except that in this case he gave the trader money, something no Indian could use, hoping to get something in return which every Indian could use. Before reservation days the trader took horses, furs, skins, and occasionally dried meat and tallow in exchange for goods. This the Indian could understand and so protect himself by refusing to trade when he thought the offer of goods unfair. But it was different with money and prices. I soon learned that if I offered an old Indian a five-dollar bill he would ask that I give him coin instead. He could distinguish a silver dollar from coins of smaller value, but since all bills were of the same size he could make nothing out of them. On rare occasions when an old Indian got possession of a few silver dollars, he would lay one on the counter and make a purchase, then put down the next dollar and so on to the last. The trader might charge too much or short weight the customer, but the latter knew that he was getting something for each dollar.

But when the Major began to give out bank checks the Indian was wholly at the mercy of the trader. Ten dollars worth of goods could be given him in return for a hundred dollar check, because all checks looked alike to the Indian. Even if the trader was honest, the Indian had no way of knowing it, and so distrusted everybody. My impression of the traders I met was that most of them maintained fixed prices and credited the Indian with the full amount of his checks. Again, when they bought his hides, horses, or cattle, the amount set down in the book was regular. But do not overlook the important point which is that what the Indian had to sell was priced much below the outside market and what he came to buy was priced to return a profit of two hundred per cent or more. An educated Indian told me that he was once required to pay fifty cents for a common sewing needle and that, when he protested, the trader defended the price on the ground that the freight rates were so high.

There was no competition because the reservation traders were licensed and so had a monopoly. The Indian could not leave the reservation without a permit and so the Major saw to it that he had no opportunity to spend his money at the nearest town. Stealing out to trade was prevented by the simple device of keeping the Indian in debt. The Major punished him if he did not turn in his check on his debt to the trader; in fact, he would force the Indian to turn in horses or cattle to bring his credit up whenever the trader so demanded. It was a vicious circle from which the Indian could not escape. Also note that the Major was the trader's best friend.

The Indian trader was sure to be aggressive. Two that I came to know were illiterate, but made up for this deficiency in aggressiveness and hard sense. In that country one could hire somebody to do his reading and writing but rarely could a dull wit hire "a live wire" and avoid being pinched out. The lure of big profits attracted aggressive, intelligent men, but the license hurdle gave off a political odor. Not infrequently, the trader was a young man backed by a near-by capitalist. If the latter lost his grip, the young man made his fortune. For example, under my observation an outsider bought out a trader and brought in a young man to operate the store. The former trader was the postmaster, receiving a small salary and rather high rent for a small corner of the store. Since the new owner was not a resident, he had the young man made postmaster with the understanding that his fee from the Postal Department was to be turned in as cash receipts. In due time, the young postmaster complained to Washington that he was coerced, and in consequence, his financial backer had his license to trade cancelled. Then there was nothing to do but sell the stock of goods to his former employee at his own price. By a little "wire pulling," the young man got a license to trade and so was handsomely set up in business. The local white people felt that the young fellow did the right thing, though I have some doubts about it.

On large reservations the trader would employ one or two clerks and a bookkeeper. Most of the bookkeepers I met came from Missouri. In fact there were so many Missourians in the Indian country, that the usual question to ask a stranger was, "Are you from Missouri or the United States?" If the former, he was in favor. Many of these Missourians were unique characters, like bookkeeper McJoy, a nervous, reserved man with a grand beard, who lived in a little room built on the outside wall of the store with a connecting door so that, like a priest, he could shuttle in and out of his sanctum as occasion demanded. He presided in a kind of wooden cage in front of a huge book in which was recorded the economic fate of every Indian family-man. When an Indian came to trade, he first presented himself to McJoy who like Saint Peter in judgment, called for the Indian's name, then opened the book and demanded what he wished—credit, of course. If McJoy shook his head, the Indian knew the book of fate was closed against him. His next move would be to appeal to the trader himself, and if the Indian could promise that a horse or a steer would be delivered in due time, McJoy would grudgingly make an entry in the book and give the Indian a credit slip to present to the clerk. Poor old grim McJoy had seen better days back in Missouri, but he rarely mentioned the subject, though once he confided that he had a kind of nervous break-down and was advised to seek an easy, quiet berth out in the open. Well, out in the open he was and could live the quiet life if he had a will for it. Once McJoy volunteered a contribution to folk-wisdom to the effect that some otherwise good business men were useless on a bookkeeper's stool. He was doubtless correct, but every man around the agency was certain that such a spot was the only place where old McJoy had any business to be. In fact, he looked so out of place when off that stool that everyone hurried on so he could resume his perch, and, of course, for the same reason, no one invited him anywhere.

The reservation trader's store had its peculiarities but it was the lineal descendant of the frontier trading post where for two hundred years Indians had been in con-tact with white men and European goods. Those were the grand old days when a beaver skin was more im-portant than the English pound for it was the standard of value. Then the Indian had no trouble with coins or checks, he could either make a robe out of his beaver or cash it in for goods. For the reader's information we offer a table of prices in beaver, prices the Indian could understand. But those were the days when the Indian roamed at will and there were no reservations.

A HUDSON BAY COMPANY PRICE LIST—1781

An Indian desires in trade, most of all, a (York) gun, hatchet, Brazil tobacco, knife, file, powder and ball, powder horn, kettle, cloth, and beads.

Hudson Bay Price List

	Beaver		Beaver
Glass beads—1 lb. .	2	Vermilion—lb.	16
China beads	6	Pistol	7
Brass kettle	2	Sun glass	1
Cloth—yd.	3	Gartering—yd.	2
Blanket	7	Lace—yd.	1
Tobacco—lb.	1	File	1
Shirt	2	Hawks bell (12) ..	1
Stockings	2	Sword blade	1
Powder—lb.	1	Needles (12)	1
Duffel—yd.	2	Hatchet	1
Knife	1	Brandy—gal.	4
Gun	14	Thimbles (6)	1
Comb	1	Steel (3)	1
Flint (16)	1	Thread—bb.	1

In my day a few of these ancient traders, long retired, lived among the reservation Indians, for example, a Canadian known to the whites as Sammy. Doubtless he had an Indian name and a Christian family name, but locally no one needed to know more than Sammy. It is doubtful if he knew his exact age, though he claimed to be approaching 90. He left eastern Canada as a boy to learn the Indian trade, took an Indian wife, drifted into the States, where later he was caught up in the reservation system as a squaw-man. He was not over talkative and a little shy, but could on occasion be led into telling of the days that were.

In pre-reservation days he followed the Indians about with a couple of wagons stocked with goods.

Once he was forced to leave a wagon behind because of a broken wheel and upon arriving at camp engaged several young Indians to bring it in. On the way back they had a running fight with some hostile Indians, beating them off, saving the wagon, but one of the young men was mortally wounded. When the news reached camp, the chief took Sammy by the hand, led him to his tipi and advised him to stay there. Later the young man died and his male relatives began to blame Sammy, grief soon giving way to a lust for blood. They wanted the chief to give Sammy up to their vengeance, but he refused. He asked Sammy to give him two guns, —these he showed to the threatening mob, saying they were for the deceased's family, that Sammy's heart was sore for their sorrow, that he loved the unfortunate young brave as his son and that he now gave this demonstration of his grief. Handing the two guns to the grieved family, the chief said, "Now, the matter is settled. You have his presents." When I remarked, "how strange that you should be blamed," Sammy shook his head and said nothing. After all, is it strange? for though we do not demand the life of an employer when the life of a laborer is lost, we may want him put into jail, or at least sue him for damages.

After the Indians were settled on reservations, Sammy opened a little store. Many Indians were still wild, for Sammy could relate numerous exasperating incidents. Thus one morning a half dozen young Indians entered in war paint and armed, they sprang upon the counter and stood there in a row. Sammy knew his Indians, so he regarded the situation as dangerous, for before him stood a mass of human dynamite ready to explode at the first jar. He asked them what they wanted, but no reply was made. If there is such a thing as a 100% poker face, the old time Indian had it. All Sammy could do was to wait patiently and show as much unconcern as possible. The situation continued without change for about an hour, when luckily the head chief came in to trade. Sammy pointed to the living statues on his counter and said, "What does this mean?"

The chief gazed fixedly at the young men for a few moments, then said, "Get down!"

They did, promptly. He then pointed to the door and the rascals filed out.

I asked Sammy what these disturbers had in mind, but he shook his head. He said no Indian ever offered to talk about it and he knew better than to mention it. Even the chief made no further comment. Sammy had other grim memories of the trade and some close calls as did every one living on the frontier, but he survived, so why relate them now. He was an illiterate squaw-man, but he had rugged individualism and plenty of character. Though his life was cast among the Indians and his children to the third generation were of that strain, yet he steadily followed what he considered a proper road for a white man and when he spoke the white man's language, he always referred to red men as "them d—d Injun." And after hearing many of his adventures, I was disposed to agree with him.

The history of the trader is so intimately a part of the history of the Indian that many times while loitering around the agency I let my fancy run to picturing the pageant of the Indian in trade. Columbus is accorded lasting fame because he found a new world, but what he really found was a vast market for European goods, a market which the English, French and the Dutch were quick to enter. In Mexico and Peru the Spanish found a sedentary people with gold and other accumulated wealth so that looting and forced labor were the easy roads to riches, but the Indians of the United States and Canada had neither wealth for the white man to loot nor a society docile to rigid social discipline. Though his women raised a little corn and a few vegetables, the Indian man was above all a hunter and a fighter. Yet as the Europeans saw it, the material needs of the Indian were unlimited, as when a bit of iron was wealth and a kettle the height of luxury. Even a needle was revolutionary. The Indian was ready to give generously for these new tools, so the trader took in exchange any and everything he could market at home, deer skins and furs for the most part. The skill of Indian women in tanning deer skins was and is still unsurpassed; there was a ready market for all she could produce. Furs of the beaver were in demand in Europe, so in due time great fur companies arose, such as the Hudson Bay Company, still in existence.

Yet all this happened a long time before the birth of the Indian reservation; that anathema to the Indian, often spoken of as his degradation, came much later. I am sure this is too harsh a view of the reservation system though it was as stern and sordid as most sectors of human society prove to be on close inspection. However, in contrast with what went before, it presented a picture dark enough to deserve our pity. It is easy to see that the Golden Age of the Indian was the period of the fur trade; it was a time when he lived his own life, and was free to raise his standard of living by increasing his production of fur, which he could exchange for amazing things, and some of the fashions set in these early days of trade still survived on the reservation.

To look upon the fur trader as a missionary may seem the height of absurdity, for how could such hard, cheating, lying personalities have anything in common with the pious religious enthusiast? Nevertheless, the trader, more than anyone, represented civilization; his role was to sell the practical aspects of civilization to the Indian. Thus the trader did all he could to raise the standard of living, to spur the Indian to new levels of production, stood for the notion that it was the man who should produce and dominate his woman, and instructed the Indian in the use of new mechanical devices and the sanctity of the contract. Unconsciously he was far and away the best preacher of the new life. Occasionally he did resort to oratory as, for example, Perrot, one of the earliest French traders to visit the Fox Indians:—

"I see this fine village filled with young men, who are, I am sure, as courageous as they are well built; and who will, without doubt, not fear their enemies if they carry French weapons. It is for these young men that I leave my gun, which they must regard as the pledge of my esteem for their valor; they must use it if they are attacked. It will also be more satisfactory in hunting cattle (buffalo) and other animals than are all the arrows that you use. To you who are old men I leave my kettle; I carry it everywhere without fear of breaking it. You will cook in it the meat that your young men bring from the chase, and the food which you offer to the Frenchmen who come to visit you." He tossed a dozen awls and knives to the women, and said to them: "Throw aside your bone bodkins; these French awls will be much easier to use. These knives will be more useful to you in killing beavers and in cutting your meat than are the pieces of stone that you use." Then, throwing to them some rassade (beads): "See; these will better adorn your children and girls than do their usual ornaments."

A little thought will convince one that a few such traders could so change the material life of Indians that one generation would scarcely know the other. Even in colonial times it was a different Indian who stood forth with the tools of the white man in his hands, in contrast to the wild savage who welcomed the first explorers. In the earliest of Indian wars these so-called savages shot the settlers with guns furnished by white men, brained them with tomahawks made in England and scalped them with trade knives. With one hand the colonial trader equipped the Indian with the most improved weapons, holding a gun in the other to repel his attacks, all of which sounds like the latest munitions scandal. It is true the trader was not concerned with the soul of the Indian, but he did labor unceasingly to make him an up-to-date fighter and a producer of goods, and when we note that for some 200 years Indians had been in steady contact with trade, we should not be surprised to learn that the reservation Indian was quite a different Indian from the one who met John Smith in Virginia.

In the old days the trader set up his store far out within the Indian country, or even followed Indian camps from place to place with a pack train, so the question is often asked, why in these early days the Indian did not knock the lone trader on the head and seize his goods? The answer is not far to seek—grim economic necessity. The Indian needed knives, axes, guns and powder. Once having realized the superiority of these new appliances, he would have no others. Having experienced the joys of liquor, he regarded a big drunk now and then as the only adequate compensation to toil and exposure. He learned quickly that no trader would venture into his country unless guaranteed protection. And when we damn the white man for breaking into the aboriginal heaven some people fancy, and forcing his debasing habits on Indian life, we are following the age-old custom of setting up an ideal in disregard of reality. Also we overlook human nature, of which the Indian has a generous supply, for when a tribe had a place to trade, enjoyed the feeling of power and security their new weapons gave them, they regarded trade as a necessity and were rarely willing that their hostile neighbors should enjoy this same trade. So the tribe without a trader was forced to seek one. Delegations journeyed to the main posts of the trading companies, pleading for a trader in their territory, offering as inducement protection and guaranteed profit.

Thus the Indian was caught up in a situation where keeping up with the Joneses, not to mention self-preservation, drove him relentlessly in the pursuit of power and wealth. If some irresponsible individual looted a trader, the leaders of the tribe were required to make good the loss before trade was resumed. We should not forget that in the old days these tribes were little nations and as such mere producers of certain raw materials, whereas all their necessary fighting equipment must be obtained by foreign trade; they had neither the skill nor the knowledge to make an axe, a kettle, nor gun powder. A few years of trade and the whole economic level of the Indian changed from one of independence and self-containment to one of dependence. He became a kind of worker, without, however, the evils of congested living quarters. And his standard of living had risen to a much higher level than before. So the Indian having been a frequenter of the store for a century or two before coming to the reservation and all this time the store having been the most real and lively contact with the white man's culture, it was natural that there should be stores upon the reservations and that around them was centered the life of the reservation Indians.

Just how the reservation store looked to the Indian we shall never know. So far as I could see, they looked upon it as both a friend and an enemy—a hard, stern reality. At times they seemed to grasp the material philosophy of the situation, but often wavering in uncertainty, just as many white people have been doing when faced with such matters as the killing of little pigs and the plowing under of rows of cotton in order to create unusual abundance. It is hard to hold one's attention to the idea that such a thing can be sensible when so many are in want of food and clothing. Well, so with the Indians, who often wavered when contemplating the trader hoarding in a great house hundreds of blankets, coats and shoes, not to mention heaps of food, vastly more than he could consume and so of no earthly use to him, while all about were poor Indians shivering from cold, and hunger, yes, hungry always. The Indian could not quite rid himself of the feeling that something was fundamentally wrong at the heart of the system, which on the other hand his common sense told him was the reality of life. Sometimes he appealed to me, as spokesman for the new culture, to set his wandering thoughts right, but I could not, for the reason that I found my own explanations failing to ring true. And so, as an old chief once said, "What is the good of having so much, if nothing can be given away."

7

Exploits of the Indian Police

SOONER OR LATER, if a stranger at the agency, you became aware of the Indian police. This was chiefly because they stood around staring at you; true, ordinary Indians did that, but when you noted a large glittering star on an Indian breast you suspected something more back of his traditional stolid countenance than mere primitive curiosity. You felt that you were being watched. Yet there was nothing inspiring about the appearance of these police. No Indian of my day looked as if he felt at home in white man's clothes. They rarely fit; the trousers might be oversize and the coat too short. The traders were usually to blame for that; some of them would sell a man's coat to a boy and congratulate themselves upon their salesmanship. Yet the Government did little better if we are to judge from the uniforms worn by the police. They were of good blue cloth, liberally supplied with gold buttons and usually in good order, but they rarely fitted, giving the impression of a slouching, misshapen human body. The policeman's boots were the high heeled funny kind worn by fastidious cow-men and when walking, their wearers tottered along like Chinese women with bound feet. Of course, no feet brought up in moccasins could get on well in such gear. Perhaps this did not matter because every policeman had a horse which he rode at all times. However, the characteristics so far noted were secondary, the essential lines in the picture were defined by an oversized six-shooter, a heavy broad leather belt full of shells, and an enormous black hat. A repeating rifle usually swung from the saddle. In short, one's first impression of an Indian policeman might include little more than heavy armament and a poker face.

My first acquaintance with the force was both amusing and informative. Arriving at a large agency late one afternoon, promptly presenting my credentials to the Major and registering in the book he kept for that purpose, I was soon settled in the little hotel. At dinner I sat beside the school superintendent who invited me to visit the boarding school about one-half mile away. I gladly accepted and spent an enjoyable evening with the teacher and employees. In due time I took my leave and walked back toward the hotel. It was a black night, but a few tiny flickering lights guided me. The agency buildings were arranged in a kind of quadrangle and as I neared the outer line a man, concealed in a shadow, stepped out and stood peering into my face. Having seen policemen on arriving at the agency, I slowly comprehended that I was now in the hands of the law. Not knowing Indian, I tried English, but there was no response. Finally, after what seemed an interminable suspense, the policeman uttered what sounded like a grunt and gestured for me to go with him.

Presently we came to a rude building before which a lantern on a post flickered fitfully. Inside was another lantern on a kind of bench behind which sat another policeman, while two others sprawled on a couple of plain benches. The man behind the lantern proved to be the Chief of Police and greeted me in English. I began to explain excitedly, but he interrupted smilingly to say that he recognized me, having been standing by when I left the Major's office, and that he had read what was written in the registry, where I stated my business, etc. He was the first smiling Indian I had seen, but I soon found that most of them could smile.

The Chief of Police explained that he would send a man to escort me to the hotel and, when I remonstrated, laughingly remarked that there were several other policemen to pass, each of whom would bring me back to him; I then thanked him for his consideration. When I arrived at the hotel, the landlord had locked up and gone to bed, but my escort pounded vigorously on the door with the butt of his huge revolver. This brought quick results and soon, snugly in bed, I felt that the agency was the safest place in the world.

Several agents assured us that the Indian police were efficient, if properly handled; in fact, too efficient. To a white man, rules and orders are abstractions, or ideals, the enforcement of which is on a 50% level, but the Indian policeman entertained no such irrational ideas; to him orders meant what they said, and rules were rules. Graft and leniency were contrary to his notion of the police function. New agents, not understanding all this, were often embarrassed. I recall one such incident. Information came one evening that some ten miles out, a certain white man with an Indian wife was on a drunk and threatening to kill his family. He was said to be a bad man when running amuck. The new agent called in a policeman and ordered him to arrest this man. Thinking it necessary to be emphatic, he said, "Bring him dead or alive; do not come back without him."

Before the lone policeman arrived at the scene, an Indian had killed the desperado in self-defense and the family had laid out the corpse. The policeman astonished everyone by announcing that he would take the body to the agent. Neither remonstrance nor threats availed; the policeman would take the body or fight to the death. "Agent's order," he asserted. So he borrowed a wagon and started on the long, slow journey alone. About four o'clock in the morning, while it was still dark, he drew up in front of the agent's house, unhitched the team, gave them some hay, then thumped on the agent's door. When the agent looked out the Indian, pointing over his shoulder, said, "Him there in wagon," turned on his heel and went to the barracks, with the feeling of a hard job well done.

As with all police so with the Indian force, much of their time was taken up with the petty, sordid misbehavior of their fellow men and women, but in addition, they acted as an information service. They generally knew about expectant births, took note of the circumstances surrounding deaths, detected the beginnings of illicit intrigues, noted illness, want, etc. On all these subjects they reported to the Major according to his desires and instructions; if on certain matters he indicated by as much as a look or gesture that he wished to be ignorant, his police were ready to isolate him, but their own ears and eyes were open still.

I came to know an Indian named Bear-foot who, though then retired, had formerly won renown as a policeman. His reservation was in the cow country and was troubled by rough white men who strayed in now and then to terrorize both whites and Indians. The strong-minded Major promulgated a rule that any white man entering the agency grounds must turn in his guns for safe keeping until he departed. The reasonableness of the request led all honest visitors to respect the rule, but one day the test came. A certain bad man came in to make good his boast that his gun would not be checked. He rode boldly into the quadrangle, tied his horse to the rack, entered the trading store, perched upon the counter and boasted his defiance. The trader cautioned him, but to no purpose. The situation was promptly reported to the Major. Bear-foot was on duty, so the Major ordered him to take a squad of police and arrest the cow-man. Bear-foot said he would go, but alone. He entered the store as if wholly unconscious of the cow-man's presence and when directly in front of him, turned his back and asked the clerk for some tobacco. While the order was being filled, Bear-foot quickly turned upon his heel, caught the cow-man by the shirt collar with his left hand, poked his revolver into his ribs with the other as he jerked him to the floor. To seize the cow-man's gun was then easy, after which he motioned for him to rise and march ahead to the Major's office.

The Major explained the rules to the chastened cow-man, and said, "Next time you visit us come directly here and check your gun." As the cow-man left, Bear-foot followed, and when out of hearing range of the Major, stepped in front of the man, saying in broken English, "Me policeman, many other policemans here. Next time no wait, all policemans shoot you on sight." So far as known that cow-man made no second visit.

You have all read of the wild days when cattlemen fought each other for the range, tore down would-be farmers' fences and burned their houses. Indian lands were seldom respected because Indian agents were exposed to political and business pressure, but the Indians registered their complaints in Washington with such persistence that something had to be done about it. Accordingly, when the wire fence came into use, reservations were fenced. For one thing, it made work for the Indians, but the cattlemen used wire cutters to open these fences so their cattle could be driven in and left to graze. In due time one Major decided to stop this game. First he recruited a lot of extra police and established a fence patrol to keep the wires up. Of course, wires were still cut, often by show of force, the Major having wisely ordered the lone fence riders not to fight. Yet when ready, he organized a few flying squads of police with a system of signals by which they could swoop down upon offenders. Scarcely had this system been put into operation when a scout sighted a large herd being driven toward the fence.

We now shift our position of observation to the approaching herd. About a dozen well armed and efficient cowboys were in charge. As they neared the fence they saw a squad of 20 Indians deploying so as to meet them head on. The cowboys rode up close to the fence and so did the Indians, unslinging their repeating rifles. The foreman of the herds approached the fence with his wire clippers, a sharp command rang out from the Indian captain and the foreman hesitated as he saw twenty rifles aimed at him. Then in unmistakable English was heard, "Cut wire, you die."

The cow-men hesitated, consulted and withdrew, but swung the herd at right angles to the fence. The Indian police followed on their side. After dark the herders made another attempt but were fired upon before they had even a chance to cut a wire.

Written history itself testifies to the efficiency of the Indian police, as for example in the attempted arrest of Sitting Bull. During the Ghost Dance trouble, Sitting Bull was believed the chief conspirator, and the agent of his reserve received orders from Washington to put him under arrest to prevent his taking command of certain Indians preparing to fight the whites. The police were of his own tribe, but they unhesitatingly proceeded to their duty. Sitting Bull's sympathizers resisted, and in the fight Sitting Bull was killed. Several policemen fell, but though outnumbered, they held their ground until reinforced. Many white authors have denounced these police as traitors and murderers, but nothing could be more unjust, for like all good police, they merely obeyed orders, some of them making the supreme sacrifice. Congress was asked to pension their widows, but white agitators saw to it that nothing was done. Perhaps it is just as well to be consistent, because at no time has the nation even considered the important services the Indian police have rendered. Certainly it has not appreciated the fibre of manhood which in those days found expression in police duty.

Again, when the Ghost Dancers threatened Pine Ridge Agency, the police remained loyal. After General Miles took charge of the agency, he detailed a second Lieutenant to command the Indian police. This West Point graduate was shocked at the ignorance of these Indians and their unmilitary bearing. So several times a day he lined them up in the quadrangle for drill. One day as they were in line, doing their best to follow the commands of this youth, the Chief of Police, now treated as a sergeant, saw some hostile Indians crawling in a ravine toward some hay-stacks. Several times before this, these police had frustrated attempts of hostile Ghost Dancers to set fire to those stacks, so the Indian captain shouted a quick command in Indian and everyone dashed toward the stacks, pouring a raking fire into the ravine. The surprised Lieutenant was left standing alone wondering what had happened. It is said that General Miles saw it all; he was highly amused, and after the hostiles were repelled, called the Lieutenant off with the remark, "Don't drill them; you may spoil them." The Indian Chief of Police he complimented highly, saying, "from now on you take orders from me only." It was some years afterward that this Indian gave me his own version of the incident and expressed great satisfaction at having once shaken hands with so great a soldier as General Miles.

When reservations were first established, the army

was expected to serve as police, but these initial experiences of Indian agents with United States troops as policemen were discouraging. In 1877, the Commissioner of Indian Affairs voiced the sentiments of his agents in recommending the displacement of soldiers by Indian police. He mentioned the newly established Canadian Mounted Police as proof of his contention that a small body of efficient police could keep our entire Indian population under control and prevent many tense situations, otherwise resulting in war. Anyway, soldiers were trained to fight, and not to act as policemen. To quote this commissioner, "I would recommend that the force be composed of Indians, properly officered and drilled by white men, and where capable Indians can be found, that they be promoted to command, as reward for faithful service. The army has used Indians for scouts with great success, and wherever employed the Indian has been found faithful to the trust confided to him. I would also recommend that the police force be supplied with a uniform similar to the style of clothing which I shall hereafter suggest to be furnished for all Indians, with the addition of a few brass buttons by way of distinction. The employment of such a force, properly officered and handled, would, in great measure, relieve the army from doing police duty on Indian reservations. I am thoroughly satisfied that the saving in life and property by the employment of such a force would be very large, and that it would materially aid in placing the entire Indian population of the country on the road to civilization."

As an illustration of satisfaction with the newly established Indian police, we offer the following from the agent of the Apache Indians in New Mexico. He writes, "The Indian police system is my great hobby in the management of wild Indians, and my police have really done more this year than I had expected of them or claimed for them. On the 9th of October General

Kautz, at my request, ordered all the troops away from San Carlos and the abandonment of that camp. This was something I had long desired; and although no more unfavorable time could have been selected for their removal (pending the transfer of the Coyotero Apaches), yet, as the general chose that time, I did not object. The troops at San Carlos left on the 27th of October, 1875, under the command of Lieutenant Carter, Sixth Cavalry, United States Army. We had now no other defense than our Indian police, and I will mention a few of their exploits, which will sufficiently prove their faithfulness and efficiency.

"On the 24th of October I received information that a number of Indians had left for the Pima villages. I immediately dispatched Mr. Beauford with a small police force in pursuit of the truants. Mr. Beauford returned on the morning of the 27th, bringing with him twenty-seven prisoners, who were furnished lodgings in the guard-house. I may mention here as a significant coincidence, that as Mr. Beauford came into the agency with these prisoners, Lieutenant Carter moved out of camp with the troops, leaving us unprotected.

"On the 22d of December a very prominent chief, named Disalin, became enraged and fired two shots at Mr. Sweeney, one at Mr. Beauford, and one at an Indian; and in less than two minutes the Indian police had put a dozen bullets through Disalin, and he was correspondingly quiet.

"On the 26th of February, 1876, I issued the following order:

"Clay Beauford,
    "In Charge of Indian Police:
    "Sir: It having been reported that there are some renegade Indians prowling about the western border of this reservation, you are directed to take fifteen Indian police and ascertain the truth of these reports by a scout in that direction. Should you find the renegade Indians, you are

directed to use your own judgment as to an attack with a view to capture their camp. Should your force be too small to effect the capture of these renegades, you will report the facts in the case to me without delay, or should you be near a military post, report the circumstances to the commanding officer, asking his assistance.

"John P. Clum,
"United States Indian Agent."

"This party was gone from the agency seventeen days. They killed sixteen renegades, and brought in twenty-one women and children as prisoners.

"On the 8th of June, 1876 (as I have already reported), a detachment of twenty police brought in to me Pionsenay and thirty-eight others. No other prisoners were taken.

"I could mention other instances of most valuable services performed by the police, but I think enough has been said to secure for them general commendation, insignia of office, and plumed hats. The very purpose of an army is to devastate and destroy; hence in times of peace they should be far removed."

I have praised the work of Major Wood who set up a form of tribal government on the Piegan Reservation. What I omitted at the time was that he learned of a former soldier society which acted as police. Most buffalo hunting Indians maintained soldier societies to police their camps, buffalo hunts and to enforce law and order. Early white observers comment upon the efficiency and fearlessness of this body. Major Wood encouraged the chiefs to reinstate this institution as police to carry out their orders. Naturally, with all its ancient prestige revived, this body functioned efficiently. Whether due to this experience or not, in due time Washington called for police on every reserve. The system was not successful everywhere, but worked best where the Indians were numerous, and as may be expected, best of all among the buffalo Indians who had maintained a similar organization in aboriginal days. Among the Dakota for example, when the chiefs were called into council on the new plan, they suggested appointing members of the former soldier society, and thus unknown to himself, the Major recognized an old and tried institution. Every tribesman understood what these new police were to do and that they would set about their business fearlessly. To resist them would be not merely a crime, but sacrilege.

There is an interesting story about the first supreme test of the newly organized police on a certain large reservation. The Major was a man of iron nerves who ruled largely by courage and the force of his personality. When the order came from Washington to organize an Indian police force he was skeptical. To him it was just another of those fool ideas periodically disturbing the serenity of the Indian Service. Nevertheless, he called in the head men for a talk. That they thought well of the idea increased his misgivings. Unsuspected by him, the head men designated a former leader of the native camp soldiers as the best man for the chief of police, and so in due time, the flower of this once powerful and venerated body was enlisted. It was sometime before their uniforms and equipment arrived, but at last all was ready. However, no use was made of these new police except to stand guard around the agency and to recover government horses and cattle when they strayed too far afield; but all this time the native head of the force was training his men to their job.

Finally a new order came from Washington. The Indians of the Plains had a famous annual ceremony called by white people a sun dance. In one spectacular feature of this ceremony a few men tortured themselves by tying ropes to sharp sticks thrust into the skin of their breasts and dancing until they were torn loose. Naturally this was frowned upon by the Government, and so it was not strange when eventually orders were issued to agents to prohibit all sun dances.

The Major in question looked upon these instructions as useless; to his mind, nothing short of two or three regiments of troops could do it. Nevertheless, he welcomed the order, not because he thought it could be enforced, or that he really intended to make an attempt, but because it offered the main chance to show up the utter folly of appointing an Indian police force. At that very hour he knew the Indians were forming a great camp out on the reservation to begin the annual sun dance, so he called in the Chief of Police and read him the order. The Chief had it repeated several times and required double assurance that it came from the Great Father. He then left to order out the force. In about an hour the Major was informed that the troop was ready on parade and that the police wished him to look them over. The sight which he beheld was astonishing. Uniforms had been discarded for breech clout and moccasins; their faces and bodies were smeared with war paint, and feathers and other symbols of the original camp soldiers were in evidence. In fact, about every trace of civilization had vanished except repeating rifles and revolvers. Even the horses wore war paint, scalp locks and feathers.

The Chief addressed the Major, recounting that when they joined the force they promised to do their duty, that now they were assigned to a difficult and dangerous task, that they would not shirk, that the chances were that some, perhaps none, would return, that they now took their leave of him, but not a man of them would return alive if they failed.

The horsemen filed away to the weird strains of a camp soldier song. Needless to say, the Major began to relent, but it was now too late.

The troop approached the great camp of their tribesmen where the chiefs were in control and every Indian armed. Their appearance was unexpected. They first rode briskly around the outside of the camp circle shouting war songs and war cries, they deployed into the circle and fired a volley into the air. Then in a loud voice the Chief of Police began a harangue, the substance of which was that all were to disperse at once to their usual camping places and that no sun dance was to be held, that this order would be enforced.

There were mutterings, tense moments and hesitation, but the troop stood fast, singing war songs and ready to fight to the bitter end. Every Indian saw not the authority of the Government, but a revival of the old camp soldier band; they knew what those songs meant, that though they could overcome the band, the killing would not be on one side only. Soon a few tipis came down, then more, until eventually all Indians had left the camp ground. The troop returned quietly to barracks, washed off their war paint, put on their regulation uniforms and took up their monotonous routine of duty.

Needless to say, the Major was converted. His police soon rose to such a level of prestige, that every young Indian on that reservation hoped some day to be considered worthy of a place in the troop.

The history of the reservation police among the Plains Indians is the one bright spot in an otherwise gloomy series of events, but it merits our attention because we here for the first time achieve some degree of insight into the obstacles to the harmonious adjustment of Indian life to white ways. In this case the adjustment was spontaneous. Indians and white men held different notions as to the sources of police authority. The soldier societies possessed rituals with religious sanctions, to flout which was sacrilege. Hence for an Indian to defy the power of his police was more than a crime for it insulted the unseen powers as well. White people, on the other hand, looked upon their police as doing the will of the Government, not of their Gods, and hence to defy them would at most be treason. Yet in manner of functioning, both white and Indian police operated alike, they enforced the orders of their superiors. Thus in the old days an Indian Chief acted under authority of the tribal council but it was he who gave orders to the police. When the Indians were placed upon reservations they were told that now the Major was their only Chief. When the Major chose Indians for his police, they understood what was wanted, and what is more, were conscious of long established ideals of courage and loyalty. It was because of these common elements in the social lives of these two diverse peoples, that the institution of the Indian police was a conspicuous success. Sociologists sometimes speak of such spontaneous adjustment between two different forms of society through overlapping institutions as the manifestation of pattern phenomena; that is, societies like Indians and whites, each have a number of cherished social patterns through which they function. Many of these may have nothing in common, in which case they clash, but others, as in the case of the police, may happen to have enough in common to make easy adjustments to the new order of life. In short, the success or failure of our random national Indian policy depended upon happy accidents bringing similar patterns together. This seems to have happened so seldom that the efforts of even the most conscientious officials were about as futile as twirling the dial on a safe without knowing the combination.

The Mounted Police of Canada are famous. They spread their control over the Canadian Indian country even before western reservations were formed. The old time mounted police deserved all the praise showered upon them; they were just as efficient as the present mounties but were men of a different background and faced more difficult problems. Three or four of these red-coated fellows would ride into a large camp of free-roving armed Indians, demand of the Chiefs that certain offenders be turned over to them to conduct to prison; strange to say they usually got their men and no one was killed. I visited a few Canadian reservations in the time of which I write, noting how the mounted force stood behind the Indian agents, relieving them of police responsibilities.

My first contact with the Canadian Police was when I passed over from a United States Indian reservation to a Canadian one. My Indian camp followers were afraid of the "red coats." They even made me uneasy by their pessimistic remarks. However, at the custom's post of entry I was courteously received and given a pass, which strange to say, was nothing more than a few lines scrawled upon a tiny bit of plain paper. This I folded to make still smaller and when my Indians seemed to weaken, I would exhibit this bit of tissue as the magic that would carry us through. I knew that a white man leading a party of Indians into a foreign country would at least attract the attention of the "red coats," but for a day we toiled along across open grassland where now are farms and villages, so new is that country—without seeing a "red coat." In the evening we camped on the flood plain of a little stream.

Presently, one of my Indians caught sight of a four-horse team in the distance with two outriders, which his practical eye knew to be a patrol. It was apparent that they were headed our way; in fact, they were coming straight on. When within some 200 yards they stopped, all their horses were unreined to crop a little grass, while one of the stately, trim "red coats" approached us with military strides. My Indians were sure there would be trouble now. The greeting was prompt and the questions direct. Where we were headed? Where we crossed the line? etc. But before I had completed my answers the officer said that he had heard of our being passed-in, that he was Sergeant Addington, that his horses and men needed a rest, so he would visit awhile. I offered him a cigar, but he preferred his pipe. He was an educated man, had been to New York when on leave, read good magazines, asked about the latest plays, etc. After a time I noticed that two men still sat stiffly upon the wagon seat and asked why they did not dismount. With a sly smile the Sergeant said, "They are chained to the seat—two horse thieves."

Presently he took his leave, invited me to visit the post and so began a pleasant and profitable acquaintance with the men of the force. My Indians marveled at the magic power of that tiny bit of paper, which though it remained hidden in my pocket did the work; to them no other explanation was adequate.

Everyone should have experienced a thrill looking at those stately, efficient Canadian Police. The United States Indian Police were efficient enough but they rarely looked it. Probably but two men ever saw anything inspiring in the appearance of the Indian police: the old-time agent who looked out with surprise upon his troop, naked, in war paint and feathers, singing death songs, setting out to stop a sun dance, and the General who saw a troop spontaneously desert their military drill-master to make a successful charge against an Indian attack on the agency. How could Indian police, motivated by the culture of their fathers, look inspiring in the misfitting gear of a town constable?

Though a profitless pastime, most of us enjoy dreaming of what might have been. So suppose that after the record-breaking explorations of Lewis and Clark, the United States had set up a police force like the Canadian Mounted, stretching their authority from the Mississippi to the Pacific, what would have been the result? We all know how it worked in Canada. Wild, roving

Indians were brought under control with but one serious war. Had there been such a force in our Great West the bad man of the frontier would have been far less conspicuous and there would have been no Indian police. Yet this is a vain dream. Our government would not have tolerated such a force and even if committed to it, would certainly have filled it with temporary political appointees. The lawlessness of the whites even down to early reservation days amazes us. In the 80's many reservations were law and order havens for the surrounding districts because they alone maintained a fearless police force. I once spent some time on a reserve near the two ends of which were towns, which if not wholly lawless, made Indian life look like true civilization.

Man is a social animal, he does his best in a crowd. We have heard a lot of talk about rugged individualism, but even the devotee to this philosophy must have a group to support his attainments. It seems to me the history of the Indian police demonstrates the truth of this, for even the police of the Plains Indians were conspicuous only on the large reservations, where they were numerous enough to form a troop. I suspect that pride of the force, the acquisition of traditions and high ideals, cannot be expected among a few lone men.

The Plains tribes of aboriginal days knew better than to designate a few lone men as the body to enforce the necessary regulations in the camp and on the hunt. Instead, they organized a society,—a kind of club,— provided the members with a tipi of their own from which women were excluded. Their faith and courage were fortified by ritual and song, sanctioned by the great unseen. Their status carried with it certain obligations, with dignified and correct behavior. They must look and act the part. Their leaders must deserve their respect. Thus, there was a pride in their office; to fail was more than a disgrace. It is easier for such a body of men to achieve distinction than for a lone policeman, for each member of the force knows that there are many comrades standing behind him, who have the same ideals as he and who will be equally smirched if he falters. Here and there an agent of a large reservation sensed all this and threw just enough solemnity and mysticism around the oath each policeman was required to take; provided a separate building and a barracks, in which by contact and fellowship they developed the pride of the force and the determination not to fail.

The police usually had a mess, exclusively their own, and reminiscent of the old Indian days when their women handed food through the forbidden door of the "soldiers' tipi." I remember one of the dining arrangements for the Indian police. The cook for this police mess was a white man who learned his trade following the cattle round-ups. Thus he belonged to a class peculiar to the cow country, characterized by a highly standardized cooking technique, rigidly limited in scope; beans, bacon, fried eggs, potatoes, flap-jacks, were the main dishes. Such of these cooks as I met were set in their ways, rarely quite sober, used bowie knives to cut up food and as badges of authority, and were everywhere looked upon as socially inferior but dangerous. As one veteran of the West once remarked, "such cooks were tough characters, best let have their own way." Of course they had to be efficient in their peculiarities to keep their jobs, but since they were trained to cook in the open, following the herds, they were misfits when put into a shack, and if kept there, degenerated.

Such was the cook for this police mess. He was said to be a Mexican, but was never known to admit it or to give any information about himself. He wore a blazing red flannel shirt even in the hottest weather; for a cookhouse he had the meanest sort of a shed, but his fame rested on his method of calling the meals. A long cross-cut saw was suspended near his kitchen, upon which he could beat out a surprising composition. It began with a boom, like a military march, but soon floated away into a kind of soft, sweet chime. At the agency his musical performance was awaited just as people living near a famous carillon await the masterpiece of the day. One of the white reservation employees said he always stopped to listen, because so seldom did even the echoes of music reach the reservation. Where that Mexican acquired his art, what fine emotions quivered beneath his red shirt as he played, no one could guess, for on this as other personal matters he was silent as the sphinx. Like all things on a reservation this came and went, for later when I came back, the Mexican cook was gone. I learned that he had left one pay day—whither no one knew—and horrible to relate, his successor delegated an Indian to preside over the saw, who merely pounded it. Too bad that everywhere and at all times even the simplest values in life on an Indian reservation should be so tenuous.

8

Riding with the Agency Doctor

THE OFFICIAL medical officer on a reservation enjoyed the title of "Dock." Always and everywhere one merely thought of his sphere and function as sufficiently defined by that term, just as Major stood for another function. Dock usually knew vastly more of Indian life than any other official, but possibly because of professional inhibitions said the least about the subject. Nevertheless I always went to him for advice because he was the one person in the situation with whom one could talk as man to man.

One day Dock remarked dryly that the wild plums were beginning to turn, but the significance of the remark was lost upon me. Naturally, I suspected that it was about the time of year when plums should mature, but he promptly changed the subject by inviting me to accompany him on a trip around the reservation. I had often wished for just such a look in on Indian life. It was a large reservation, so about ten days would be required to complete the tour. At the appointed time, I appeared at Dock's quarters with my bed-roll. He was stooping over a kind of trunk filled with rows of bottles—never had I thought it possible to put a drug store into so little space. The bottle holders seemed to unfold like a pocket map and I hoped to see how they would look when all were opened out at the same time, but the opportunity never came. Having thoroughly checked the bottles, Dock opened the other side of the trunk, revealing saws, knives, forceps and scissors. I was naive enough to ask if he anticipated a surgical case. He was a tolerant person and so merely remarked that anything might happen. True enough, it was a foolish question, how can a doctor know what the next call will require?

Our traveling equipment was a kind of buggy with a rear extension like peddlers once used, large enough to receive the precious drug store and our bed-rolls. Two strong black horses furnished the motor power. Because of tradition rather than need, Dock took a repeating rifle, but the only use he found for it was to confuse running coyotes by dropping bullets in front of them, the puff of dust serving to turn the runner, only to face another puff and send him off in another direction. It gave me a good deal of satisfaction to see this impudent smarty of the plains meet his match and sometimes I wished Dock would give one of them a taste of lead, but being a superb marksman, he never hit one by accident. I never met a man with such hunting skill who killed so seldom.

It was plains country and as usual the roads, if they could be called such, followed the higher ground. It was soon evident that every Indian knew Dock's buggy miles away, for ere long a galloping horseman appeared far out upon our flank, every now and then waving his hat. As soon as Dock caught sight of the rider, he stopped the team. This was the first of a long sequence of hails. When within speaking distance, the Indian brought his horse to a walk, uttering a few brief sentences in his native speech. It signified nothing to me, but Dock evidently recognized a word or two, for

he said we must turn out to see a sick child. We followed the lead of the rider for a few miles to a small
cluster of log cabins and tipis, sheltered behind the low
terrace of a little stream. There was a sick child,
though seemingly not dangerously ill. One Indian girl
could speak a little English and from her Dock learned
that there were several other children ill and that all of
them had eaten green plums. I assumed that Dock
knew as much anyway and that the questioning was
carried through out of deference to me. As may be
guessed there were many similar calls ere the trip was
ended.

Like others of his profession, Dock had a number of
patients on his list in various stages of tuberculosis and
other chronic diseases. Upon these calls were made.
There were no obstetrical cases for the good reason
that the culture of this tribe did not sanction the presence of a male on such occasions, but so far as I could
learn this was the only limitation to Dock's services.

There were two calls for what may pass as surgery.
One of these was upon a young man with a dislocated
jaw. For two days an Indian doctor had sung songs
and prayed, but to no purpose. The patient was stolid,
but plainly in great pain. With my bungling assistance,
the rounded end of the lower jaw was forced into the
cup-like depression where it belonged. The other case
was that of a youth accidentally—so it was said—shot
in the thigh. The doctor probed the wound, obviously
exceedingly painful to the boy, but he made no
sound.

We all know how the mere sight of a drug store may
start a headache or an advertisement convince one that
his liver is diseased. Being illiterate, the Indian escaped
some of these fears, but I noted that a peep at the rows
of bottles in Dock's chest was sufficient to remind these
supposedly fortunate children of Nature that all was
not well within. By signs, each would indicate the part

of the body he thought misbehaving. Had I been scientific I should have listed these and thereby discovered where the Indian localized his aches and pains, but the wide range of such bodily locations seemed to run parallel to what an equal number of white people would point to as the seats of the pain. Dock agreed with me on this point, though he believed the Indian far less honest, whatever he may have meant by that.

Dock met these requests by tiny vials of camphor, of which the patients were to smell twice a day, or a few tiny pellets unmedicated; if an Indian complained that these had been tried before without results, a little ammonia might be substituted for the camphor. Like the white man of the 90's, the Indian judged medicines by their kick.

The Doctor and the Major were seldom friendly, but for the most part preserved a kind of armed neutrality. Of course, the Major was supreme in theory, but medicine was more of a mystery to him than it was to an Indian. He dare not rule on that subject. Then at any moment he himself might fall into the hands of this under official, be ordered to bed or perhaps quarantined. The Doctor's appointment was far less political and his term of service much longer. Thus a new Major often found himself linked up with a Doctor so long in the service that he knew vastly more about the situation than the Major could hope to learn and whose responsibilities to his patients were unlimited. No Major could feel entirely at ease in such a setting, and not infrequently was heard to say that Dock was conceited and impractical, whereas Dock pronounced the Major as ignorant and stubborn. In one place, I heard that while the Doctor reported each year the number of tubercular Indians observed, the Major considered the number absurd, refusing to transmit the Doctor's reports to headquarters or to approve requests for aid and better facilities. Of course, in the end, the

Doctor won out. However, these official clashes were far less interesting to me than the attitude of the Indian. From the first he took kindly to white man's medicine, assuming that men who possessed fire arms, steel tools and liquor could effectively treat the sick. Often the fur trader became a doctor against his will.

For example, from the diary of a veteran trader by the name of Alexander Henry, who lived and traded among the Indians of northern United States and the adjacent parts of Canada for many years around 1800, we extract the following:

"Medicines they have few or none, except some simples they use to cure wounds. They are perfectly ignorant of internal applications, and seem to have no medicines for the relief of any inward complaint. Notwithstanding their own ignorance in quackery, they are perpetually begging medicine from us, and place the greatest confidence in whatever we give them, imagining that everything medical which comes from the trader must be a sovereign remedy for all diseases. I have often done wonders by giving them a smell of *eau de Luce* (ammonia), as something warranted to cure all kinds of internal maladies. Next morning after drinking they generally swarm into the house for medicine to relieve the effects of the liquor, and we often have some diversion by assuming a solemn countenance, and letting them taste or smell some kind of trash; and the more poignant the application, the greater faith they put in its efficacy."

The Annual Reports of the Commissioner of Indian Affairs occasionally contain statements indicative of medical problems on reservations. Some Indian physicians were by no means patient or tolerant toward the Indians under their care, and I recall one instance in which the complaint is made that after forty years of general practice among white people, the physician now tending the Indians, remembers no class of people among whom medical practice had been so difficult.

For one thing, if the Indian patient did not show improvement after the first dose of medicine, he refused to take another. Naturally this was disconcerting to the physician. However, he complained of other difficulties, since if he should leave a bottle of cough medicine and the taste was not found too bitter, the patient was likely to drink it at once. Again, if the patient was found in pain, suggesting the use of liniment, and a bottle was left to supply him for a long period, the chances were that the whole bottle would be dashed upon the patient's skin in the hope that relief would be immediate. All of this indicates the antithesis of the favorite expression of one doctor which was, that life in the Indian service was one continued round of pleasure. No doubt when he uttered this bit of homely philosophy, he had in mind such experiences as we have just enumerated.

Another doctor seems to have been shocked with the unsanitary life he observed when first assigned to a reservation, since he writes that—"The people are troubled by pulmonary diseases to quite an extent. This I attribute not to a weaker organism than the whites have, but to the fact that during the last generation they have changed their mode of living to an extent hitherto unknown to any class of people with whom I am acquainted, or have ever heard of. A lifetime ago these Indians were roaming the plains, subsisting, without Government aid, on game, fish, and berries, and such edible roots as could be gathered from forest and prairie. They were living a free, outdoor life, winter and summer, in their skin lodges, inured to hardships that would seem, even to them now, appalling. They were able to withstand, in their bearskins, the extremes of summer's heat and winter's cold, and pulmonary disease among them was practically an unknown quantity.

"All this is changed; the game that subsisted on the

plains has been swept away as the crumbs from the festal board; the skin lodge is gone; the free, roaming life of this athletic race has passed away. They are living on reservations in small cabins built upon their allotments; in winter time made as tight as possible; heated to a degree almost unbearable by a white man. Here they gather, old and young, male and female, sick and well, breathing the vitiated air, further contaminated by the fumes of the red willow; usually without floors, always without beds, they sleep on the ground, and as the fire dies, the death's-head grins on them in a form of quickly contracted pneumonia. Of sanitary laws in the past they knew nothing, or from their mode of life needed to. But under the changed condition they must be enlightened on this subject, or the death rate in the future will be greater than that of the past."

Another difficulty which sometimes troubled the physician was the tendency to bury the corpse immediately after death. Most of the doctors known to me were of the opinion that in some cases the individual was not dead, but merely unconscious, and the annals of the Indian Department actually report such instances. For example, "The second case was that of an old Indian, aged about sixty years, who was suffering with an aggravated attack of la grippe, who got up early one morning last winter, when the thermometer stood at about 40 degrees below zero, and went out in his bear pelt, without even moccasins on his feet, to get an armful of wood with which to build his morning fire. A quick congestion of the lungs seized him, and he toppled over insensible, and was quickly brought into the house by his family in that condition. They sent in for a coffin, and told me of the circumstances of his death. Thinking it might be a case merely of suspended animation, I sent the agency physician out to render such assistance as he could, and report. On his return he reported the case as that of suspended animation;

said he could only detect life by holding a looking glass to his mouth, and finding moisture thereon by his breathing. He said he told the Indians that the man was not dead, and instructed them to rub him and restore animation by that process. I sent him out the next day. When he got there he found the man was buried."

I heard of a case which had a happier ending than the one just cited, since in this instance the supposed corpse came to life upon the way to the burial place and remonstrated with the pallbearers. Not only did this man fully recover, but because of the belief that he had really died and then came to life, he was forever after considered one of the greatest medicine men of his tribe and could tell interesting stories of what he saw in the happy hunting grounds during the brief interval between his supposed death and his revival.

If the reader has any doubt as to whether Indians were willing to be treated by the white doctor, they need only scan the agency reports to observe that in some years the number of patients treated was practically equal to the total population. In earlier days when the Indians were first settled upon the reservation, there was still a good deal of fighting among themselves and with hostile tribes, and the physician of that day had plenty of practice in surgery, since one of them reports that during a single year he treated more than one hundred arrow wounds, not to mention cases of stabbing and wounds from bullets.

One fortunate aspect of this doctoring by white men was the absence of commercialization. With us the chief worry is the doctor's bill, but at no time had the white man demanded pay of the Indian, his was the Good Samaritan's role. The most hardened old fur trader would ruthlessly cheat the Indian in a trade, but at the same time treat his wounds or try to save the life of his child with never a hint of pay. This is the one bright spot in the sordid record of Indian contact. When military posts were set up in the Indian country, the medical officers of the army dispensed freely to such Indians as came to notice and, of course, when reservations were formed, doctors were assigned to them. All was free for the asking. No wonder an Indian rarely caught sight of the agency doctor without feeling the urge to present his tongue in return for a box of pills or a vial of camphor. Yet the reader should not take this to mean that the Indian had turned his back upon the doctors of his own color, for like most people, he held to an abiding faith in the wisdom of his ancestors. He usually tried to play safe by appealing to both white and red doctors. That both failed he saw proof on every hand, but in the supreme hour of trial he turned to the traditional healers among his own kind. What else could he do?

It may be an anomaly to say that men, who rode so boldly to battle, feared death, but I was everywhere impressed by the terror a slight illness could create. Even in my day I believe most Indian men would have fearlessly approached the firing line, had there been one, and gone to their death without a regret, but the mere mention of illness would make them uneasy. I suppose the explanation lies in their past, for I recall an Indian song which ends with the refrain, "that nothing can be so bad as to die in bed." Perhaps such a death was considered abnormal, or a disgrace or a kind of treason. Not infrequently in the annals of reservations one may read that a man believing himself sick to the death, began shooting at everyone in sight until he himself was killed. In one instance, a doctor, new to the service, frankly told a patient that he was on the road to death and that nothing could be done about it. The Indian went home, armed himself and set out to kill until the end, several Indians and a white school teacher falling before a lucky shot ended his murder-ous career. In pre-reservation days such an Indian would have gone on the warpath, continuing until killed by an ememy; perhaps on the reservation this pattern could be realized in no other way than by running amuck. Experienced doctors in the Indian service knew better than to tell an Indian death was near.

I began this digression by considering the attitude of the Indian toward the reservation medical service and before passing to other subjects should record here that the white doctor was usually held in high regard. In the wild tempestuous days of the 70's and 80's, the doctor could go about his mission fearlessly even at times when no other white man was safe. As I noted above, the doctor asked nothing in return for his services, his whole approach was kindly and sympathetic, the result being that no Indian ever thought of the doctor as in the same class with other white people. It is true that the Indian is a good judge of character and might think less of a medical misfit, but when a man of merit occupied that office, the Indian valued him accordingly. Anyway, to the Indian mind, the doctor and his office stood as the symbol of what was best in white culture, the one outstanding example of true philanthropy. Rarely did the church and the missionary rise to the same level in his pagan regard.

The reader may have heard some disparaging remarks about the doctors in the Indian service for which there was some excuse. At least I met up with a few poor specimens of the healing art who had no more right to practice than a deaf and blind man; had I fallen ill in one of their reservations I should have preferred to take my chances with the Indian medicine man. Some apologizers for the presence of such medical incompetents said the explanation lay in the low pay offered by the service, but this did not appeal to me. True the salary of the agency doctor was $100 per month; yet since he paid no rent and all his equipment

was furnished, the return was better than for many
country doctors. So I saw nothing in that argument
and after all many of the small town doctors I have
heard about were no more efficient than some of the
Indian service misfits I have in mind. For one thing the
isolation on a reservation offered some doctors the
opportunity to cease reading journals and otherwise ac-
quainting themselves with the advances in their profession. Some took to drinking. One or two I knew became notorious for sex offenses, young Indian women
offering abundant opportunities. I recall one rather
amusing incident; a doctor began calling upon a young
girl whose mother could talk a little English. The obvious trifling on the part of the doctor so aroused the ire
of this upright mother that she appeared upon the
scene one evening with a six-shooter, giving him the
choice of marrying the girl or keeping away. The doctor chose to decamp, his speed accelerated by a few
bullets spattering at his heels. The Indians so enjoyed
the story and so industriously ragged the victim that he
resigned. But why recall these unlovely exceptions in
the Indian medical service, for there were real men
among them, a few whose acquaintance I valued and
whose memory I cherish, though all have passed on to
their reward.

Occasionally an unusual person found his way into
the Indian service, and though the doctors seemed the
most standardized of all employees, this fact alone
threw every variation among the medical personnel
into high relief. The most unexpected case of aberrant
medical behavior coming to my notice was also the
most interesting. The doctor was young and just out of
the medical school, but had a flare for social problems.
So in due time he invited all the Indian doctors to a
feast. Of course, they were suspicious, but with the
Indian even more than the white man, the lure of a
good dinner is irresistible, so they came. It was merely

a friendly get-together—one doctor to another, so to speak. Finding the new doctor's food good and his manners pleasant, they were more than ready to accept other invitations and so it came about that the discussions turned professional and a kind of medical association was organized. Each conceded they had special powers, but that no rational objection could be raised against cooperating, since if both Indian and white worked toward the same end, more lives should be saved. This went so far that the Indian doctor would send for the white doctor and each treat the patient; in fact, the Indian doctor would see to it that the treatment proposed by his white colleague was faithfully carried through. What could be more promising? Yes, it was too good to last; the Indian service was no place for a man with vision. When it was discovered that a civilized doctor was on friendly terms with pagan doctors and tolerating their methods, the church people were horrified, even the Major, a case-hardened politician, was indignant and went on record that such a white doctor was no safe person to treat the sick.

All sorts of ridiculous charges were made as, that the doctor was about to give up the use of regular medicines, that he had become a devotee to pagan worship, that when he had a white patient, he proposed to call in a troop of Indians to beat drums, sing songs, dance and perpetrate filthy and disgusting practices. All of which were ridiculous. It was the old familiar story, try to meet the Indian half way and the specter of paganism would be conjured up to your undoing. However, this worthy young man was saved the disgrace of an undeserved dismissal because he braved a blizzard to make a distant call; the storm beat relentlessly upon his team, until the poor horses could go no farther, but undaunted, the doctor set out afoot with his medicine case in hand. No human saw the fight he made, but some days later the wind uncovered the doctor's lifeless body within a half mile of the sick Indian's cabin. Maybe the Good Lord had use for this precious soul in a more grateful world—let us hope so. The Indian who told me the story took a harsher view of the matter, feeling that even the white man's God was against the Indian.

In the days of which I write there were neither hospitals nor nurses; the doctor saw his patient lying on the floor of a cabin or a tipi and left the family to its own nursing devices. Hospitals would have been useless anyway for most Indians shunned a shelter in which there had been a death. To their way of thinking, to enter such a building was to invite destruction, hence to have dragged a sick Indian into a hospital would have scared him to death and so defeated the purpose of such an institution. Long after I ceased to frequent reservations, hospitals were built, but as expected, the Indians were resistant. I hear that on one such reserve the Indians held out until a few years since when they were persuaded to look upon a hospital, not as a place where people lived, but as a building for the sick. This shift in the point of view did the trick, by saving the face of these sticklers for tradition. Among most tribes as among many white communities, no one was anxious to approach a corpse and a rattling skeleton was frightful enough to start a panic. Once a trader planted a few water-melon seeds and when the fruit was up, allowed the Indians to taste it. They were so excited over this new luxury that they urged the trader to plant a large crop, volunteering to assist. Accordingly, a large square of ground was cleared and seeds planted. Unfortunately, the Indians were so deeply interested in the plants that they tramped daily over the plot to watch them grow. No amount of protesting by the trader seemed to check their curiosity, so it was evident that no melons would mature unless the Indian could be kept away. Remembering that they feared human bones, the trader brought a few skulls from a burial place, placing them upon sticks in different parts of the plot. The method was effective, for after that not an Indian came near the melon patch. So a fine crop of melons matured and the trader had visions of a handsome profit, but when the time came, the Indians refused them at any price, saying, they grew in a graveyard.

Every now and then I became aware that the native doctors longed for some of the secrets of the white medicine man. They envied him the great array of bottles and mysterious instruments, but no inducement seemed to move the white doctor to instruct his red brother in the principles of white medicine. Occasionally some shrewd Indian tried to stock up with medicines by playing sick and saving up the pills and powders freely doled out by the white doctor. This method had its merits, since if the Indian could simulate one type of illness and save what the doctor prescribed, he would thus know what drug to use for that form of sickness. It seemed easy and so it might have succeeded if it had not been for the suspicious Indian police. Once Dock was tipped off by the police that a certain Indian was giving his patient pills and powders which resembled those doled out by the Government and then Dock remembered that many times this old Indian had called in to say that he was ill and accordingly received such medicines as Dock thought he needed. True, Dock usually worked off harmless stuff on this faker, noting that there were no visible symptoms. Nevertheless, no one likes to be made a fool of and so Dock bided his time. Sure enough, the old rascal turned up, groaning and pressing upon his stomach. As soon as he entered, Dock appeared alarmed, grasped the patient, hurried him to a couch, shouting to his assistant to be quick, for the Indian was near death. A large dose of seidlitz powder was forced into the patient's stomach, who was then induced to swallow a lot of water. The result can be imagined, spouting like a geyser, the terrified Indian sprang for the door and when last seen was still running at top speed. Dock assured me that this Indian never called again and, though ultimately seriously ill, stubbornly refused to have anything to do with white man's medicine.

One day I found Dock at a strange task. Seated in the middle of the floor, he was examining small objects resembling matches, casting some into an iron pail, the others into a traveling case. As I watched, the mystery grew, and in response to my expressed curiosity, he explained that these were vaccination points. Noting that the number of these points seemed enough to inoculate an army, I showed concern, my imagination picturing the inconvenience of quarantine, but Dock said there were no cases on the reservation at present. However, small-pox had appeared upon a reservation 300 miles away, and that as a precaution, he was inspecting his stock of points, rejecting those seemingly dead. When I voiced relief to know that the much dreaded disease was so far away, Dock countered to the effect that within three days he expected cases, because according to his observations small-pox traveled about 75 miles a day. What he meant was that roaming Indians with good horses, could travel at that rate. Everyone has heard of how in pioneer days small-pox carried off thousands of Indians. Dock would have it that the small-pox germ was so fond of Indian flesh that it would leap great distances to reach its victims. However this may be, there was no disease the Indian dreaded more; in the old days its appearance was the signal to dispersal into small groups, in fact, the best possible procedure. Incidentally, Indian history records that there was little resistance to vaccination, the Indians' record in this respect standing superior to the white.

We must now take leave of Dock and the odors of his medicine closet regretting that his place in this monograph is a modest one, for whatever may have been the shortcomings of the Indian medical service there is little to apologize for, since in contrast to the sordid graft and incompetence obvious in many places, this branch of the service was conspicuously beneficent and humane. A fitting ending to this chapter would be a tribute to the old time reservation doctor, but having neither the ability nor the touch of the "Bonnie Brier Bush," we can do no more than cite that classical tribute to the old Country Doctor. We have in mind several agency doctors equally deserving, who in the blackest night, the most stinging cold, would set out for a journey of hours and hours, in response to calls to relieve the distress of ignorant illiterate Indians in rude shelters. To them there were neither distinctions of color, sex nor station in life, the call for aid was enough. It mattered not if many times lost in a blizzard, carried down stream in a swift flood or stuck in a treacherous bog, all such trials were accepted, and if perchance, one went down to rise no more, he would rather have it so, than to end his days in idleness. No wonder my Indian friends put these doctors into a class apart from other white men.

9

The Indian Court

THOUGH IN MANY respects the Indian court that was
established in the 70's and 80's soon became the most
important institution on the reservations, it was often
the least in evidence. A stranger could easily spend
weeks about a given agency, observing and dipping
deeply into the life that came and went, without dis-
covering the court's existence. It came to my attention
quite by accident when a trader introduced a dignified
Indian as "The Judge." On inquiry, I learned that there
was a court then sitting and gladly accepted the judge's
invitation to attend.

The courtroom was plain; a few rude chairs for the
officials, rough pine seats for those in attendance. The
aroma of the Indian pipe was everywhere, giving the
feeling that, for once, I was standing in a government
building in which the Indian could feel at home, even
as a prisoner. The judge to whom I had been introduced and two venerable colleagues, all bearing themselves with even more dignity than an outstanding Indian habitually assumes, took their seats behind a rude
table which I rightly assumed to be the Bench. No one
announced their entrance as in a white court.

Aside from their impressive countenances, what particularly impressed me was their clothes. They wore full black custom-made suits, of the type donned by white men only on special occasions; white shirts, rolled collars, and, instead of moccasins, well blackened shoes. Shortly after they had taken their positions, the Major entered—a sure sign that an important case was to be heard. An attending Indian policeman, his heavy pistol sagging at his loose belt, left the room, returning soon after with two women, one of whom came forward bold and defiant, the other hesitating and timid. The first proved to be the chief offender so the proceedings began with her. No one went through the formula of asking her name, etc., as in a white man's court. I suppose that in a place like this, where common sense rather than hoary ritualism was the order of the day, that question did not arise. No doubt, I was the only person in the room ignorant of her name and identity. Later, I learned that a good English translation of her name would be Standing-woman.

Standing-woman was an impressive figure, tall, obviously strong and muscular as an athlete. Her countenance was rather hard, and her eyes flashed defiance. Over her head was tied a large faded, but clean handkerchief, her dress was of red dotted calico cut in Indian fashion, moccasins on her feet, and of course, the ever-present trade blanket. The other woman whose name I did not learn, was perhaps a little older, thin enough to suggest an underfed and slightly dissipated existence. Her countenance was blank, her clothes in disorder and by no means clean, but the most conspicuous feature was a large white spotless bandage encircling her head and face. Obviously she had just been treated by the agency doctor.

The proceedings opened with a question from one of the judges, and since the Major was present it was necessary to have everything interpreted—fortunately for me.

Judge: "Did you beat this woman over the head with a water pail?"

Standing-woman: "I did."

Judge: "Why?"

Standing-woman: "She came around making a fuss. I told her to go away, to leave me alone. She continued until I beat her over the head with the water pail."

Judge: "Are you living with the husband of this woman?" (the one with the bandaged head)

Standing-woman: "Yes."

Judge: "Why?"

Standing-woman: "She had a good man who worked hard, but she was lazy and always nagging. I am a good woman and work hard; I needed a good man so I took him into my house. Then this woman came around making a disturbance, so I beat her over the head with a water pail."

There was a deliberate pause, then a second judge asked:

"Standing-woman, did you have a previous husband?"

Standing-woman: "Yes."

Judge: "Where is he?"

Standing-woman: "He was lazy, no good, quarrelsome, so I ran him away."

Judge: "Where did he go?"

Standing-woman: "To live with this woman," pointing to the one with the bandaged head.

The judges went into a huddle for a brief discussion, but soon returned to their seats. One of them asked the policeman if the two husbands were waiting and upon being assured that they were, requested their presence. So the two men were brought in, taking their places beside the women. The four now stood in a row. Standing-woman with her new man at her left, next on her right the bandaged woman, and then the former husband of Standing-woman. One of the judges then addressed each man in turn as to his future intentions; each declared that he intended to continue under the present arrangement. Standing-woman next declared that her intention was also to abide by her *fait accompli*. Finally, the woman with the bandaged head was asked if she preferred to live with the man on her right; since she had the last turn, about all she could do was nod her head.

While the judges engaged in further consultation, the Major turned to me, asking how I would decide this case. My reply was that the whole matter seemed to have settled itself; the only thing remaining was to enter into the agency record two divorces and two marriages. It so happened that the judges recommended such a procedure, in which the Major concurred. Then one of the judges lectured the culprits upon their unseemly conduct, recalled to their minds the traditional ideals of virtue, and admonished them to live in peace. Nothing was said about the bandaged head, perhaps the judges believed a little letting of blood was necessary to real social adjustment. I left the court, doubting the legality of the procedure but fully approving it and admiring the bold short cuts taken by these illiterate judges. In our courts, a judge, several lawyers, a jury or two, no telling how many witnesses, a few stenographers, and a few clerks would have labored several weeks to untangle a similar situation.

"Tell it to the judge," may be an ultra-modern phrase, particularly in tabloid journalism, but it expresses such a basic human relation as to make easy its translation into the most primitive of unwritten languages. Among the aboriginal Indians of North America, the phase would have implied standing face to face with the highest human wisdom backed by that of the gods. The ancient Semites looked upon their Supreme God as a great judge, and while the Indian did not lean so far in that direction, he knew that if his society frowned upon his behavior, he must make answer, sooner or later, to its leaders, and through them to the Great Unseen. In aboriginal society, rules were made to be obeyed, but like many such rules in all kinds of societies, it was often difficult to make them apply to the complicated situations in which one must actually live. So, even in the aboriginal scheme of things, the judge steps into the picture to interpret the rules and fix the penalties. In other words, there were judges in America long before Columbus was born.

Some agents on the reservations wisely took advantage of the fact that Indians had always had judges, and accordingly drew the arbiters of the reservation court from the native ranks. There were, of course, agents who refused to appoint Indian judges and who heard and decided all cases without native advice. That this did not work out so well in many cases was probably due to the differences of opinion that lay in the two conflicting culture backgrounds, rather than in differing capacities for administering justice. For example, most Indians of that day put far less value upon time than the white man. A week or a month meant little to the former and a great deal to the latter. A jail sentence for an Indian might easily mean better food than he got at home and freedom from all responsibility of providing for his family. In old times Indians were punished by destroying their property, by cutting the tails of their horses as a badge of disgrace, and sometimes by whipping them with horse quirts. But the accompanying disgrace and ridicule engendered by each and all of these were the real penalties. The jail, on the other hand, was merely a white man's house, and so carried with it no traditions of disgrace. Of course, in time the Indians came around to that point of view, but even now to many Indians a jail sentence does not mean the same thing as it does to a white man. And if anyone should wonder at this, let him not forget that it took centuries to condition white society to abhor the jail.

The agent rarely knew enough about Indian life to understand any of these things, so one can imagine what tragic mistakes he might make when judging cases without the advice of responsible Indians. As a rule intelligent Indians knew a great deal about the white people and so would have judged many white offenders justly, whereas most agents would have made themselves ridiculous dealing with Indian offenders. Of course, if he possessed the proverbial wisdom of Solomon, an agent might get along without Indian advice, but many stumbling blocks would lie in his path, not the least of which would be the problem of language.

Every now and then, these language difficulties would work to the advantage of the Indian, as in the amusing incident once told me about two Indian men who amicably exchanged wives. All parties to the trade seemed pleased, but according to white law this was a serious offense. So they were arrested and ordered to assume their former relationships. When they refused to comply, the agent conceived a good punishment would be to lock up each man with his original wife. But what actually happened was that the agent got things mixed up in his struggle with the language and locked up the men with their new partners instead of with the old ones. It was great fun for the Indians, who kept it to themselves. The erring couples were released from jail some weeks later after promising to live together in the future. No doubt this agent congratulated himself on his ingenuity and the success of his original method for the reconciliation of estranged couples.

These incidents are not given to create the impression that when an agent decided to be the judge he invariably made a mess of it, but because no one cares to hear about the uniform and wise decisions many of them handed down. In any case, the Government expected the agent to review the decisions of his judges and revise them if necessary. This had the additional virtue of providing a method of appeal when Indians felt they had not received justice in their own court. I note in the official reports that some agents complained because the decisions of judges were too harsh. For example, the verdict might be a long jail sentence, whereas the agent thought a short one sufficient. Yet a wise agent was sparing in his review of cases, otherwise the morale of the judges would weaken.

There was one thing, however, that every agent insisted upon: that the judges cut their hair short. Some time previous to my visit, an order had gone out from Washington that no Indian could be employed by the Government nor elevated to office until he visited the agency barber. Not only was his hair to be cut short, but cut in the prevailing white style and kept cut. Such an unreasonable decree caused endless strife, of course, and benefited no one but the barbers. But agents, taking the hint, filled their reports with statistics of so many haircuts, proud of having used force to bring about this reform. When an Indian was so unfortunate as to be arrested, the barber was promptly called in to cut off his glorious black hair.

Why the Government should have set itself so uncompromisingly against male long hair, I do not know, unless the why for this fanaticism lay in the fact that long hair stood before the white mind as defiance of paganism against Christianity. I suppose all long-range government is stupid, but what could be more inconsistent than to demand that all police, judges, and other Indians loyal to the United States should cut their hair and then at the same time impose this indignity upon the criminal and thus give it the quality of a social stigma? At the time, I should have liked to know what the judges thought about this, but later happenings convinced me that they had become reconciled to such inconsistencies.

One case where the haircut rule was not enforced stands out in my mind. This exception occurred in an agency where two Indian boys about twelve years old had committed a theft. In the trader's store there was a showcase containing chewing gum and candy from which on occasion these boys were given a treat. But these were rare events in their none too exciting lives. Since burglary was an almost unheard of crime at the agency, windows were seldom locked, and so it was easy to steal a few handfuls of chewing gum. The two boys were quickly apprehended, convicted and condemned to labor on the agency driveway. I pitied these poor youngsters, doggedly hacking at weeds with hoes too large for their strength. How their muscles must have ached and their blistered hands stung when at night they curled up in the lonely lockup! I was interested to observe that each wore long braids of hair, and, on inquiry, learned that the agent had been humane enough to order that the usual haircutting be omitted. This was one of the finest things I ever heard about that agent.

Although the Indian judges I saw in court looked more at ease than most Indians trying to conform to white ways, I could not escape the feeling that they would have been happier sitting on the floor as they did in their homes. Of course, here again, Washington and the agent would have been horrified at the idea of a judge so seated, but I suspect that the defendant up for trial would have been more impressed, and at least have felt that the gods of his fathers were sitting with the judges. However, it was in such outward inessentials only that Washington could work its will, for none of these judges spoke English. They conferred in their tribal tongue and questioned the prisoners and witnesses in the same. Of law books they knew nothing, but they did know that their people were still enmeshed in tribal customs, and that the moral status of their people must be preserved or at least slowly eased over into white social patterns. They had taken an oath to perform their duty and they understood their responsibilities.

But let us return to the court; the judges are sitting. An Indian policeman presents a clownish-looking Indian whom I suspect of being near the feeble-minded level. The judges ask the policeman why he arrested the prisoner. The statement is brief enough, merely that the prisoner rode into the agency at a gallop, shouting war cries, saying he had something to tell the Major. The policeman knew a drunk when he saw one, so he ignored the message to the Major and put the hilarious fellow into the lock-up. Signs of recent operations by the barber are noticeable.

One of the judges asks the prisoner what he has to say for himself. As I shall need to remark more than once in these narratives, the Indian's mode of discourse is different from ours; if one chooses to speak for an hour, no one interrupts. The judges usually respected this custom so long as the speaker seemed to be honestly trying to give the information desired. In this case, the speaker was perhaps insincere, because he told how, when riding toward the agency, he saw a bottle in the trail containing something suspicious, but that he rode on. Then it occurred to him that it might be whiskey, which some Indian would find, drink and get into jail, so his duty was plain. Returning, he picked up the bottle, intending to take it to the Major. However, as he rode along there came to him the thought that the bottle might not contain whiskey, so he pulled the cork and sniffed. Yes, it smelled like whiskey, so he replaced the cork and rode on. Later came the idea that other liquids might smell like whiskey and yet not be whiskey, in which case the Major would ridicule him. (No people can be more sensitive to ridicule than Indians.) Naturally the bottle was opened once more and a swallow taken. Again he said this certainly is whiskey, and should be taken to the Major at once. Yet as he rode on he did not feel as if he had had a drink, perhaps, after all, this was not real whiskey. So he took another pull at the bottle and was soon convinced, for now he was feeling fine. He whipped up his horse and headed for the Major's office. He said he had done his best and almost got to the Major's before the police stopped him. Neither the judges, the policeman nor the few other Indians waiting around showed any change of countenance during or after this long narrative, which was at times enlivened by good and even humorous acting.

The judges sat silently for a brief interval as if to make sure the prisoner was through, then went into a brief huddle, after which one of them uttered a few words which the interpreter passed to the clerk as "Three weeks."

The most important aspects of all courts are the personalities who sit on the bench. This is probably true for all grades of society, including Indian reservations. I soon learned that my best chance for enlightenment on aboriginal life was to sit at the feet of the men who sat upon the bench. So I made it a rule to cultivate the friendship of these judges, and had little difficulty in winning their respect. On one reservation three judges were unusually helpful, and even spent part of their time between cases planning my next lesson in tribal customs and history. Their chief concern seemed to be that what they handed on for the written record should be correct to the smallest item. It was an inspiration to work with them, and as my day of departure approached, there were regrets on all sides—there was still so much to learn. My obligations to them were so great and my appreciation of their personalities so real, that I sought advice as to how, in keeping with the dignity of their position, I could do something adequate to the time and place. A wise

RESERVATION LIFE IN THE GAY NINETIES

HERE the Indian is the artist, drawing according to his own ideas and traditions. Paper, pencils and crayons were not familiar to him; he usually worked upon the covers of tipis and upon skins of the buffalo and deer, drawing where there was plenty of room and in the large. Small sheets of paper cramped his style and presented new problems on orientation. Traditionally the Indian drew animals and men in profile; backgrounds were neither colored nor shaded. In the old days the Indian spread a large skin upon the ground and moved around its edges as he drew. Given a piece of paper he often turned it as he worked, so the reader should turn the page accordingly to see things as the Indian visualized them.

Photographic reproduction eliminates the colors and so fails to do the originals justice, for this we apologize both to you and to the Indian. We hope that when the reader looks at these drawings he can imagine the flat strong colors of Indian costume and the sparkling sunlight effects as reflected from the pinto horses. We hope the pictures selected will reflect the life of the time and the aesthetic mysticism of the Indian.

These are Dakota Indians drawings made about 1890, collected by Rudolf Cronau and now in the American Museum of Natural History, New York City.

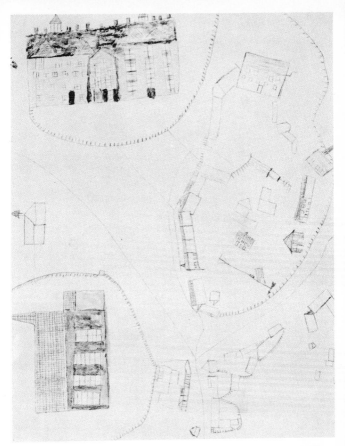

1. Ground plan and building detail of Pine Ridge Agency. The flagstaff and windmill, with water tank, mark the official quadrangle where the Major presided, surrounded by offices, warehouses, police barracks, doctor's quarters, etc. The school and the church are shown in detail. The traders' buildings are outlined in lower right. Like many Indian drawings this one must be turned from time to time to bring the objects into the positions intended.

2. *Once as the artist was driving a U. S. freight wagon along the trail to the Agency, he passed two buffalo bulls fighting. Though faulty in perspective the artist caught the mannerism of an Indian driving four horses.*

3. The Indian of my day could not forget the buffalo. They were life to
him, but what is more, they stood for the past and were his only hope for
the future. The picture is in the setting of bow-and-arrow days, but after
the horse came. No Indian could draw such a picture unless he had seen
many buffalo.

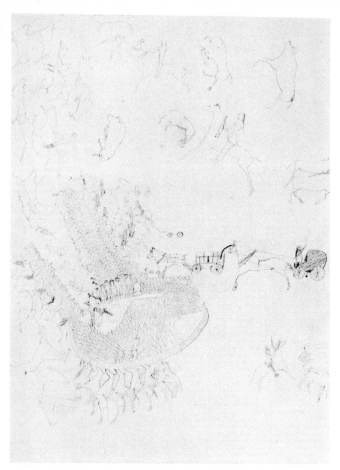

4. To the Indians a Cattle Issue was almost as exciting as an old-time buffalo hunt. We see the cattle in the corral, white men counting them out to waiting Indians, out in the open, Indians shooting down running cattle. The buggy means that the Major is on the ground.

5. *The Indian did his courting in the open, throwing his blanket around his lady love; one of the most familiar scenes around an Indian camp.*

6. *An Ultra Fashionable Turn-out. Parasols became fashionable in the gay nineties. Young men and girls rode double. As may be expected something like the modern horse show spirit dominated.*

7. *A Medicine Man's Vision. The thunder God, or Bird, riding the heavens on an Elk-horse, sends a bolt to earth killing an Indian. The scales upon the body of the steed symbolize hail, in turn a demonstration of power.*

8. *Men forced their attentions upon women by riding in front of them. This is an example of the Indian way of drawing either in profile or full face; but he was best in profile.*

THE PHOTOGRAPHIC RECORD

THE WRITER took many photographs but since most of the personalities he valued highly and who flit in and out of the following narratives refused to face the camera, those given here merely reflect the atmosphere of the time. In those days cameras were not what they are now and moving pictures were crude and impractical at best. The standard glass plates were heavy, cumbersome and almost impossible in camp and on the march. My friends, Col. John G. Worth and Walter McClintock, have given me many interesting photographs of Indians in the Nineties, a few of which I have used here as credited.

My greatest obligations are to the sincere personalities, mostly aged Indian men and women, whose kindness, sympathy and patience gave me some little understanding of their world, their disappointments and their forlorn hopes. Then I must not forget my many white friends on and about the reservations, especially the agency doctors to whom I am especially indebted for insight into the human side of Indian existence.

1. Indians waiting for rations of beef at one of those so-called sanitary slaughter-houses.

2. *Indian Leaders and Officials, Pine Ridge, S. D., 1891: Buffalo Bill, center rear; Young-man-Afraid-of-his-Horse, center front; Kicking Bear, to his left; J. G. Worth, next on right; Short Bull, next left rear. Other important Indians are Two Strikes, Crow Dog, High Hawk, Two Lance, Good Voice, Thunder Hawk, Rocky Bear and American Horse. Photo by courtesy of John G. Worth.*

3. Part of the original police force at Pine Ridge in 1879. Fifty police were recruited in that year to control 7,200 of their fellow tribesmen. The writer came to know several of the retired surviving members of this force. Photo by courtesy of the United States Indian Service.

4. Ill fitting uniforms disguised the efficiency of the Indian Police of 1900.

5. Always the older women were working with skins.

6. *Three ways of transporting baggage.*

7. *Every Indian was glad to move out of a log cabin into a tipi when spring came. Photos by Dr. G. L. Wilson.*

8. *Hotel accommodations for the Doctor and the writer: the patients sat on the ground outside waiting turns.*

9. *The most characteristic feature of the reservation landscape was the shade. In this case pieces of cloth draping the posts were offerings to the sun.*

10. *Indians were always welcome at the writer's tent. Polite Indian men always sit cross legged, respectable Indian women never do so.*

11. One of the vanishing types dressed for a sitting to the portrait painter.

12 and 13. One medicine man inside his tipi, the other posing outside. Note the sacred medicine bundles hanging up. Lower photo by Walter McClintock.

14 and 15. A sacred sweat house is built and then consecrated by devout medicine men and women. In the rear of the procession is the holy woman of the sun dance, for which function the most virtuous and noble woman in the tribe is selected. No greater honor could come to any Indian woman. Blackfoot Reservation, 1903.

16. A distinguished medicine woman calls upon the setting sun to guard the footsteps of a little girl, to give her health and long life.

trader suggested giving the judges a dinner. As this seemed by far the best solution, invitations were extended and accepted by their Honors, Pine-tree, Four-guns, and Running-wolf.

At the appointed time the first to arrive was Four-guns. I had been mildly surprised by his civilized apparel and that of his colleagues in court, but that was no preparation for the dignified figure I now beheld resplendent in a Prince Albert coat, white tie, spotless creased trousers, shiny shoes and carrying a gold-headed cane. I had never seen a red man look so stately and correct. Next came Pine-tree, shorter in stature, a bit jerky in manner, but elegant in similar costume; finally, Running-wolf, a grand old man, heroic in stature, who also looked perfectly at ease in the costume made famous by a distinguished prince and later a king.

Needless to say, I was considerably taken aback at this turn in affairs and embarrassed beyond measure at not having changed my own clothes. Who could have expected these old-timers to appear in such garb; and what was the more remarkable, to exhibit such easy habituation to this phase of white culture.

Running-wolf was quick to sense my discomfiture. He said, "We understand that you are far from home, traveling light and so not equipped for formal occasions. Therefore, you could not be expected to appear in dinner dress." But it was different with them, he explained. For since they had these clothes at hand, it was their obligation to wear them out of respect to their host.

The dinner proceeded deliberately, but without conversation, though when spoken to, a brief but respectful answer was made. But when cigars and coffee were served, Four-guns, so far the most frigid of the party, went into action. Pushing back his chair he arose, calmly surveyed the room, then said:

"I have visited the Great Father in Washington. I

have attended dinners among white people. Their ways are not our ways. We eat in silence, quietly smoke a pipe, and depart. Thus is our host honored. This is not the way of the white man. After his food has been eaten, one is expected to say foolish things. Then the host feels honored. Many of the white man's ways are past our understanding, but now that we have eaten at the white man's table it is fitting that we honor our host according to the ways of his people.

"Our host has filled many notebooks with the sayings of our fathers as they came down to us. That is the way of his people; they put great store upon writing; always there is a paper. But we have learned that though there are many papers in Washington upon which are written promises to pay us for our lands, no white man seems to remember them. However, we know our host will not forget what he has written down and we hope that the white people will read it.

"But we are puzzled as to what useful end all this writing serves. Wherever white people come together there is writing. When we go to buy some sugar or tea, we see the trader busy writing in a book; even the white doctor as he sits beside his patient writes on pieces of paper. The white people must think paper has some mysterious power to help them on in the world. The Indian needs no writings, words that are true sink into his heart where they remain; he never forgets them. On the other hand, if the white man loses his papers, he is helpless. I once heard one of their preachers say that no white man was admitted to heaven unless there were writings about him in a great book.

"There are still many things we have not explained to our host. As handed down to us, the Great Spirit made the world. He made two great bodies of land, separating them by water. Then he made many kinds of plants and living creatures, different in these two great lands. However, in the course of time, he thought it best to make people to enjoy all these wonderful things. There being two separate lands, he decided to make two kinds of people—Indian and white. We know there are black people in the white man's world, but the Great Spirit had nothing to do with them; they were invented by white people as slaves to do their dirty work.

"The Great Spirit first made the Indian. He said to him, 'You are the one I love the most, you are my favorite son.'

"Then the Great Spirit was wrapped in thought for a time, but finally called for the Indian to stand forth. To him and his descendants was to be given all this land of America, to enjoy to the end of time, but he and his descendants were to follow the straight road. Further, the Great Spirit spent several days instructing the Indian as to how he was to live, all of which he was expected to remember and pass on from generation to generation without change. When the Great Spirit completed these instructions, he placed the Indian in this new land.

"Then the Great Spirit remembered that there was another large body of land on the other side of the great water. To live in that land, he created the white man. When this, his second son, stood forth, he also was instructed as to how he should live in order to possess and enjoy the land, but before sending him on his way, the Great Spirit sat in silence for a long time. At last, he sorrowfully admitted that this, his second son, had such a poor memory that he feared for the outcome. So he decided to have all these instructions written down in a book. In due time the book was ready, but before handing it to his son, the Great Spirit again relapsed into silence. It was plain from his countenance that he was sad. At last he raised his eyes, his face expressing shame and sorrow, because this his second son could or would not tell the truth. The Great Spirit knew his descendants would be known as liars forever and ever.

"Hence, no one would believe these white children when they claimed the Great Spirit was the giver of their book. Therefore, the Great Spirit would sign the book."

Then the speaker, looking straight at me, continued, "Naturally, the white man possessing a book in which was written the way of life and signed by the Great Spirit, had a great advantage over the Indian, eventually surpassing him and overrunning the whole earth."

The speaker lapsed into silence; I, being unable to think of anything to say, tried to assume the impassive countenance of my guests.

In due time, the venerable Running-wolf arose. His manner indicated that neither wit nor humor were in his mind. His remarks were brief, but touching. In substance, he stated that when an Indian died, he went to the land of his fathers, at least he was sure that such was his destination. Most white men went to another place, but he believed that his host was different from most white men since he was anxious to learn more and more of the Indian way. He said that last night he had a dream—a holy dream, the kind which is prophetic. In that dream he saw himself in the heaven of his fathers. Then he saw the writer walking up the trail with notebook and pencil. He believed that his own days were numbered, but that after a time he should meet again with his host. He hoped that it might be so.

After a pipe around, we shook hands and wished each other well. It was the last time I ever saw these three venerable judges, so sedate in their ultra civilized clothing yet so redolent of the philosophy of their fathers. Their bones now lie on the hills of their country; may they rest in peace.

If anything were to be inscribed on a stone or tablet to these Indian judges it should read: "Of all men, masters in common sense."

10

The Indian at School

OUR FOREFATHERS were so sure that the schoolhouse was the gateway to right living that they put the young Indians to school as soon as they could lay hands upon them, and whenever Indians were forced to sign treaties giving up most of their lands they were promised schools.

Naturally at the outset there were no schoolhouses, but as soon as a treaty was signed, a show of good faith was made by appointing a school teacher. For the most part these were conscientious, honest souls, these teachers, who boldly set out to meet dangers they knew not of, actuated by a faith in the great gifts the new education was to bestow upon these poor red children. These early enthusiasts deserve honors as much or more than the missionary because their task was still in the formative stage. In our day the system had seen to it that teaching the Indians was merely another government job, so to find a real educational enthusiast in the service was a rare event.

Almost upon my first try at the Indian country, while still in the green-horn stage, I arrived at the railroad town nearest the reservation I expected to visit. Entering the post office to mail a letter I noticed a large poster calling for bids for supplies for a United States Indian School. All this was new to me so I read it through. What such a school was like I could not imagine, because it wanted to buy 50 tons of hay, several wagons, a lot of potatoes, a cargo of flour, barrels of sugar, boxes of soap, towels, sheets, brooms, hardware, boots, shoes, etc., to a bewildering end. Nothing was said about the thing one usually expects to see in a white school. Even in my innocence I began to think, what a fine chance for a rake-off by some local merchant. At the end, in large letters was: James Terry Scipio, Superintendent, United States Indian School.

The name brought back old memories; could this be Jimmie of boyhood days? At first I dismissed the idea but the question refused to down. Then there came to mind a long scar Jimmie had on his cheek, where once he fell against the side bar of a reaper and cut a nasty gash. So upon returning to the hotel I casually asked the manager if he knew James Scipio, and of course he did. I mentioned once meeting a man by that name who had a long scar upon his cheek. "That's him," was the reply.

So I planned a surprise on Jimmie. It had been a long time since I had seen or heard of him. As youngsters we had not been real friends, and met but occasionally after passing into adolescence and a year or two beyond, then we each stepped out into the world and neither met nor heard of each other afterward. But I had Jimmie's number, as they say; in this new country where everyone had made a new start, an old friend from back home was not always welcome, because he knew too much. Really I cared little about Jimmie's reactions, since here was a chance to see an Indian school. So I hired a livery man to drive me to Jimmie's place, some ten miles out.

The school was not very impressive; several new looking brick structures, a couple of barns, some hay stacks, a power house, etc., but round about no trees, no lawns, nothing but an ugly wire fence. I was directed to the office, where I asked to see the Superintendent. After some delay he appeared; it was Jimmie, I could see that, though he was disguised in a three-day beard, a bushy head and slovenly dress, tobacco juice streaked from the corners of his mouth and his breath smelled like an alley saloon. It was plain that Jimmie was either coming out of a spree or just starting in upon another, and what is more, he was not expecting visitors. After some prompting he realized who stood before him. The shock sobered him up and then embarrassment set in. It was obvious that he wished my appearance had been less sudden. Yet he rallied quickly, suggesting that I dismiss the driver and visit a while, explaining that he was fighting off a cold with whiskey. Then excusing himself for an interval he returned shaved and cleanly dressed.

Learning that I had never been in such a school before, Jimmie conducted me about answering questions graciously. In the main he seemed glad to see me, but obviously not at ease. When he questioned me as to what brought me into the country, I was probably not explicit because interested in learning all I could about how such a school functioned. Perhaps I was too keen and too systematic in my questions. I did tell Jimmie that I was headed for the reservation where I expected to loiter around awhile, to study reservation life. He learned bit by bit that I knew some of the officials at headquarters in Washington and that I carried a document giving me permission to enter Indian reservations.

Afterward I learned that all this puzzled Jimmie so much that he dispatched a messenger to the reservation to warn the Major that a Big Cat might be around. But

I want to be fair to Jimmie, he was "a regular fellow" in the community. He and the Major at the reservation were in the cattle business on the side and I heard that he had stock in the local bank, was a partner in a general store, etc., like many other men round about. Perhaps his partner in the store would get the contract to furnish the school supplies. Obviously he was getting on. So far as I could judge he was the boss of the school and a good disciplinarian. Some of the larger Indian boys had to be subdued occasionally and Jimmie was said to have a heavy fist. The teachers and employees "toed the mark," so it appeared, one person remarking that "it was hard to put anything over on Jimmie."

I asked some questions concerning class work, but Jimmie preferred to talk about food, clothing, beds and how often his charges tried to run away. Yet he had an interest in these red waifs; having blown a cornet in the band back home, he trained up the older boys so that he had a real kid band. He had them play for me and though the music was simple, I could see that these lonely, homeless Indian boys enjoyed playing. I was glad for them, since that was about their only chance to be happy. A glance at them working under compulsion in the harness shop, feeding pigs, washing dishes and scrubbing floors, revealed the saddest child faces I ever saw.

Though not inspired by the boarding schools, I saw they were doubtless a great advance over those originally set up. In 1875 an agent wrote frankly of the school placed under his charge, as follows:

"I found the school poorly attended, no interest manifested by the pupils, and but few of the children attending regularly; no effort made to teach the importance of cleanliness, nor any attempt at inculcating instruction as to the parental relation, so essential to be understood by children. As soon as circumstances permitted I commenced reforms.

I caused the children to wash and comb their hair before entering the school, and provided dresses for those in want from the annuity goods. A programme of exercises was also adopted, dividing the time and allotting a certain amount to each study. Vocal exercises were added for opening and closing each session, consisting of hymns of praise to their Creator, which the children sang with great taste and correctness. Cutting and sewing are also being taught the girls, which is an important and most necessary part of their education, no knowledge of this ever having been brought to their notice; and I am glad to state that the female pupils especially pay an earnest and respectful attention to everything taught them, and that they are now making rapid progress; also that the school has increased in numbers and efficiency. Yet a number of the boys are irregular in their attendance, and consequently make slow advancement. This is not altogether owing to a want of disposition on their part to attend, but is attributed to the roaming propensities of their parents, who must have an occasional hunt, at the end of which time the child returns to school, having forgotten everything previously learned. The only remedy for this is a boarding-school, where the children can be kept, and trained to an attendance; and besides, our language can be taught them by this means, as the child never cares to use our tongue so long as he inhabits the wigwam, for there he has neither encouragement nor desire to acquire it. So soon as the agency is removed to the new location I shall submit estimates for a boarding-school, to accommodate twenty-five pupils, the male portion of which can be instructed in agricultural labors and carpenters' and blacksmiths' work, and the female portion instructed in housework, needlework, and cooking. This is the only practical method in which to inculcate and impress the minds of the coming generation with the superiority of civilized over the uncouth and precarious course of life in the wigwam. This appears to me to be of the utmost importance, as our strongest hope lies in the coming generation, for the more civilized and intelligent they are the fewer vagabonds and criminals will there be to burden the coming communities with which the immediate future will populate this fair country."

Many such pleas for boarding schools reached Washington, leading eventually to such establishments as I have described and about which there is now so much difference of opinion. Perhaps there was no other solution among parents to whom both the clock and the calendar were strangers. Anyway, this agent was a realist, not content to merely make recommendations, but with soap, scrub-brush and comb seeking to civilize his charges. Jimmie once remarked that the chief obstacle to educating Indians was dirt.

On subsequent visits I found Jimmie less distrustful, but from time to time he revealed some anxiety lest I tell too much when in Washington. Eventually Jimmie retired from the service to live on his ranch and has since died. I met many other school officials, none seemed quite so dynamic as Jimmie, and though some were better, some were worse. Through it all I came to feel that running a school of this type was about like operating a juvenile penal institution. All of the inmates wanted, above all things, to go home, none of them were in school by choice. On some reservations the entire Indian police force was often necessary to return a runaway to school.

Once only was I present on the day when all the children to enter school were delivered to the Major for transport to distant government boarding schools, but that was enough. The older boys and girls assumed indifference, having made the trip before. Each had a bundle, usually an old flour sack, in which were their meager belongings. As the school furnished everything, they needed little. One tiny girl clutched a white puppy but at the last minute an Indian policeman gently separated them, obviously government regulations did not tolerate pets at school. I thought of Jimmie—he was always popping into my mind—because he told me that he compromised on the rules by permitting each little pig, calf, and colt on the farm to be the pet of some Indian child, even though the animals could not be handled. Strangely enough, upon inquiry, I learned that some of these departing children were destined for his school. I hoped this little girl was among them.

Three large spring wagons now appeared into which the older children climbed without hesitation, but the little ones clung to their mothers weeping until their father or other male relative tore them away and lifted them to their seats where they were held by the older children. The mothers wept, some of the children screamed as the horse trotted off, and fathers preserved their dignity by looking another way. Well might these parents weep, since by the law of statistics some few of these children would return in coffins, and Indians are no more logical than we, at least each sorrying parent would be sure that had their child remained at home it would not have died. But why waste tears over this scene, are not many weeping white children sent away to school? I said as much to the agency doctor, who stood by to see that all were fit for the ordeal, but with a solemn shake of the head, he said, "Yes, but these are not white children."

As I returned to the little agency hotel to reflect upon the events of the day, I tried to follow in imagination the careers of these children in the schools they were to enter. What changes would the school make in them other than the superficial? Would they enter as Indians and emerge as Indians still? I recalled an enthusiastic Father at a mission who took photographs of the children when they entered his school and again a year after. One pair of such photographs I recall vividly. A boy about ten years of age was brought to the mission school by his parents. Like most Indian parents they were inordinately fond of this little fellow and so dressed him for the occasion. His face was painted, he wore a decorated skin shirt, beaded leggings, and moccasins. His carefully braided hair was set off by a few eagle feathers and in his hand he carried a fine pipe with a decorated stem, to use in praying to the pagan powers in whom he had been taught to trust. He stood erect, with a fearless, proud look. The second picture showed, first of all, a serious, downcast, slightly drawn face. His short cropped hair was carelessly combed. His clothes were plain black, slightly over-sized and his shoes were clumsy. Most conspicuous was a stiff collar, far too high, and a necktie meant for an adult. The good Father bubbled over with enthusiasm as he pointed to the two pictures. To him the first stood for all that was evil; the latter, as the indices of a Christian. I could not share his joy, for the boy looked so much healthier and happier in his original state. I secretly suspected that there was still a pagan heart concealed by those plain black clothes and that if the boy lived to return to the reservation, he would let his hair grow long, own a beaded shirt and a blanket, and on occasion pray to the pagan gods of his tribe.

Most of the white men about reservations had little sympathy for any kind of an Indian school. They considered them an inexcusable waste of time and the taxpayer's money. To their way of thinking the answer lay in the blood, once an Indian always an Indian. However, this was an extreme view, for though it was true that often the returning boy took to the blanket and to feathers, he possessed some knowledge of white ways and was conditioned by useful experience. As I saw it the girls were the greatest sufferers in a return to reservation life. At school they had clean beds, good food, comfortable clothing, and many of the luxuries pertaining to white ways. Many of them entered a boarding school at eight and remained until they were seventeen. Then suddenly they were turned back to the reservation, immediately forced to take husbands and begin life in tipis or shacks, without the equipment they had learned to use. I watched some of these tragedies; in a few months there remained merely a sour-faced, dirty, ragged squaw. It was at such examples that local white men pointed in scorn as evidences of the folly of education. I tried to be open minded, regretted the sorrow and disillusionment of these girls, but being white, felt that after all they had experienced something different, something better, than had they stayed at home. Certainly their standard of living would have been no higher had they merely grown up under their mother's care. I questioned some of the women, long out of such schools, and found without exception that some of their most treasured memories were associated with the school; there was always some white teacher each of them idolized. What more can be said of our own schools?

Perhaps I should repeat that these casual peeps at the passing show are in no sense studied judgments on Indian policy, they are but fleeting glimpses of life as I saw it and what I am moved to say about them may be far from just. I admit that I rarely visited a school room, partly because I was not interested, but chiefly because I found the place depressing. Even at play the Indian children seemed to lack spirit. Once I watched a group of small school boys pitching horseshoes. They were dressed in ill-fitting black clothes, weighted down with those enormous black felt hats peculiar to Indians. Their movements were slow and hesitant, each handling his horseshoe as if it were dangerous. I asked their overseer about it, and learned that these boys would not play the games provided, unless forced to do so. No wonder! I asked if he had tried Indian games; with a blank look he said the government rules specified what games were to be played. Perhaps it never occurred to him that Indians had games of their own.

Again Jimmie comes to mind. He did not always obey the rules, that may be why he never quite trusted me, but with all his faults he seemed to feel for his charges. Time has softened my judgment, but I still wonder how he got into such a school in the first place, why he wanted the job and what he thought about it all. The last time I saw Jimmie was not at school, nor on a reservation, but at a county-fair on Indian day. He was there leading his school band, his boys resplendent in their bright new uniforms. Their playing and marching was the climax to the day's recognition of the Indian. I treasure this picture of Jimmie, lustily blowing his cornet when not waving it as a baton, the boys proudly doing their best, while Indians and white alike cheered them heartily. Somehow the memory of that scene seems to blot out the drab pictures of Indian schools. Perhaps after all Jimmie was in the right place, things being what they were. What did it matter if these Indian boys never heard that Washington crossed the Delaware, that dog was a noun, and bark a verb, that there was such a thing as least common denominator, if they learned a good deal about how white people acted, especially a lot about Jimmie, for he was just an average white man such as they would needs live with when they returned to the reservation. Perhaps all of us expected too much of the Government Indian School, because we failed to see it as an outpost of white culture in the raw.

11

The Black Robes

The Indian's habit of standing about, staring at white folks, was not something peculiar to reservation days, it is an old time habitual attitude, a quiet cold-blooded appraisal of persons and events. Such loitering about was often disconcerting and also shows how clearly the Indian was present not as a part of our national life but apart from it. In the same way the Indians gazed at the Pilgrim fathers, the Virginians and all the other invincible invaders of their world. From the first they noted distinctions in dress as indices of function, and one class, the fewest in number, stood out from the rest, the preachers and the priests. These were promptly named the Black Robes, though sometimes spoken of as holy-men or medicine men. Yet in spite of all this objectivity and analysis, nothing in the ways of the white people was so perplexing to the pagan and near pagan Indian of my day as the white man's religion.

Most of the outstanding personalities I met discussed the subject at one time or another, sincerely seeking some understanding of the phenomenon. This did not mean that they were ready to embrace the faith, in the white man's meaning of that term, for doubtless they would have remained pagan still, but they believed there must be some real worth in the religion of a people so numerous and so mighty. "No people," said one of my friends, "could do the things white people do without help from the unseen." I fancy most of the missionaries would have said "Amen" to such a remark. It seemed to me that the wiser Indian heads were troubled not because their minds were feeble, but rather because they were too rational. They seemed to have little difficulty in grasping two of the leading concepts in Christian teaching, ethical ideals and the preparation for a life of joy in the next world. To the latter objective they subscribed wholeheartedly, though their ideas as to how such joy and satisfactions were to be obtained were not wholly orthodox. Strumming a harp and using a golden stair did not appeal to them, but walking in an easy trail and shaking rattles while the hosts were singing did seem quite worth while. Even their ancestors taught them to expect such pleasure in the land to which the dead go. Ethical teaching was welcomed in theory. No Indian I talked to had anything but praise for the ten commandments, though Old Wolf Chief thought the list should have been expanded somewhat, especially since it was intended to apply to white folks.

Where then, was the confusion? In the application of these ideals and the rivalry of churches. When the Indian came to compare his daily experiences among lying and cheating white men, with the beautiful ideals he heard from the missionary, his mystification was complete. Why on the one hand he was daily urged to take up the white man's road and then scolded for doing as white men did, was the eternal contradiction. Many of the Indians came to suspect that even the missionary was trying to steal away the good things in their aboriginal life and then give them not the good things of white culture, but a few useless glittering precepts. Although I searched far and wide I found no pagan who believed but that selfishness and deceit were the basic principles in white culture. Even many of the professedly Christian Indians had periods of wavering doubts that all was not as it should be, some solving the problem by assuming that though the white religion was alright, the present generation of whites was hopelessly wicked. One old pagan said he could not understand why the white man's god did not destroy all the white people and start over again. I made no attempt to explain away these confusions, my abilities not rising to the level of the difficulty.

The other puzzle was as between Catholic, Methodist, Baptist, Episcopal, Mormon, Quaker, etc. To the Indian's mind there was nothing strange in having so many denominations, because there were many cults among his people, but he could see no sense in the fanatical notion that a person could belong to but one of them at a time and be required to denounce the other at sight. Why these sects should hate each other so, was quite beyond his understanding.

First, last and always the Indian was tolerant and respectful of personal beliefs. I recall that one of the early Jesuit missionaries, writing to his superior at home, told how he experienced little difficulty in inducing the Indians to be baptized, but when told that they must drop all other religious practices, they failed to understand. One of my Indian friends, a professional interpreter, on occasion performed pagan ceremonies, entering into the spirit of them with such enthusiasm and sincerity, that it was a pleasure to see him officiate. At the same time he was a member of the Christian Church, frequently interpreting, line by line, the sermons delivered by the white pastor. One Sunday the pastor failed to appear, so my friend took the pulpit and preached a sermon, first speaking in English, as did the pastor, then as interpreter translating his own words into Indian. I suppose he felt it necessary to perform in this unexpected way to avoid violating the ritual. That would be the pagan way of looking at it. All Indians put great stress upon formal procedure; for example, several Indians who could speak good English refused to talk with me except through interpreters.

I did not question my friend about his curious performance in the pulpit but a few days later ventured to ask if he really believed what he said in the pulpit, since to my mind it flatly contradicted what he said and did in ceremonies. His face showed surprise at the question, then pain, and finally resentment. I promptly apologized, but he said what hurt him was to discover that I was like other white people. He had thought me capable of taking the Indian point of view, but it was now clear that there was an impassable chasm between us. White people, he said, thought one could believe in but one religion at a time, whereas the Indian saw good in all of them. So he was a Christian and a pagan at the same time and proud of it. True enough, it was just as impossible for me to consistently react as an Indian, as for him to always think as a white man.

I do not mean to imply that there were no devout and orthodox Indians, for even in my day there were converts who were fanatical in their adherence to the church. There were minorities of church-going Indians tending to form blocs in their opposition to pagan practices. However, to a surprising extent paganism still survived, perhaps because of the difficulty the Indian had in seeing anything consistent or honest in the ways of the white man. This is a harsh and disconcerting view of our cherished civilization and is unfair, as everyone will agree. It is not true that our civilization is one of deceit and falsification, but it was none the less a tragedy that these interesting aboriginals found it difficult to see it otherwise. The local white people returned the compliment, as it were, by declaring the culture of the Indian vulgar and stupid; it was difficult for them to see it in any other light. So perhaps we should not take all this too seriously because in the matter of misunderstanding the score stands about fifty-fifty.

When expressing such wholesale condemnation both Indian and white were generalizing since in relations between individual Indians and whites there are many exceptions; honesty, charity and nobility characterizing their friendly association. I always found Indians quick to recognize virtue and worth in an individual of the white race, going much further in this respect than would the white man, few of whom ever extended full recognition to a worthy Indian. So it came about, that whereas Indians found little to admire in our civilization, they did now and then meet a white person in whom they not only had confidence but whom they admired. Among such were Father Marquette, Father De Smet, General Anthony Wayne, George Bird Grinnell, and General Hugh Scott.

The Catholic Church established missions on all the large reservations. These were imposing institutions; most conspicuous among the mission buildings was the church, then a school building, a dormitory for the Indian children who lived in the mission, a house for the Sisters, one for the lay employees and finally a building to house the Father and the priests, with a few guest rooms. But this was not all, because the farm was provided with the necessary outbuildings, including a series of shops for the carpenter, blacksmith, leather worker, etc. There was always a quiet dignity about such a place, no one seeming in a hurry, but yet everyone busy. A stranger to the system might not realize that these missions were largely self-supporting, producing enough food and salable farm products to finance the institution.

I recall my first visit to one of these missions. Night came down upon us as we were passing the place so my guide suggested that we apply for a night's lodging. I rememberd some of the romantic literature read in my youth, particularly in the works of Sir Walter Scott, how in the troublesome days when robbers stalked boldly through wood and clearing, the traveler's spirits rose at sight of a monastery, because there hospitality was the order of the day. So we approached the mission with confidence. The Father in charge met us at the door, his greeting was cordial, in fact he appeared to be highly pleased. He called a serving man to conduct my guide and the horses to their respective quarters, remarking that I should give myself no concern, since they would be at the door when I elected to depart.

The good Father first conducted me to a large living room, indicating that here I was free to "make myself at home," as he expressed it. Then I was shown upstairs to a large bed chamber. The Father explained, in a business-like way, that dinner and breakfast would be served at such and such hours, that he must be excused for a brief interval to attend services in the church. This gave me time to look about, observing that the furnishings were plain but substantial, the whole having the appearance common to Catholic missions. Perhaps this standardization was so ordered that as the sisters and priests were moved about from one place to another they would not experience homesickness. To us the living quarters in these institutions always seemed a little grim and austere.

I learned that the Father dined alone, a practice which no doubt enhanced his dignity and made discipline easier. So when dinner was announced he conducted me to the dining room where we were attended by two men. The amount of food upon the table was disconcerting, the grand piece being a large beefsteak prepared in true New York style, something rare around Indian reservations. As the meal progressed the good Father remarked that my steak should be eaten before it cooled and when I suggested he take his portion first, he reminded me that the day was Friday, adding that the steak was for me. There was about a square foot of it.

After the meal we returned to the living room and around a box of cigars talked about the work of the mission and the Indian problem. This mission was still relatively new, having been organized and built under his jurisdiction. I learned the barest outline of his biography; born in the Isle of Rhodes, trained in Rome, and after a brief service in St. Louis, assigned to his present task. He plied me with a good many questions concerning Indian policy, none of which I could answer, his chief difficulty being to understand why the United States Government refused to support or even encourage mission schools. I tried to explain that the country was founded by Protestants whose dominant fear was that the Church would get a grip upon education and thus have one hand in the government till, that even today the average American was "gun shy" on church education. Being neither a sportsman nor versed in the habits of hunting dogs, I fear he missed the point.

He lighted a candle to conduct me to my bedroom and before leaving remarked that in the morning there would be a distressing clanging of bells but that I should not mind, that he would call for me when breakfast was ready to be served. Sure enough I was aroused by the bells, and looking out in the gray of the dawn saw the Father hurrying to the nearby church, into the front door of which the Indian children were passing in two well formed lines.

I spent a little time in the garden because I learned that the man in charge came from New York. He told how he had entered the service as a youth, vowing to devote his life to gardening. For many years he had been here and was obviously proud of his achievements. There were long rows of vegetables, for his was the duty to produce food for the whole establishment, including the Indian children. With delight he pointed to a plot of growing pop-corn where he raised enough to give the children a cracker-jack party each Christmas. I wondered if the children got as much joy out of it as did the gardener. He raised a few choice flowers too, because he thought the beauty of them would elevate the Indian children.

Somewhat in contrast were the efforts of the Protestant churches. They rarely undertook to maintain a school on the reservation, leaving that to the Government. So their plant consisted of the dwelling for the pastor and a little frame church, neither of which were impressive. Naturally the pagan Indian rated the Catholic mission higher because it was prepared to care for him when ill and above all he knew that when he called, good food and lodging were his without asking. Rarely could he expect a hand-out at the door of the Protestant pastor. Of course, when the Indian began to attend church he took a somewhat different view but one hard old personality summed up the matter by remarking that the white people seemed to have two kinds of holy men, those at the mission (Catholic) and those at the agency (Protestant); that he preferred the former, since when he called he was fed, if his child was ill they would nurse it, and when one of his family died they would help with the burial. On the other hand when he called upon the holy men at the agency, he was greeted coldly with, "what do you want?" no food was offered, etc. For his part he wanted nothing to do with the white man's religion, but he respected their holy men according to their deserts. He was, at least, frank.

Many harsh charges have been hurled at the missionaries, blaming them for everything seemingly wrong on the reservation, but like most such statements this is going quite too far. Most of the blame should be laid to the drivers of the economic and administrative steamrollers which crushed down everything before them in spite of the churches, and don't forget the bootlegger plying his trade in the wreckage. In the onward swing of these tragedies the few missteps of the missionary count for little.

I regret not having given more attention to the Christianized Indians but being antiquarian by nature I found the pagans fascinating. I thought I knew what a Christian was like regardless of his skin color. Yet I could not help making casual observations. For one thing Christian Indians lived in better houses, had better wagons and finer horses, dressed well and in general gave one the impression that they lived on a higher economic level than the pagans. I am not sure that all this prosperity was due to their having joined church; perhaps it was the other way around, having become more like white men economically they became church goers as a matter of course. Yet I did meet some prosperous pagans.

I remember an occasion when an Indian friend of mine took me to call upon a blanket wearing Indian who had just built a modern house with up-to-date decorations and furnishings partly out of the income from his profession as medicine man but chiefly from the rental of certain farm lands allotted to him. He received us in the parlor, sitting in a fine mahogany chair which stood on an oriental rug. After we had visited awhile, my companion asked permission to show me the attic. Our host consented but did not go with us. We climbed a narrow dark stairs but when our heads rose above the floor level, we looked in upon a new world, for here was the replica of an aboriginal lodge.

Resting upon the floor of the attic was a large

wooden tray, filled with earth, tramped down hard like the natural floor of a lodge. At one side of this earthen floor was a small raised square, or altar, upon which were painted symbols in red and in its center a tiny fireplace, with ashes indicating the recent burning of incense. On the wall behind hung a large bundle of sacred objects. Around the sides of the attic floor were pallets of blankets all ready for the medicine man, his assistants and the singers. Even the drum and the rattles were in position.

This thrifty old Indian knew how to make money in a white man's world. He lived in a beautiful modern house, in every way like that of a well-to-do white man, save that tucked away out of sight in its attic was the essence of living paganism. At least once a day the family climbed those narrow stairs and, shut in from the white man's world, gave whole-hearted devotion to the gods of their fathers.

In one respect the zealous church going Indians were trouble makers, though many of my readers may think their acts laudable. Once they became enthused with the idea of forsaking all Indian ways, they formed a vociferous minority, appealing to Washington through their respective church organizations to forbid all pagan practices and social gatherings based upon the old life. It seemed easy for church people everywhere to believe that the power of the Government should be used to stamp out all the old life because inimical to the life of a Christian. They forgot that our constitution says every one shall have liberty to believe what he can about religion and even if they did recall that fiat, they declared all the original beliefs and practices of the Indians were not religion at all, but crimes to be dealt with in the usual way. Reservation politics were more or less mixed up in this, too; the feeling of the Church Indians that they were superior and should run things, their ability to get the ear of influential white

persons, all presented an opportunity not easily ignored. They were still a minority, of course, and the
Catholic Indians rarely pulled with the Protestants.
Somebody is reputed to have said that man is a political animal, and, if this is true, the Red Man is no
exception.

Some of the church going Indians annoyed me by
wanting to tell how religious they were, how completely they had put the past out of their minds and
how silly and stupid were the beliefs of the pagan
Indians. Such boasting seemed somehow naive. True I
have heard white people boast of their religion without
jarring my sensibilities, so it must have been the crude
way in which these Indians did their boasting that riled
me. I could not help wondering what was really "in
their attics," so to speak. Once in Australia I was introduced to a full-blood black who had gone to college
and was now an ordained minister. As the meeting was
in a museum, devoted to the exhibition of aboriginal
pagan life, I welcomed the opportunity to ask his aid in
interpreting the objects shown in the cases. He was not
only willing but helpful, until we came to a case where
objects used in "black magic" were on view. Here he
balked, put his hands before his face and turned away.
Not only did he refuse to look at them but to talk
about them as well. When I began to argue the question on the ground that he was a Christian and so
knew these things were harmless, he broke off the conversation with the assertion that he feared them still.
The opportunity never came for me to try out some of
these boastful Indian converts but I have little doubt as
to the result. One of the priests at a mission regretfully
admitted that most of his Indian flock died in the
pagan faith of the past.

I knew one Indian pastor. Being curious to know
about his pulpit methods I eventually got him to talk.
He was frank to say that most Indians knew so little of

white civilization that the beautiful parables and teachings of the scriptures were meaningless to them. So he substituted appropriate excerpts from the tribal mythology. There was sound sense in the method, but what would his white superiors have done had they known what was going on!

But his most illuminating statement was, "In war with the white people I found their God the superior. I then joined the church and am a pastor in it, and shall be until I die. I have done all I was able to do to persuade my people to live according to the teachings of the Christian ministers. Before I joined the church I was a medicine man and owned a medicine bundle. I have it yet and am afraid to offend it, because when I die my spirit may go to the spirit land of my tribe."

12

The Old Post Carpenter

ON MY FIRST VISIT to a certain small reservation I noted a frame building with a sign, "Carpenter Shop." Wondering what could bring a carpenter to such a place, I made a friendly call. On a crude work bench sat an aged man smoking a home-made corncob pipe, his face wrinkled and weather beaten, what little hair remained, full white. As to age, I should have guessed eighty, though it was obvious that he could still do an average day's work. His equipment was simple and old-fashioned, an open door revealing a small back room with a bed and stove, suggesting that he lived alone. From the first I knew that here was one of those rare memories of the unwritten frontier soon to be lost forever.

Of his history I learned in time. He was born in lower eastside New York, soon orphaned, lived by selling papers, until tall enough to pass for a youth, when he got a place as a cab driver. While still barely sixteen, he saw a recruiting sergeant's stand and stopped to listen to the soldier's efforts to sell the army to the passing prospects. The story interested him because it promised adventure in distant lands, fighting Indians, shooting buffalo, good clothes, no work, etc. When he heard the sergeant say that one must at least be 18 years old, his heart fell. Later on, it occurred to him that he might even be that old, and probably no one could prove the contrary. So he applied. The sergeant took his height, and finding that satisfactory, asked no more questions; so our new acquaintance bid good-bye to the Bowery, once and for all.

After a preliminary try-out at a nearby post, he with other recruits, was shipped to St. Louis, then to Fort Leavenworth where a year was spent in learning to be a soldier.

His first real duty began at Fort Laramie, Wyoming. After all, garrison duty for the infantry was drab enough, unless Indians attacked the fort; but Laramie was too strong for that. Most of the fighting he knew about came by hearsay. Soon after his arrival, he made friends with the fort carpenter, and being young and never before offered a chance to play with tools, gave a helping hand whenever he could. Evidently he had some mechanical skill from which it naturally followed that he developed a liking for the trade. He noted that the fort carpenter was in a different class from the enlisted men, for though under orders from the Commandant, he seldom drilled, was for the most part free from the tyranny of officers, especially the young up-starts from West Point. So when his time was served, he applied for an assignment as carpenter, and with his appointment to this service began a life career, up and down the Indian country, now to one fort, then to another, finally taking a similar position in the Indian service, where he was now making his last stand, doing odd jobs about the agency. Relatives, he knew of none; being for the most part illiterate, he wrote no letters. Whether or not he was the father of some loafing half-breeds, no one knew, but it was evident that he never recognized such relationships, if they existed. He was not over-talkative, but on occasion, would become reminiscent, and when in the mood for it, a skillful narrator. Some of his tales I record here, but with apologies, because they do not reflect reservation life of the time of which I write and so belong to a more remote past. Nevertheless, they do give the antiquarian feel which pervaded most friendly talks around the old agencies. Even the Indians when not denouncing the service, spoke in terms of the past, and the white people around seldom found current agency affairs inspiring enough to talk about. So antiquarianism was the order of the day.

The first tale by the Carpenter was an account of the celebrated Wagon Box Fight, which was from hearsay, since he was not a participant. Consequently, I omit further comment because the details of this exploit are fully presented in the appropriate literature, how a few men behind some wagon boxes with breech loading rifles and plenty of ammunition defied the power of the Sioux. Perhaps this fight should go down in history as the turning point in Indian border warfare, since from this time on the invention of new mechanical devices placed the Indian in hopeless inferiority. His mobility and skill in hidng out might for a time postpone the inevitable, but the end was in sight. However, one day the Carpenter greeted me with the promise of a story in which he was an actor, though an unimportant one. It was, as he put it, another instance of his bad luck not to see a real Indian fight. Every now and then he referred regretfully to the fact that though his entire life had been spent on the frontier, he missed all the exciting events. It was to substantiate this generalization that he offered the narratives which follow.

The Big Medicine Gun

We were stationed at a post in the Missouri country when Indians were running wild. True, the chiefs were supposed to have signed many treaties and to be good United States Indians. They usually were good during the winter, hanging around the military posts for a hand-out of rations and an occasional bottle of liquor. Many of them were not above prostituting their women to add to the family purse, so peace was for the Indian woman worse than war. However, there was method in the Indian's way, for in the spring he took to the open, raiding and killing, running away from the soldiers whenever possible, but in the autumn as the air became snappy and snow threatened, the chiefs would be seen approaching the post with peace pipes in their hands. They would be graciously received by the Commandant, would make long speeches, declaring that once and for all they had put war behind them, and that henceforth, they intended to hearken to the words of the Great Father and respect his wishes. The Commandant speaking for the Great Father, would express his satisfaction with a hand shake around. Then would follow a hand-out. Later rations would be issued to the needy and all was peace and harmony once more.

The soldiers were content to have it so, since campaigning in winter had its disadvantages. Then we should not blame the Indian until we see the other side of the picture, for when spring came the soldiers were just as keen for excitement as the red skin. Almost invariably when they rode abroad, they fired upon every Indian they saw. It was, in fact, the open season for human game.

It was late in the summer before the government steamboat arrived from St. Louis. As an innovation two light field pieces in knock-down form came in with the supplies, and accompanied by two gunners. No Indians were about and so none of them saw this new equipment. During the winter, it remained in storage. The Indians were now at peace, of course, and in and out of the post daily, but as spring approached they disappeared completely. The Commandant now put his defenses in order, got out the artillery, and doubled the guard.

One day a scout brought word that something was in the air for some five miles away a great camp was forming; further, he saw signs which led him to suspect that a surprise attack upon the post was intended. A low ridge near the gate would make it easy to conceal several hundred mounted Indians and, if the gate was open, a quick charge might carry them in, or if not, they might scramble over the palisades before the alarm was given. If they were quick enough, the chances for success were good. Careful scouting confirmed this suspicion and finally one day it was reported that mounted Indians were massing just over the ridge. Everybody was quietly ordered into position under cover and the gate sentry ordered to appear listless. However, while they were waiting, the Commandant remembered that the field pieces had not been tried. So he asked a gunner if he thought he could place a shell over the hill among the assembling Indians. He thought he could, if someone gave him the direction and the distance. This information was supplied by one of the scouts.

So a shell was sent over the ridge. The test proving satisfactory, the Commandant ordered the guns trained to sweep the approach to the gate and then awaited the attack. But nothing happened. After a time a scout stole out, soon returning with the information that not an Indian was in sight.

It was a disappointing summer; the Indians seemed to have gone out of the country, gone so far afield that there were no skirmishes. Yet one day in the autumn the chiefs were seen approaching with the peace pipes. All now went on in the usual way, the pipes were smoked, speeches were made and all were one happy family. Finally, the Commandant made a speech telling how he knew that the Indians were one day hiding behind the hill and how he had all his soldiers ready, thinking that at last he would have a good fight, but that he waited and waited to no purpose.

After a brief silence the head chief said, "A man who can shoot through a hill to kill a man and a horse has too strong a medicine for us to fight."

Breech Loading Guns

After joining the Indian service, the Carpenter became acquainted with an old chief who in his young days aspired to be a real war leader and from him had many interesting anecdotes. It seems that this chief began his career in the days of muzzle loading guns. He watched soldiers drill and fight until he understood some of their technique. He was authority for the statement that the Indians disliked to charge infantry because of the bayonet. If mounted Indians tried to ride down infantry, they usually came to grief because the first line kneeled with their bayonets outward while the rear lines shot over their heads, but the chief noticed that when Indians on foot faced a line of soldiers, the fire was in volleys, after which all loaded at the same time. This gave him an idea which was to induce the soldiers to fire a volley, then rush them with the tomahawk while they loaded. At the first opportunity to try this technique, it worked fairly well, but the second time was disastrous, since in the meantime, unknown to the Indians, the United States army was equipped with breech loading rifles and fixed ammunition. So when one day the chief saw a small body of soldiers in skirmish formation far in advance of the main body, presenting just the situation he thought right for his new method of attack, he formed his Indians in a line and approached the soldiers. The troops withheld their fire until the Indians were close, then the usual volley was given; immediately the guns were broken to load. The chief thought this meant that their guns had burst and so ordered a charge with tomahawks, but the soldiers continued to fire which so surprised the Indians that a quick retreat was ordered. In fact, they ran as only Indians can run. Their losses were heavy, but when the survivors felt safe, they sat down to rest and to discuss this mysterious affair. Some were certain that a powerful medicine was at work, a magic, which broke guns, but shot them off again. One Indian thought this might be the white man's Sunday or Big Medicine Day. However, others, more realistically minded, thought it was a new kind of gun, which they must demand of the traders, and as usual in such situations one humorist suggested that this was a Sunday gun, that the soldiers spent the whole week loading so they could shoot on Sunday without working.

The Carpenter said that every time the chief told this story, he laughed long and loud over what he regarded as a good joke upon himself.

In a way, this narrative reminded me of something I heard in New Zealand where during the war between the natives and English soldiers, the latter surprised a village because the natives assumed that the soldiers, being Christians, would not fight on Sunday. In this case also the misfortune was taken as a joke.

The Coffin War

On another day when I dropped in for a little visit with the Carpenter, he was busy over a long pine box. I suggested that it looked like a coffin and was told that my guess was a good one; that there was a hurry call from the Major's office to furnish such a burial box to an Indian family in which there had been a death. He then volunteered some information as to the mortuary policies of the Indian service. It seems that originally, few of our Western Indians deposited their dead in the ground. The truth of the matter was that they looked upon the white mode of burial as cruel, an attempt to doom the soul of the deceased to a subterranean existence. To their way of thinking, man was made to live above ground and the proper way to treat the dead was to place them upon the hills, in trees or other desirable points of advantage from whence the spirit of the departed could easily survey the world round about. To interfere with the freedom of the spirit, was according to their philosophy of life immoral and antisocial.

Naturally the Indian service held a different viewpoint, to them no civilized people would treat their dead in such fashion, and so one of the first steps in civilizing the Indian was to order that the graveyard be patronized. For the most part, the Indians ignored the order, but the service offered them a bribe in the way of free coffins. Many Indians accepted the coffins, but set them upon hills or in trees.

At last the Carpenter finished his task and stood the long box on end outside his little shop as a sign to the waiting Indians that it was ready for delivery.

Then he seated himself upon the work bench, lit his pipe and said, "this reminds me" and so we were off on another adventure. After leaving army service, he got a job as carpenter at one of the newly created agencies, where Indians were still Indians and where several companies of soldiers were kept to keep the peace. An order from Washington had been issued that coffins were to be furnished the Indians for the asking, and occasionally, one was called for. One day, it occurred to the Commandant that there might be a run on the post for coffins in which case it would be well to have a supply on hand. So he ordered some of the enlisted men to spend part of their time making coffins under the direction of the Carpenter.

The men enjoyed the work, singing and joking as they sawed and hammered. Every now and then an Indian or two would stand at the doorway quietly as only an Indian can when wishing to appear stupid and disinterested. As just said, the soldiers had great fun. Coffins of different sizes were made and now and then some one would ask who this one was for, and then another would say it was for so and so. This went on for some time and the pile of finished coffins mounted higher and higher. By and by the Carpenter noticed that no more Indians were around. Everyone began to notice it and to wonder what mischief was in the air. Finally, one evening, as the Carpenter was walking outside the stockade, a few bullets shrieked past his head followed by several reports from a near-by ravine. The sentry over the gate reported later that he saw a few Indians scamper away up the ravine.

The Commandant had been through many Indian wars and to him this incident meant trouble. Accordingly, the post was put in a state of defense and that very night a sentinel was fired upon twice, a sure sign that the post was now besieged. Everyone in the fort had to be cautious since a mere peep over the palisades would draw the fire of hidden Indians. The Commandant had never experienced so determined an attack nor one so long sustained. By day and by night occasional bullets found their way into the post and some of them drew blood.

It was apparent to all that little by little the garrison would be worn down to a state of helplessness. One night a terrible storm broke over the valley, in the midst of which two soldiers set out to steal past the Indians to bring help. Later the garrison learned that they succeeded, but a few days after the storm, firing ceased and no Indians could be seen. The Comman-

dant suspected a ruse, but a few night scouts failed to
locate a single Indian. Then a few mounted men ventured out to the tops of the surrounding hills, but the
Indians had left the vicinity, so a second set of mes-
sengers was sent out to forestall the expected relief
expedition. Further scouting revealed that all the Indians had left the reserve. Later on the Commandant
learned that smallpox broke out among the attacking
Indians and as usual they moved off rapidly in all
directions to escape the dread disease. Yet this did not
explain why the attack was made in the first place.

It was more than a year later before these Indians
were rounded up and forced back upon their reservation. In the first talk with the head men the Commandant took them to task for their sudden outbreak,
telling them how the Great Father had made them
many presents, how his soldiers had not disturbed
them, etc. To this, the Indian spokesman replied vigorously, he would not say that the Commandant was a
liar, but there were those under his command who
planned to kill all the Indians. The leader of these evil
white medicine men was the maker of coffins (the
Carpenter). He it was who planned their death. When
the Commandant denied this and made light of these
foolish fears, the spokesman presented other argu-
ments. Had not all the white men been set to making
coffins? Had they not seen that the coffins were of
different sizes, had not some of their people who could
understand a little English heard the workmen say that
a certain coffin was for this Indian, calling him by
name, and so on? Had the workmen not boasted that
soon these boxes would be filled with dead Indians?
Further, there was among these Indians a very tall
chief, taller than any man in the post and one day the
watchers saw a coffin made long enough for him. Even
the Carpenter had said he would keep it for this chief.
All these doings spoke for themselves, the Indians

could not be fooled so easily. So what could they do but go to war to kill these evil white medicine men before it was too late?

Then another head man spoke, pleading that the Commandant require the Carpenter to cease working his evil powers. They knew that he was a great medicine man, because though their best marksmen had shot at him, not a ball found its mark. Further, it was he who sent the smallpox among them to break up the siege and to fill the coffins; he who caused a great storm so that scouts could get through to bring help. They were ready to acknowledge that his power was great and hoped that he would now let them live in peace.

The Commandant told the Carpenter that it was up to him to make a speech. Never having done such a thing, he broke into profanity, but promised the Indians that he would make no more coffins for them and that those he had made would be kept for dead soldiers.

"And," said the Carpenter, as he knocked the ashes out of his pipe, "so ended the coffin war."

The Fossil Hunters

Like many others around the agency, the Carpenter seemed perplexed as to my occupation, though unlike them he gave no hint that I was under suspicion, probably because he was not involved in the economic and political life of the reservation. However, I happened to drop in on an occasion when he was reflecting on my status, for his greeting was, "Are you hunting fossils?" I assured him that I was wholly ignorant of that subject. When I countered by asking if he ever collected such things, he answered in the negative, but that years ago many such collectors were in the country, sometimes with large well organized camp outfits. The excuse he then gave for bringing up the subject was that from what he had heard the Bad Lands of South Dakota were the best places to go for fossils, that one could pick up life-like replicas of wolf-heads, turtles, and buffalo horns. However, when questioned closely, he admitted this was mere hearsay, though he had once made some crates and boxes for a Professor from the East into which he saw packed away backbones and ribs, certainly not belonging to any animal now living in the country.

This Professor seemed to be a fearless sort of fellow because no matter how ugly the Indians might act, he would push out into their country unarmed. His party would usually consist of a cook, a guide, and a few college students. The Professor would search all the cutbanks and hills, locating fossils for the students to chisel out by slow hard work. One summer the Professor was advised not to go into the Bad Land country because the Indians were angry over a land dispute with the Government, but he paid no attention to these warnings. As it turned out the party met no Indians on the way, and once well into that forbidding country thought they had little to fear. Yet one day, two students, far from camp, industriously pecking away at the rocks, were startled to see an Indian riding up. Across his saddle in front was a repeating rifle, held by one hand in a position for quick action. His countenance was stern, his approach bold. There was nothing the students could do but resign themselves to their fate.

When within about 15 yards the Indian stopped his horse, looked for a time fixedly at the two boys. Their hearts began to pound but outwardly they feigned indifference. Presently the Indian said in good English, "Where is your camp?"

The boys believing they were lost anyway decided

not to betray the others, so they declared that there was no camp, that they were alone in the Bad Lands.

This brought from the Indian an emphatic "You lie!" Then fingering his rifle, he said, "Come, out with it, where is your camp?"

The boys were about to lose self-control but still manfully stuck to their resolution, once again denying that there was a camp.

The Indian, now angry, raised his rifle, saying, "For the last time, I demand an answer."

One of the boys began to weaken, so he said, "Why do you want to know?"

The reply was as astonishing as unexpected, "I came to pay my respects to your Professor. I was once a student of his at the University."

Many years afterward at a university gathering I heard a similar story attributed to Professor Marsh, a veteran fossil expert from Yale University. Perhaps after all the Carpenter was speaking from contemporary knowledge.

13

The Enigma of the Squaw Man

ALMOST WITHOUT EXCEPTION, when traveling on the reservations, if I called at the home of a white man with an Indian wife, my host sooner or later offered apologies. Such unexpected behavior led me to wonder about the social and economic implications. Obviously the squaw man was aware of the contempt in which he was held by those of his kind married to white women, but let me take you on a visit to some of these enigmatical homes on the old-time reservations.

On a certain reserve, I often heard about the ranch of Sid Lee and was advised to find an excuse to spend a night there. In due time it became convenient, and following the directions given, I came in sight of Sid's place. It was an impressive plant, with numerous corrals, many wire fences, a string of cattle sheds, a row of log stables and several clusters of one-story log cabins. Fences guarded the property on all sides, but an open roadway led to the stable yard, where a young English-speaking Indian met me. He informed me that Sid was not at home but was expected soon, and that it would be quite all right for me to remain for the night.

He thereupon led the way to a row of log cabins and, opening a door, showed me my bed. It was a bare bunk-frame, and there was nothing else in the room except a broken-backed chair and part of a mirror on the wall. Of course there was nothing wrong about this—it was a good dry cabin, one could bar the door and slide into his bedroll as elsewhere—but it was not quite what I had expected. While looking the place over, I heard a commotion at the stables; someone was being bawled out in strong language. Next there were vigorous strides and the jingling of spurs. The door flew open, and a tall, muscular, dynamic man stood before me.

Without pausing for an introduction he said, "Come out of here!" I was taken aback. "This is no place for a gentleman," he went on. "You are to go to the house. I apologize to you for this insult. These d——d Indians never learn anything."

Obviously this was Sid. Later he explained that he was so angry at his Indian employee that he forgot to be polite, that he had heard of me and that I was headed for his ranch. (In time I learned how impossible it was to approach his place without being spied upon and without one's presence being relayed to Sid.)

The ranch house was a series of log cabins arranged around a court. Not having the privilege of exploring the whole place, I cannot describe it fully. It appeared that there were at least twenty units or rooms. We entered directly into a large living-room surprisingly luxurious, beautifully polished wood floor, good oriental rugs, correct up-to-date furniture and a grand fireplace. But Sid led the way to a side door which opened into a perfect bedroom, resplendent with bird's-eye maple furniture and, best of all, a real bathroom. This was luxury.

Sid excused himself on the ground that it was necessary for him to see about my grub. It was pleasant to lounge in a great soft chair before the wood fire which someone, possibly Sid himself, had kindled while I was in the bedroom. About an hour later, Sid returned with the brisk announcement that we were to eat. We crossed the open court and entered a large room, severely plain. In one end was a huge wood-burning range flanked by shelves bearing cooking utensils, toward the other was a plain table covered with oil-cloth and literally packed with food. There was a large platter containing some twenty fried eggs, another covered with ham and slices of bacon, then dishes of beans, fried potatoes, stacks of bread, etc. It was a large table, as may be expected, but what held the attention was that only two chairs were set, one on each side.

Sid motioned me to a chair opposite the range, where I sat facing him, the wealth of food between us. To say that I was perplexed is to put it mildly. For what, in the name of all the great Indian medicine men, could two men do with so much food!

Seeing my hesitancy, Sid said, "Take some eggs." I took one.

More emphatically, "Take some eggs!" I took another, remarking that two fried eggs were about my limit, to which Sid replied, "H—l, I intend to eat half of them and expect you to eat the other half!"

I was hungry, terribly hungry, but I made a sorry showing. Sid had been riding the range all day without lunch, and how he did eat! Noting that neither cooks nor waiters were in sight, I inquired as to who was responsible for this meal. To my surprise, he apologetically admitted that he had done the most of it, not daring to trust those d——d Indians when he had company.

Eventually we returned to the living-room, settled ourselves before the fire, and talked. Among other things I remarked that I was interested in bead work, upon which Sid asserted that the "Old Woman" had some. He left the room at once and soon returned with a young Indian female. She giggled as Sid presented her, then sat down upon a couch. She looked like a full-blood, too well fed and too lightly employed to show a pleasing figure. Her dress was plain but clean, and her face was pleasant. She began taking beaded moccasins, etc., from a bag, and, realizing that it was up to me as a guest to carry the thing through, I selected a few objects. I asked Sid what I should pay, but he said that it was her property. So I bargained a little, then paid what she asked. She quickly thrust the remaining objects into her bag and withdrew.

Sid began to make apologies. He said that his first woman died recently, that she was not much to brag about, but the best to be had; that the younger generation of Indians was not up to standard, and though, for his present wife he had taken the best one he could find, she was a poor substitute. "But," he said, "what is a man to do in this country but take an Indian woman?"

I agreed that the natural thing to do was just that, though privately I reasoned that unless Sid married an Indian woman he could not live on the reservation and operate a ranch there. All the riches of his ranch were by legal fiction the property of that Indian girl, but in reality owned by Sid. He paid no rent, no taxes and could stock the whole reservation.

We talked of his children to whom he seemed greatly attached, three girls and a boy. They were in a boarding school in California and had not been to the ranch for a long time. Sid went out to see them regularly, was trying to bring them up as white people, and hoped that they would find a place in a white world. I would like to know how this noble experiment came out.

When bed-time came Sid announced that he expected to leave early in the morning, far too early for me, but that his white ranch foreman would fry me some bacon, etc.

So, like all the characters in these reservation sketches, Sid takes his turn upon the stage and vanishes into the wings. I never saw him again, but learned that eventually the Indian office forced him to reduce the size of his herds, an outcome which he doubtless expected, and that finally he was liquidated, left the reservation, presumably to live with his children. No doubt his going was a misfortune to all the Indians whose living depended upon him, but since he was exploiting Indian land in the name of his wife, the law was certain to get him sooner or later.

Not infrequently when I inquired about a white man I had not met at an agency, the answer would be a sneer, "Oh, he's a squaw man," or "Oh, he is a good fellow in a way, but one of those d——d squaw men."

One need but note the emotional slant to these expressions to understand the social position of these white derelicts, and their embarrassment when we called at their homes. The unconventional wife could rarely speak a word of English. Why should these white men have made such sacrifices? This is the question we often asked ourselves. Sid's case was exceptional; his chief motive was economic. Yet every squaw man of reservation days exploited his woman in a way, because, if industrious, he lived on her land, raised cattle and horses in her name; if lazy, he lived on the rations she drew by her ticket. But it was not the fact that these white men were slick enough to get their living from the Government and the Indians, that roused the indignation of their conventionally married fellows, for they, as officials or traders, were grand masters of that game. The iniquity lay rather in not playing the game in the conventional way. Further, living outside the pale of social respectability, the squaw men made friends with their Indian male relatives, and without official approval informed them as to their rights and the true state of affairs at the agency. Need we say more?

History shows that the mere marrying of Indian women is an ancient and honorable custom, for did not one John Rolfe, landing in Virginia, initiate this by marrying the daughter of a Chief? Captain John Smith must have liked Rolfe, because he consented to be his publicity agent and in the story of Pocahontas produced a classic still the admiration and the envy of all press agents. Yet Rolfe had his troubles; King James did not approve of the idea, for though quite willing to receive Pocahontas as a Princess, he balked at recognizing her husband and thus elevating him. The question in his mind was "Why did not the Chief, as the father of Pocahontas, consult him: he would have picked out a man of royal blood. And how dared one of his subjects marry a Princess without his consent?" So the first squaw man had his troubles. His King frowned upon the marriage and his less fortunate brothers hated him for his luck. Yet, Rolfe had something in the way of compensation for he won immortality and gave to the F. F. V.'s a line to be proud of, which is more than can be said for the fellows who married those white "jail-birds" sent over to the Virginia colony. Historians tell us that we live by precedents, and if so, this explains the whole thing. Because since noses were turned up when Rolfe took an Indian wife, every squaw man from that day to this has of necessity been an object of suspicion. Yet the historian may be wrong, for as a schoolboy, we accepted Captain Smith as a hero, we adored Pocahontas, but failed to enthuse over Rolfe. Perhaps there is something constant in human behavior after all.

The second picture to intrigue me was in different colors.

Squaw men were not always white. But if a man of color married an Indian woman, no one seemed shocked. White people merely felt sorry for the woman, apparently believing that while the white man always married down, in the other case the man always married up. Somehow this shifting in values always left one in doubt, because many Indian women we knew seemed to have married down when they took their white husbands.

I heard a lot of talk about Ping Shoo's Hotel, how the beds were immaculate and meals unsurpassed, and was advised never to pass up a chance to spend a night with this famed "squaw-chink." Like an oft-repeated advertisement, this propaganda broke down my initial resistance, and I came to have a secret, guilty longing for the luxuries of this hostelry, guilty because I was out to see the Indian country, not to visit in Chinatown.

Fate was kind, for one day I saw in the distance a two-room log cabin, and drawing near, read in crude black letters, "Ping Shoo Hotel," on an unpainted board over the door. Entering, I found myself in a common room, on one side a rough table, with board benches, on the other a rusty stove and a few broken chairs. Obviously, this room was dining hall, lobby, and office combined. Presently an inner door opened, and a typical Chinaman entered, saying "Hello." He looked like the laundry man around the corner back home, in fact dressed just like him.

I asked if he was Ping Shoo and he assented, but ignored my remark that I had heard of Ping Pong, with, "Wantie eat and sleepee? Good, takie chair, suppy quick." With the last word he vanished through the door.

This gave opportunity to look around. The cabin

stood alone, without fence or tree. Hearing chopping, I looked around a corner at a sizable wood pile, and saw that Ping was swinging the ax. Presently the familiar odor of wood smoke was recognized, soon followed by the tantalizing odor of frying bacon. In the distance stood a tipi around which a few children were playing, which I judged were his. I could not help wondering about the eyes of these mongrel children, but even through field-glasses, they were too far away for anatomical observations.

While waiting, I began to wonder where Ping kept his famous beds. Peeking through the back door merely added to the mystery, because range, utensils, etc., seemed to fill that space. In short, all I could see was dining room and kitchen furniture and very little of that.

When the table was set, it became evident that other guests were expected, and it was reasonable to suppose that Ping Shoo's family was to join us, but not so. Presently a horseman arrived, followed by others. It was soon apparent from the commotion that these were regular boarders, and government employees at that. The supper was splendid, though served in simple style. It came in courses, but a large reserve was placed in the middle of the table from which everyone was free to take. Never in all my travels have I sat with regular boarders who uttered such praises of their cook. And in the same spirit I, as guest, was so often urged to commend the food that I seemed to be eating and making an after-dinner speech simultaneously. It was most unusual.

After the boarders left, Ping lighted a coal-oil lamp and left me to my devices, but in time he appeared with, "Go-bed?" Joyfully I accepted this invitation; now the mystery would be solved. Picking up the lamp, he conducted me into the kitchen, and I noticed for the first time a curtain across one end. Behind it was a white iron bed with fresh white sheets. It was a real bed, just like we had at home. This was what had given Ping Shoo's Hotel such a reputation.

When I took my leave the next morning, I could not forbear a try at Ping for a note to put in my field book, so asked him how he liked an Indian wife. His reply was, "All samee."

Well, hats off to Ping Shoo; he made no apologies.

You should understand that when a white man went to live in the reservation country, where single women were scarce, he had to take what he could get. And if he drew a dumb-bell, he was apt to try again. Ben Coldwater, for instance, over seventy when I first met him, had his fourth Indian woman and could boast the ancestry of three generations of mixed bloods. When I called upon Old Ben I noted a poor sort of cabin, with a sod roof and an earthen floor. It was no better and little worse than those occupied by the older Indians. Presumably, it was equal to anything Old Ben had ever called home. He desired nothing different. When occasion permitted he went on a spree, but at other times was a good talker, and many times we heard him tell stories of adventure which as examples of artistic lying, deserved preservation. He liked to gamble and now and then cheated an Indian out of a few dollars, but in the long run lost as much as he won. He was not excessively cruel to his family. He had but a few head of cattle and a couple of horses, so could not be accused of exploiting the Indians, nor could he be credited with trying to uplift them. What was conspicuously charged against him was that he was the ancestor of several exceedingly troublesome and worthless mixed-bloods. He was never heard to complain of anything, probably because he was too busy magnifying his own adventures.

Not infrequently it is asked whether these white men loved their women, or were such unions merely selfish and sordid. On the one hand there come to mind examples of life-long infatuations such as one may meet anywhere; on the other there are many instances of selfishness and greed. There was a soldier, graduate of a military school, who while on duty in the West fell in love with a young "barracks squaw." She would stay with him for an interval, then desert to another, but always he labored until he got her back. Finally, finding that the service would take him where this coquette would not go, he resigned his commission and lived with her on the reservation. She still indulged in occasional lapses, even eloping to other reserves, but each time he either induced her to come back or waited impatiently until she did. I knew the couple in their old age and the man still adored her. To me she appeared as a shrewd, naughty but likable woman.

The old-timers at a certain agency told me how a slender, lively, bright full-blood Indian girl once led the unmarried white men a mad race, now flirting with one, then another, and according to report was a frequent sex offender. One of the government clerks with a wife and children fell in love with her. The girl consorted with him and jilted him by turns, but his infatuation seemed to grow. Finally he told his wife to move out, that he could no longer do without the Indian lady. This brought matters to a head. It was too much for the Major, so the clerk was fired. Thereupon he eloped with the Indian girl, but in a short time she left him to take up her old life. The ardent lover got a divorce from his white wife, eloped once more with the girl, and married her. They then returned to the reservation, as was her right; they were a childless old couple when I knew them, living happily so far as could be seen.

Perhaps this is sufficient to bear out our general conclusion that the much-abused squaw man was a cross-section of men at large, good, bad, and indifferent. Some strong and good men lost their hearts for good when they struck the Indian country, making the supreme sacrifice, if such it can be called. Some were beastly and heartless. The great majority were just calculating, ordinary mortals.

Now look at the other side of the picture, the white squaw. The reader may be astonished that any white woman would willingly marry an Indian, but such marriages are on record. One notable example coming under my observation was that of a French woman who married a young full-blood Indian employed by a traveling show. Obviously she fell in love with him and married in a hurry. They returned to the reservation, put up their log cabin and began life in the usual way.

The man was rather dull, loved ease and fine clothes. He showed neither ambition nor power of leadership but behaved as something of a snob. The white wife, on the other hand, seemed aggressive, sensible, honorable and business-like. To see her walking about the agency was to recognize that here was a person possessed of executive ability. The white people called her Maxine.

The first time I saw her she was at the agency directing the delivery of several wagon-loads of hay to the government stables under contract. An immaculately dressed Indian standing about stiffly and doing nothing was pointed out as her husband. He must have put on a freshly laundered shirt every day, for we never saw him dressed otherwise—the only and truly stuffed shirt among Indians. Maxine was then the mother of half a dozen children, some of marriageable age. They were handsome, well dressed youths, but in Indian style. One might easily have thought them full-bloods, because of their conservative Indian behavior, especially their haughty bearing.

Maxine was the owner of a large herd of cattle,

several hundred horses, corrals, feeding sheds and the equipment for cutting and storing hay.

The trader, who like a village banker, knew the financial status of every one around, volunteered the information that Maxine carried the check-book and that her man had to ask her for an order on the trader for tobacco, etc. Further, her credit was said to be good for $10,000 any day.

In short, this is the reverse side of the picture; a white woman exploiting the lands of the Indians in the name of her husband. Strange to say, I heard no sneers from the agency white men; all took off their hats to Maxine. But the things they said about her Indian husband cannot be set down here. On the other hand, the white women at the agency had nothing good to say of Maxine; if anything, they pitied her husband on the ground that somehow he was basely imposed upon. From all I could gather, he was deeply in love with his wife, proud of her achievements, and enjoyed her wealth with a clear conscience. Though I met both many times, neither offered explanations or apologies.

Another woman I have in mind was a mulatto whom the white people called Mrs. Redclay because she was the widow of an Indian by that name. She was as poor as many Indians but lived in a neat log-cabin at the agency, dressed plainly but becomingly, spoke good English, was skilled in conversation, respected by whites and Indians alike.

Mrs. Redclay was said to have been a captive, or rather a stolen child, brought up as an Indian. Apparently she considered herself Indian and, of course, made no apologies. She received rations as an Indian widow and supplemented this by doing sewing for the white folks. Her cheerfulness and sincerity inspired our admiration. She had no complaints to offer. Several dusky children and grand-children were her contribution to the world. One of her sons was a natural leader and destined to be a chief, the white-negro-Indian blend in his case producing a countenance decidedly Indian in appearance.

But why go on with these instances, for as we see it neither the squaw man nor the white squaw needs defense. In reservation days the squaw man had to be legally married or move away, and if his conduct became too outrageous he was evicted from Indian lands and thus separated from his Indian wife and children. Few agents would lose any sleep over such forceful disruption of marriage ties; on the contrary, they would have felt that justice and propriety were advanced thereby.

Most squaw men gave to the world a flock of hybrids, and though these were legitimate in the eyes of the law, they were probably neither better nor worse than the more numerous "breeds" resulting from illegal unions. One saving grace was that the full-blood Indian seemed to see nothing exceptional or degrading in either case, possibly because though at times an incomprehensible idealist, for the most part his social realism knew no bounds. If he disliked "breeds" at all, it was only when they became snobbish and considered themselves superior because of their white ancestry.

On the other hand one did not need to tarry long at an agency to learn what the white people thought of them, for it was everywhere, "those good for nothing breeds." As one veteran Major said, "Give me the full-blood every time. He drinks less, tells the truth, has moral principles by which he stands, and a mind you can reason with. On the other hand the 'breed' has no such qualities, he is a trouble maker without morals or principles. He respects neither white nor red."

Note that the Major said, "he." I never heard an official raise his voice against the female "breed" as a class, nor could I see that she presented a problem.

True, now and then I heard of a gay lady who preyed upon white men, but there were full-bloods who did likewise, whereas the mass of hybrid girls were set to Indian ways by their mothers and grandmothers, married for the most part to full-blood men and so backcrossed, to use a phrase coined by the experts on the famous fruit fly. So far as I could observe, the mixed-blood woman was content to chop wood, scrape skins and bear children, like other Indian women. Possibly if I had really known them they would have expressed resentment over the conventionally closed doors leading to the firesides of their fathers' people, but I doubt it. Surely nothing came to my eye or ear even hinting of such a thing.

As to their brothers, well, one was inclined to agree with the Major, for to see some of them was enough to make you feel for your pocketbook. I can see one of them yet, of burly prize-fighting appearance, a bloated face, silk handkerchief around his neck, demanding the loan of five dollars on the ground that I owed the Indians something for coming on their land. Finding that I was neither frightened nor impressed, he asked for liquor, finally begging for a quarter, saying that he was a white man and that surely I would help a white brother. Fortunately, all were not like this, far from it.

Lest the picture be painted too black, let us turn to an exceptional case or two. About the second day on a certain reservation I was introduced to Cloud, obviously half-white and in command of good terse English. A check-book and a diary protruding from his pocket guaranteed that he was literate and businesslike. One of his first moves was to try to sell me a horse or two: "Got too many horses, you know. Got to sell some of them, eat up all the grass, you know." Receiving no encouragement he soon dropped the matter. Gradually I came to know and admire this man, though I had no desire to trade with him.

Upon inquiry I learned that his father had been a trader, but that from the white point of view Cloud was illegitimate. However, I was warned never to hint as much, for in times past Cloud had knocked out more than one white man for saying something he interpreted as an insult to his Indian mother. Ultimately I saw her, a very old but magnificent full-blood woman. It was an inspiration to look at her. That she adored her son was obvious, and it was equally clear that Cloud saw to it that she had the comforts of Indian life as she knew them—"Nothing too good for the Old Mother," he said.

You should have seen his home, a large two-story frame house, with a lawn, a kind of garden with a small lake in which there were real swans. Did the Old Mother live in this great house? Yes, she had a room there all her own, but at the far side of the garden, where one could look out upon the virgin hills, was a fine skin-covered tipi in which she spent much of her time around a fire of cottonwood bark. When I commented upon this, Cloud said, "Can't stand too much civilization, you know."

When I met Cloud's wife, the mistress of this house, I found her a full-blood, but intelligent and efficient. To all appearances she lived like a white woman and preferred a brass bed to a pallet in a tipi. The reader who has scanned these pages need not be told how Cloud made his money; cattle, horses, contracting with the Government, etc., but in his case it was legal, except possibly when he bribed an official. His house was always full of Indian relatives and hangers-on, but he could afford the usual Indian hospitality. His children and grandchildren were nothing to be proud of, lazy and snobbish, none of them showing much promise to carry on.

Perhaps the reader is aglow with approval for this seemingly successful career; but in time, as we came nearer to Cloud's inner life, it became clear that the outlook for him was not altogether alluring. He seemed not to lack confidence in his business ability, but he was lonely, very lonely in spirit. His white associates could not forget that he was a "breed." None of them would take him by the hand and say, "You are a man"; no one ever made him feel quite welcome. At times we suspected that his eternal bustle at business was an attempt to smash down these barriers.

Now and then he sought an outlet in another direction, a grand drunk. We felt that already Cloud had passed the high point in his career, that he was on the down grade. Year after year his herds decreased, his house and grounds fell into disorder, his wife died, he turned the place over to his children. He drank more and more, and eventually died.

The Major said, "I told you so. The eternal breed dominated in the end." It was hard to accept this statement, for many a white man has done the same thing outwardly at least. But it must be admitted that Cloud was handicapped, for "breed" he was. That, he could not forget; nor did those among whom he lived forget it. We should have liked to inscribe over his tomb, "He had no place to go."

Then we recall Sunray, who was once my guide. He also had a white father whose memory he cherished as a successful gambler, a career he secretly envied but could not follow. Sunray was bright, had done fairly well in an Indian boarding school, and learned to make harness, a trade which gave him part-time employment around the agency. But he really enjoyed taking me about and took an intelligent interest in helping me with my notes. Often around the camp-fire he opened his mind. He saw no future in his trade. What galled him most was that no one trusted him. He was loyal to me but I heard that he was tricky at times and grasping. His favorite game was to over-charge for his services. When I parted from him the last time, he seemed melancholy.

"You are a white man," he said. "You have a place among your people, you count for something. Around us here are Indians, they revere their past, they have the respect of their fellows. Here am I, neither an Indian nor a white man—just nothing."

I did what I could to encourage him, to suggest that he could be a white man if he set out to be, though I had secret misgivings about the soundness of this advice. We parted and Sunray returned to his job. But a year or two later he blew out his brains. Poor Sunray! Our ethical code frowns upon such a deed, but there always rises the question, "What else could he do?"

Enough of such depressing scenes. There were many who did live it out—average resistant souls. Here again we are looking back at the long ago, for life on a reservation today is quite a different matter. Most everywhere the mixed-bloods constitute a respectable minority and so have social solidarity. Statistics show that they are healthier, have a higher birth rate and a lower death rate than full-bloods. Also, in standard of living, schooling, church affiliation, etc., they lead. In short they have found a place in the world and deserve our respect.

14

Those Ever Vanishing Types

UP AND DOWN the Indian country roamed a few artists, in reality conservationists, since they sincerely believed that when the few old Indians died, the type would vanish forever, and feeling that here was something of incalculable value, they were out to copy, model and photograph for posterity. Many of them were so radiant with holy zeal, that they made us ashamed of our own more practical attitudes. That these passing Indian personalities were worth recording, we agreed, but there were many fine figures and faces among the younger Indians which should grow equally picturesque with age. Anyhow this idea of saving vanishing types was not new to the time and place of which I write, for as much as seventy years before, a Philadelphia miniature painter by the name of Catlin conceived of painting the passing tribes of the Missouri. He was a good painter to begin with, because his miniatures are now prized by collectors, but having been smitten with the "save the vanishing tribes" idea, he took to the wilds with pencil and brush. No one before nor since has so completely sold the idea to the world; not only did he exhibit hundreds of portraits and sketches in the great cities of this country, but took the capitals of Europe by storm when he exhibited live Indians—the original Wild West show. The number of sketches and paintings executed by Catlin almost surpasses belief: every important museum in this country and abroad possesses a collection, one American institution alone boasting over 300 canvases.

It always follows that a thing done with conspicuous success calls forth many followers. There were artists before Catlin's day who painted Indians but no colonial was troubled by thoughts of vanishing tribes; their fathers had barely managed to hold on to the rim of the continent while doing their best to extinguish the red man, even the Puritans went to church and congratulated the Deity on having seen fit to send a plague to carry off a few hundred Indians. It was only after the frontier had passed beyond the Mississippi River that the conservation idea took hold and then in the heart of the "effete" East. So following Catlin the painters held the stage until photography came into its own, for then new enthusiasts visualized a realistic record—accuracy was now to be the slogan. I met some of these photographers, one with a kind of camp studio, an enormous tent and a huge portrait camera. Of enthusiasm he had no lack but seemed to have little insight into Indian life, no notion of just what was to be done with these portraits after they were made. Even the Indians considered him so lacking in worth that the most worthwhile personalities refused to sit for him. There were poor specimens of painters, too, fired by this saving of types idea, who had been better off had they stayed at home. Thus at various times I met a round headed dumb-bell who when at home made his living painting names and landscapes upon carriage doors but who periodically used his savings to try his hand as an Indian painter. It was a pitiable sight, to see a bungler with no artistic imagination, who first photographed his Indian and then tried to fool the observer by covering up the picture with paint.

Notwithstanding the varying deficiencies of many such enthusiasts, their appearance at an agency was little short of a sensation, for if one merely announced himself as an artist, immediately all hats were off, everyone felt that now a superior person was walking in their midst. The adoration of the average American of those days for art was astonishing, perhaps it was a case of valuing that of which he had the least. Even the Indians were infected by this white hero worship and looked upon the artist as a kind of magician, though rarely overlooking the supposed commercial value of the product and driving hard bargains for their services as artists' models. One need not be surprised at this realistic attitude on the part of the Indian after a century or two of experience with trade, and most of the white men he met were engaged in trade. Further, he knew that if a white man gave service he expected to be paid and so the Indian reasoned logically that unless he received due compensation for his own services, the white man would be reaping undue profit. The only wonder is that he would sit for a portrait for a fee an artist could afford to pay, because on every hand he heard the white people speak of a painting as something priceless.

I hope these remarks do not convey the impression that no real artists visited the Indian country for such would be slanderous. Even in my own occasional rambles I met such well known masters as Remington, Deming, Burbank and Sharp, and often crossed the trails of others equally well known. If these artists only knew the joy and inspiration their visits brought to the hearts of the white residents in these out-of-the-way places, they might feel they had not lived in vain. The would-be artists were so receptive to this adulation, something they had never experienced before, that like old pampered house cats they spent their time purring rather than pursuing the game they came to seek; but not so with the true artists, who were so inspired by the picturesque personalities stalking about that they worked feverishly and wholly unconscious of the honors showered upon them, attentions which they found annoying rather than otherwise; and why not, because every day one could see more splendid art material.

The old Indian of that time had been trained to sit, stand, and walk in a somewhat conventional manner which enhanced his dignity and bearing. He practiced sitting on a horse until he knew just how to harmonize the lines of his body with those of his mount. The white man of that day gave little thought to such matters and is now so engrossed in bending over a desk or a bench that his body has lost such arts of expression as glorified the Indian. Certain of the Plains tribes practiced a style of walking which always held my attention. Each foot was placed in front of the other, the step made by swinging the foot in a graceful up and down curve. The total impression was not unlike a dance. It was such carry-overs from the old regime that moved the artists, but unfortunately most of them failed to catch the spirit of it all, probably because they were so fanatically obsessed with the preservation idea. Even George Catlin, the pioneer conserver of vanishing types, was so taken with the novelty of Indian costume and trappings that he almost forgot to draw the figure, his sketches reminding one of costume displays hung upon dummies in the windows of a department store. Many of his followers went to the other extreme in fixing their attention upon nose, cheek and ear, without regard to action or costume. Better had they all turned photographers than carry the preservation of types to such lengths.

In my day an Indian enjoyed being painted. True, he

might earn a dollar or two by it, but that, though otherwise inconsequential, he regarded as his due and necessary to save his face. He was quick to catch the idea that he would be immortalized by having his portrait hung in a gallery somewhere, but not even for that would he waive the expected fee for a sitting. I liked to watch them making up for their sittings. For example, old Thunder's Child first combed his long hair, still glossy black, carefully parted it in the middle and gathered it into two side rolls, not braids, but carefully twisted and ingeniously wrapped with long strips of red cloth. A small wisp of hair on his crown was carefully braided and allowed to hang free down the back of the head, forming what white people call the scalp-lock. Yet old Thunder's Child laughed scornfully when I called this a scalp-lock; that, he said, was a foolish idea, because even white men with short hair were scalped. I did not get the point but probably he meant to convey the idea that this way of braiding the hair was merely a matter of style. A small amount of hair on his forehead had been cut short and trained to stand up stiffly, pompadour fashion, into which he worked a paste made by mixing white clay and tallow, the result giving a pale bluish appearance to this portion of the hair. His next procedure was to tie two hair ornaments on his temples so that they hung down past his ears, reaching to the shoulders. These string-like ornaments are difficult to describe though such may be seen in museum collections. In this instance they were fashioned of brass buttons, leather, german silver wire and weasel fur. Dangling from one was a tiny gear wheel from a watch, which he stoutly maintained was a sun symbol.

The face was given an even coat of fine vermilion, mixed with tallow, the whole having the consistency of face-cream. He spent several minutes mixing this paste in his hands and then looked in a mirror as he carefully rubbed his hands over his face, neck, and ears. He was now a "red Indian" for sure. What was left of the paint was carefully applied to the backs of his hands and wrists.

The next procedure was to open a skin bag from which he took a pair of beaded moccasins, fringed leggings and a decorated skin shirt. The latter had hair fringes down the arms. Having put on these clothes he placed a bear-claw necklace around his neck. Finally, he opened a bundle from which he took a large quirt with a heavy wooden handle, striped in blue and white, and with this in hand set out to have his portrait painted.

Out of curiosity I walked along to the improvised studio at the hotel. The artist had Thunder's Child mount a chair on a packing box where he sat stiffly like a king upon a throne. The more the artist signed that Thunder's Child relax and look natural, the stiffer he sat, until in disgust the artist grabbed the decorated quirt from the Indian's hand and tossed it into the corner of the room. Thunder's Child rose, descended from his throne, recovered his precious quirt and walked out. The dignity of his leaving defies description. Had our artist been a grand master of the brush, he might have painted a great picture, but he merely swore about Indians in general. He begged me to ask Thunder's Child to return, but I knew that was useless. What the artist did not understand was that this precious quirt was a sacred object, belonging to which was a ritual and that he was desecrating holy things when he threw it into the corner.

The next day I called upon Thunder's Child to apologize for the ignorance of the artist. However, he waved my apologies aside, remarking that now since this artist had grossly insulted the powers that presided over the quirt, those powers would see to it that they were revenged. Curiously enough, while we were talk-

ing a young Indian riding by gave out the news that a
horse had run away with the artist's wife and injured
her. "I told you so," said Thunder's Child. Whatever
may be the correct explanation, he was certain that the
mysterious powers invoked had seen to it that the artist
was punished. So far as I know Thunder's Child was
one of the vanishing types that vanished, for nothing
could induce him to return to the studio.

I rarely grew enthusiastic over mere portraits,
though obviously some of them were works of art. The
Indian was usually disappointed too, because he came
arrayed in feathers, bits of fur and hair fringes, all the
distinguishing marks of merit according to the culture
of his fathers. Yet the portrait painter ignored these,
reproducing for us a somewhat stylized face in a plain
setting so that the Indian, far less accustomed to the
mirror than the white man, saw nothing familiar in the
picture. What he expected to see was his whole self
with all the gay trappings, or to appear as he imagined
he must look. Anyhow the old Indian of my day experienced difficulty in recognizing any kind of a picture.
This seems strange to us, brought up amidst pictures
but I recall how when one of these old timers was
shown his photograph he scowled at it, turned it first
one way and the other, finally in desperation biting it. I
came to the rescue by putting the card in the correct
position, then pointing out the eyes, nose, mouth, etc.
After a time he seemed to grasp it, but was obviously
disappointed in so poor a representation. Nor was this
because he knew nothing of drawing for I had seen this
same old man working with his own materials draw in
bold life-like lines the horse and the buffalo. Even aged
women, hands knotted with toil, could trace upon raw-
hide with the point of a knife much better drawings
than I could execute, but all such pictures had a style
of their own, a very different style from that of the
white man, hence the difficulty in recognition. One

photographer I met knew how to please the Indian. He would make an enlarged print and touch up the same with bright water colors, thus producing a picture in true Indian style. I was shown a number of these by their proud owners.

All the old Indians I met drew their horses, deer, and buffalo in profile. Most children do the same, perhaps because that is the easy way, and I got the impression that a painting or a photograph in profile was the more pleasing to Indians. Another thing strange to me was that whereas most every Indian could draw lifelike outlines of animals, he failed miserably with the human figure. Perhaps he gave less attention to humans, but one of my artist friends insists that this is not the explanation, claiming that the human figure is much more difficult. Well, may be, but I doubt it. Of one thing I was certain, that the younger generation of Indians either would not attempt to draw or had become perfectionists. Perhaps those who attended school were instilled with the idea that unless drawing was executed upon the highest levels it was not worth doing. On the other hand my old timers subscribed to no such fads of the new civilization but turned their hands loose to express what they saw and felt, for in no other way could I account for what these primitive draftsmen did. Now I wonder what they would have thought of the new art of today which means nothing to one even when note is taken of what the artist says he tried to draw. No doubt they would have said that the white man's world was an entanglement of foolishness.

All the connoisseurs of vanishing types met with in the Indian country were men, nor have I at any time met more than two or three women who showed any zeal for the task. I do not regard this as another argument for feminine inferiority, for it may well be an evidence of good sense not to run wild with an idea not securely grounded in fact. So it was a man who stepped into the Indian's world with a palette and a handful of brushes and it was a red man who met him at the threshold because it was his habit to stand between his women and the stranger. Two or more centuries of experience had convinced him that the white man rarely looked upon an Indian woman disinterestedly and he had accordingly built up a set of rules and regulations which forbade his women to speak to a strange man. So no matter what these artists had in mind the Indians saw to it that men sat for the portraits. On the other hand the artists themselves saw nothing alluring in the countenances of Indian women; even their figures did not appeal to them as good copy. As one of them once remarked, "when an Indian woman sits down, she settles into her place like cold molasses." In another chapter we commented upon the inspiring bearing of the Indian male, but I prefer to be silent respecting the female. A middle aged Indian woman walking somehow lacked unity, since various masses of unstable shapes appeared to be in ceaseless agitation under her loose flowing dress, causing one to wonder how such seeming lack of anatomical harmony could accompany directed locomotion, and as the reader may guess, these women are at a disadvantage in dancing. In fact it is the man who dances, women merely shake these loose sectors in their anatomy, moving, if at all, by sliding their feet. The sight is amusing but not inspiring. The artists I knew did make a few portraits of women, for which they apologized, their behavior suggesting that they were willing to concede that the Indian female type was not worth conserving.

Of course, there may be other reasons for painting men rather than women, recalling that artists have a preference for nudes and that whereas the Indian man preferred to go about in breech-cloth and moccasins, his woman was always dressed. So it was no trouble at all to find models for painting the Indian male, but the female was a problem. I heard about an artist who planned a large canvas, showing a mourning scene for a tribe formerly practicing scaffold burial; that is, four forked poles were set up and a kind of platform made of cross poles, upon which the corpse rested, wrapped in buffalo skins, forming a bundle suggesting an Egyptian mummy. This tribe, like many others, required that the women of the deceased's family show their sorrow by gashing their legs and arms. By inquiry, the artist learned that a woman thus mutilating her leg would remove her leggings and moccasins, but not expose the thigh. There was some difficulty in persuading a woman to serve as a model but finally one did consent, though in ignorance of what was expected. Everything went along smoothly, the painter completing all the figure except the legs and feet, but when the woman understood that she was to bare her feet and legs, she balked. However, after a long argument, she withdrew from the room, removed one moccasin, and returned. After one foot had been painted, she again withdrew, returning with the other foot bare. As to the leggings, there was another argument, but at last the woman agreed and presented one calf at a time.

Perhaps in closing the reader may ask as to whether the types did really vanish. Of one thing I am certain, the old life passed, the old people I knew came to adult life before reservation days and so saw the breakdown of tribal life and independence. Some of them were discouraged as to the future, but by living in the past and capitalizing their ancestral pride, they carried on. They found little joy in the new generation, which lacked purpose and morale. What white artists had in mind, without knowing it, was the passing of personalities that were original and unique when looked at from the horizon of a culture that was passing, and because the old life was passing there could be no replacements, yet these artists were but fooling themselves, for what does a portrait tell of a personality if we never knew the original? The portraits of the finest Old Indians can convey little to those of this generation. Anatomically they may be correct, but for that very reason not materially different from their direct descendants living today and to live tomorrow. The ambitions of these painters were headed in the right direction, but their chosen medium was wholly inadequate. These personalities did pass, they are gone, and so have passed many before them. I, also, should have liked to preserve them, but realized that unless one knew them in life, all their truly fine qualities were beyond representation.

15

A Camp Diary

FOR THE PRECEDING CHAPTERS we selected situations and adventures with a view to revealing the high spots in reservation life but now we give the diary of a brief visit, hoping that it may indicate what the daily life of an Indian family might be. The policy of the Government was to force the Indians to erect cabins far apart, like the scattered farm houses of the contemporary West, often scarcely in sight of each other, which is understandable since the purpose was to transform the Indians into farmers and stock raisers in the shortest time possible. Further, the hope was that to each head of a family could be allotted the land upon which he built his cabin, to which he would eventually be given title and thus the reservation pass into history, leaving in its wake new United States citizens of Indian ancestry. This was asking too much of human nature, for this policy was destined to part the Indian and his lands, leaving him a poverty-stricken derelict, dependent upon the bounty of the Government. Today we see this policy of the Government reversed and new lands purchased to be maintained as reserves, upon which the Indians of the future are to live under rehabilitated tribal organizations.

Yet in the days of which I write every family had a log cabin. It is plains country we are to visit, but along the streams were cottonwood and birch trees affording fuel and building material, consequently the Indians strung their cabins along these creeks. In mid-winter they lived in these cabins but at other times in tipis or tents, shifting them about as convenient.

A young Indian and his wife, Dick and Gertie, both graduates from a government boarding school, were engaged as guide and cook respectively, and here is the record.

July 20. I reached the agency early in the morning. No one was to be seen at this unseemly hour save two Indian policemen wearily loitering about waiting to be relieved. The little frame hotel was locked up, but by rapping on the manager's bedroom window, I got him out of bed. At last I was admitted and spent the time until breakfast reading papers that were at least a week old. Breakfast was served by a neat mixed-blood woman; oatmeal, a few miserable fried eggs and some bacon were put on the table. The change from the dining car was disconcerting. After breakfast I strolled out to the trading store where I found my old friend Jim at his usual occupation, burning paper in front of the door. He came up with an expression of surprise. In a few minutes he had given me the news, a girl baby having recently been born to him, the first after a marriage of years. Naturally this event occupied his mind. Then I met in succession all the other people I knew. While so occupied an Indian policeman reminded me that I had not reported to the office of the Major. As there is a severe penalty for such an offense, I made due haste. The Major, a retired army officer, having seen service with Washington Mathews at Fort Buford in 1868, was very formal. When handed my letters of introduction from the Department of Indian Affairs he scanned them deliberately and then proceeded to give me a long talk on things in general.

Afterwards when walking about I met the woman of Bull Shield who recognized me at once. She wore the same striped robe and had her face smeared with yellow as when I saw her last. Then I met several other old women I had known. Afterwards I saw them all sitting on the sunny side of the store smoking their little black stone pipes. My guide had a camp outfit ready for me, a new tent, bedding and provisions. While at his house writing letters, old Rock Chief came in with his usual shout. After mutual greetings we talked of traditions as to the former home of his people. Following a luncheon of bacon and eggs with fresh biscuits we packed our outfit in a wagon and all set out for Black River. It was fine weather with a steady wind from the mountains. We made camp in a deep valley where Black River ploughs its way through a rocky ridge. This is camp No. 1.

Dick pointed out some ashes and bones in a cut bank, which we must examine later. One of the cliffs here seems to have been used as a buffalo drive. (A place where buffalo were driven over as a method of hunting.) Scouting along the foot of the cliff revealed nothing save fragments of bone. This evening Dick caught five trout and his wife prepared a fine meal. Then until bedtime, we talked over old times.

July 21st. This is a cloudy morning with a cool moist wind that threatens rain, but the only regret is our inability to see the hills. Last night the coyotes barked, as usual. This morning I walked along the edge of the river bank looking for signs of former habitation but found nothing. Later Dick rounded up his horses to go up stream and fish. I went with him, spending the forenoon looking for archaeological signs in the gravels and along the banks. I passed a number of Indian cabins but the people are all out on the hills making hay. At one place I saw a few rags hung in a small cottonwood tree as an offering to the Sun. We passed a high hill where Dick recently buried two children of his stepmother. Their graves are unmarked as usual. Traces of habitation along this part of the stream are numerous, but they refer to the present regime. The remains of sweat houses are on every hand. Many cabins have been abandoned for one reason or another; these Indians do not relish long residence in one place. The afternoon was spent below camp in a thick cottonwood grove such as one meets here and there along this river. Dick did not get many fish this time. My tent looks up at a ragged ledge of rock near the top of which is the nest of a hawk. One part of this rocky ledge is filled with shells resembling the oyster but these are spoken of by these Indians as the Old Woman's finger nails, referring to a mythical character.

July 22nd. It rained this morning but soon cleared and was hot. While gathering fire wood, Gertie found a smudge stick for a medicine pipe. Since all objects pertaining to such sacred pipes are regarded as holy, such a find is unusual. Later Powder Man came over from his hayfield with his two sons. One of them is a young man, the other a mere boy. The latter wore a good suit of custom-made clothes with black stockings and shoes. His black hair was parted in the middle and braided in four braids similar to that of his father. At luncheon we were short of dishes for serving and it was suggested that the little boy wait, at which he pouted and shed tears, but did not cry aloud.

Powder Man has a good house and hay sheds near this place. He took us across the river on his wagon and loaned us a pick and shovel to examine the deposit of ashes and bones we had previously noticed in the river bank, about two feet down. However, all we found was animal bones, a bone bead and a chipped implement. The sun burned us cruelly but I did not mind for it was scientific work, you know. This evening we crossed back to our side of the river, and as I sat in my tent writing, saw Gertie on top of the cliff searching for the marks of the old buffalo drive we failed to find yesterday.

July 23rd. I arose at six o'clock and as the sun was already high took a turn down the river. Here I startled a large hawk, resting at the edge of the water. After breakfast I walked up to the top of a high hill where an Indian once slept to dream. He had erected a small shelter of stones on this height and lined it with cedar. I sat there a long time wondering how lonely he must have felt in the darkness, what prayers and sacrifices he offered and what came of it all. The etiquette of his tribe regarded it as insulting to even hint that a man had gone out to such a place, so we were barred from asking about the man who slept here, I having been told his name in confidence. Juniper and sage were scattered about, sure signs that something sacred had been involved. Perhaps this Indian came here often, like a priest to a place of retreat.

Dick is anxious to move camp—no Indian is satisfied to stay in one place long. I put him off as long as I could, but at noon today we broke camp and moved over to Wolf Creek. Here we made camp No. 2, on a small flat. The hills here are tame and there is nothing of interest. I shall always regret leaving camp No. 1 for the place was a delight in scenery and interest. Dick came in with 33 small trout and strange to say he and his wife managed to eat most of them at one meal.

July 24th. The coyotes wakened me once or twice last night and a horse stumbled through the ropes of my tent. This morning I sent an Indian to the agency for our mail. We had a quiet day until Eagle Plume came along and, of course, stopped for luncheon. He told us that a few miles down stream a woman was very ill and that three medicine men had been called in.

July 25th. Today Eagle Plume came in again with the welcome gift of some dried meat. He has a large number of horses and cattle and spends his time riding around viewing them through an old-fashioned field-glass. After lunch we drove up to see a dance house used by the young Indians and on the way back caught enough trout for supper. We passed Eagle Plume's place. His people were living out in tipis. His father-in-law walked about dressed in a shirt and moccasins which was amusing.

Our camp is beset by range cattle. They seem curious to know what is going on and come down from the hills to look at our tents, but the moment they get sight of a person they trail off. This evening several bulls gathered near here and threatened each other but we were disappointed for they all bluffed and contented themselves with throwing dust. We got our first mail today.

July 26th. This morning finds a steady wind blowing from the mountains. At times it is difficult to walk against it. This wind is cool so we are all wearing heavy clothes. The constant blowing is slacking the ropes to our tents and may get them off over our heads if it continues. Later there was a little shower of rain, but now it is warm again. Dick caught the usual number of trout today and we ate them for supper. For once we had no visitors in camp and so had an uninterrupted day. The gophers woke me up this morning by gnawing on the ropes of the tent and when I beat upon the canvas they stopped to give that ear racking squeak that characterizes them.

July 27th. Last night was pitch dark. Before bedtime we heard an animal chewing on bones near our cook place. Shouting seemed to have no inhibiting effect for each time the chewing became more audible. We all agreed it must be a large animal, probably a badger. It seemed wise not to stumble over it in the dark so Dick fired a few shots into the air which started a general alarm in the animal world; our horses snorted and jerked on their tethers, a few range steers grazing nearby stampeded and various small creatures added their feeble but shrill notes to the dwindling noise; then some dogs at a distant Indian camp began yelping and howling. It is surprising what the report of a gun will set in motion. Presently we realized that there was complete silence around our cook place. Later in the night I was roused from a deep sleep by the feeling that something was going on. It was still very dark but again I heard that unmistakable chewing on bones, gentler than before, but now inside the tent. As I turned to look in the direction from which the sound came, the chewing ceased. Then after an interval it began again. This suggested a game, so when the chewing began, I moved, then it ceased, and so on. I had suspicions. Soon the first faint rays of dawn began to lighten the gloom; then I saw a small shape with an erect tail—it was a skunk. When I lay still, he would begin chewing, when I moved, he would walk rapidly up and down the opposite side of the tent. Apparently he could not find the exit, but as it grew lighter he found the place and passed out.

I felt relieved and settled down for a little sleep, but then hearing a noise, I looked toward the point of his exit, and there was that skunk, his head and forelegs thrust under the edge of the canvas, calmly looking the situation over. That was too much. I grasped a boot, beat upon the ground and shouted, "scat!" Nothing in particular happened as the skunk withdrew. Next day I discovered that all the fish-heads and bones from our cook place were cached in a corner of the tent behind my baggage. He had moved in during the night. Perhaps I had convinced him that he was not welcome, but after a camp council we decided to move back to the site of camp No. 1, and set out promptly. As we came down the hill to our first camping place, we noticed wild gooseberries beginning to ripen. Indian-like, Dick and Gertie rushed out upon them.

We are once again settled at this fine camping place, and happy. In the evening we dug up a buffalo skull in the old buffalo drive; it was deeply imbedded, probably belonging to one of the last buffalo to be killed at this place.

July 28th. This morning I climbed the bluff to trace out the rock piles of the buffalo drive, succeeding in part. Later in the day we went to the agency for supplies.

July 29th. This is an unusually hot day for this country but there is a fine breeze. While creeping through some willows this morning I came upon a magpie's nest, but was quickly surrounded by a chattering group of those birds. It was quite amusing. Afterwards as I lay in my tent Dick and his wife began singing church hymns they had learned at school. They sing remarkably well.

In the afternoon, while I was writing up my notes a powerful whirlwind came down the valley and turned over the cooking shelter, rattling the camp stove and stove pipe around on the ground. Old Indians hold such winds in awe and even the mixed-bloods dislike to talk about them.

July 30th. Eagle Plume rode through our camp greeting us with a smile, but did not stop. Later in the day an excited young Indian rode up stopping just long enough to say that a drunken Indian had run amuck and was intrenched upon a high hill shooting it out with the Indian police. Having said as much he spurred his horse and vanished. At intervals others reined up long enough to tell us the same story with variations. I knew enough about agency life to visualize the whole reservation criss-crossed by similar riders spreading exciting stories. The last rider to pass said that soldiers had been sent for to reinforce the police, but we discounted that. However, about dark, Eagle Plume came by again with the plain facts; no shots had been fired, for after shouting defiance for a while the intrenched Indian was persuaded to throw down his gun and surrender.

July 31st. John Bird, a well-to-do mixed-blood came by this morning. I was glad to see him because he has a fine personality which attracts everyone. After luncheon we drove out to some hay camps. The first was that of Red Dog, consisting of four wall-tents. A number of women and children were about, one woman scraping a cowskin in front of her tent. Near by a travois was leaning up against a tripod of tipi poles. An old woman in mourning for her husband came out and asked us to carry a message to a relative concerning the division of the property left by her husband.

Next we came to the camp of my old friend Wolf Head, who also lives in a wall-tent. He is somewhat aristocratic in that he has a low bedstead for his tent, the usual thing being to spread the bedding upon the ground. He said it kept the bedding clean. We talked a great deal about the location of old trading posts and the traditions concerning them, while his wife brought in some coffee and crackers. There was about a gallon

of coffee and strange to say it was good. I invited him
to move over to our camp. He said he would accept the
invitation but hoped we would then seek another location because there were a great many ghosts at that
place. Many years ago a large number of Indians died
there of smallpox and the bodies were placed in the
brush near-by. According to Indian belief, the spirits of
these dead still haunt the place at night. The Major had
given Wolf Head a permit to kill a steer so he expects
to butcher tomorrow, after which he proposes to give
us some fresh meat.

We then drove to Powder Man's camp, who is quite
a man in the Indian way. We found him directing the
operation of two mowing machines and a rake. In his
camp were two tipis and two wall-tents. A little girl
was playing outside, dragging a young pup around by
the fore leg, while chewing on a piece of dry meat.
Dick begged a sack of dry meat for our camp and
bought a piece of raw hide from Strangling Wolf for a
half dollar which I interpreted as a roundabout way of
paying for the meat. On our way home we saw two
eagles.

This morning when upon the hill by the old buffalo
drive I saw Gertie wading the river with a large bundle
of firewood on her back. Above everything else it is a
woman's duty to get the wood and she takes pride in
this custom. It is as much of a disgrace for a woman to
let her husband get the wood as it is for him to carry it.

August 1st. Last night we heard a pack of coyotes
barking as they galloped over the hills and from the
noise they made judge there were at least a dozen.
After luncheon we rode along the crests of the hills
toward the mountains. On the top of a very high hill
with a fine outlook were some recent graves. In some
cases the grave boxes were set upon the ground and
rocks piled up around them, in others the boxes were

sunk until the top was on a level with the ground. Over one a heap of stones had been raised. A woman's legging and a few trinkets scattered about gave indication that the coyotes had been at work. The old Indians thought it wrong to cover up a corpse because then the spirit could not get out.

We passed on to the forks of Black River where Dick showed us an old pit in which camas roots were once baked. On the way home he shot at a badger, a hawk and an eagle, but all were too far away to be in danger.

August 2nd. Last night some small creature came into my tent and gnawed paper. Nothing I could do seemed to scare him away but when a match was struck, the first crack of the head silenced him.

At noon I watched some range bulls. One herd of cattle was on our side of the river and one on the other. The bulls on our side began to roar and throw dust on themselves, then those on the other side did the same. It was one continual flow of sound for about two hours, after which they ceased as abruptly as they began. Late in the afternoon a cold wind came up and in a few minutes I heard Gertie chopping wood for the camp stove. Her tent was fitted with a smoke hole so that in case of need the stove could be moved inside. Before long we all gathered around her fire. The sheet iron stove shone red with the heat and everyone soon felt comfortable. Even Gertie put off her shy reserve long enough to tell me something about medicine women and their doings.

August 3rd. This morning I heard shrill sounds from above and presently perceived two eagles fighting high up in the air. After a time one seemed to have enough of it and soon passed out of sight. Last night I was again disturbed by something chewing paper. I lighted a candle and waited; presently a fieldmouse appeared. I seized the sacred pipe smudge stick Gertie found one day and thrashed the ground vigorously. With a sharp squeak of alarm the mouse scampered away.

Not having a chance to send out mail for a week I decided to go to the agency. The wind was cold and sharp like a winter day. While at the agency I met an old mixed-blood Cree who had known Larpentere, a veteran of the fur-trade, and was interested in what I remembered of that old trader's journal.

August 4th. The morning began with a clear sky and a hot sun. During the night I was awakened by a hooting owl. Wolf Head rode over before lunch. As yet he had not joined us, having been called away to treat a sick woman and could not leave her until today. In some respects he is quite a doctor. While we were talking, Powder Man came down with about fifteen pounds of beef, he having butchered yesterday. This man has a fine personality. He and Wolf Head had an argument over the usage of certain symbols in sign writing. At the end they were still in disagreement.

August 5th. This is a hot still Sunday morning. Last night a coyote wakened me with his weird howl. Then I lay awake for some time. It is surprising how still it can be at night in the open, but now and then you hear a faint sound from some of the wild creatures that pursue their occupations in the night, occasionally the night hawk squawks its indescribably explosive note, all is still again. About noon two wagon loads of Indian women visited our camp, to eat and to talk. One woman had a little bead work and the other a small painted tipi which she set up. It was a nice toy with otters painted around the side but I had no use for it. The women got their dinner, of course. Wolf Head came over for a visit. In the evening some Indian boys came for a stray horse and made a show of roping it; but after a great deal of chasing around drove it off.

August 6th. Wolf Head and his woman moved camp today and pitched their tent by the side of mine. We now have a camp of three tents. His woman is a typical Indian, yet they live in a wall-tent, use a camp stove and conduct themselves in many respects like white people. Yet in their tent is the tell-tale tripod with a medicine bundle. Every Indian must have one of these tripods even though he have nothing to hang on it save an old pair of leggings.

August 7th. Last night Wolf Head sat by our camp stove narrating old myths. This morning we noticed that his wife had put up a second tent to serve as a kitchen, another indication of the advance of civilization among these people. During the day Wolf Head suggested that we change camp because he heard an owl hooting during the night. None of these people like to hear owls, they think they are the spirits of dead medicine men. While up on a hill I saw Wolf Head's old woman giving him a bath in the river, scouring him with a bar of laundry soap. He claims that his "medicine" requires him to take a bath once a day. This evening we heard him singing in his tent after the old woman took in the medicine bundle from the tripod outside.

August 8th. Wolf Head is an early riser like most old Indians. Before daylight I was awakened by the lightest of foot-falls. Peeping out I saw Wolf Head facing the east, gazing at the brilliant morning star just coming into view. He raised his hands in the way that I had seen him do when praying to the sun. For a long time he stood thus, then turned slowly toward his tent. Later in the day I asked him if his people ever prayed to the stars; in a matter-of-fact way he said that they frequently did. I thought best to let it go at that.

This morning we had a clear sky but a steady cold wind from the west. Wolf Head was going about in breech-cloth, moccasins and blanket helping his wife tighten the stakes to one of their tents. Yet before noon the wind shifted resulting in a very hot day for this country. Powder Man came down for dinner and brought us the mail—the first since last Friday. He and Wolf Head had a great time telling war stories. This evening we had some sport. While Wolf Head was sitting before my tent, talking in the sign language, Dick came along with some grass wrapped in a piece of burlap. He sat down to join in the sign talk, placing the bundle of grass on the ground. Wolf Head's dog came up and began to bark at it. Then Dick tied a rope to the bundle, jerking it around. The dog was furious, yet too much of a coward to go up to it. Finally Wolf Head's woman caught the dog and threw him upon the bundle, at which he ran up the hill and barked down at the terrible bundle from a safe distance. Old Wolf Head found the scene so humorous that once he rolled over upon his back and shouted.

August 9th. The mosquitoes troubled us a little last night. Old Wolf Head has been talking to us of spiritualistic performances. Once he asked if I should like a ghost to go around with, and being told that I would, he said that he would go to some burial place and get bones for me to carry, then ghosts would always be with me.

Strangling Wolf came to visit us. He is quite a skeptic. While we were sitting in Wolf Head's tent he pointed to the medicine bundle hanging there and made signs that it was worthless. He also explained in the sign language that he had many cattle and that if these medicine men would work like himself they would have something worth talking about.

This evening I climbed up the ledge of rock overlooking our camp. From there I could see out over the rolling hills for a long distance and it was a fine view. The valley of Black River is worth seeing even though it be a small stream passing through a grass covered country. After I came back Wolf Head began explaining how in the old days dogs were muzzled to keep them from scaring the buffalo. He cut a hole in a piece of paper and slipped it over his dog's nose, explaining that if it were a piece of soft tanned skin, it could be tied around the dog's neck, thus holding the dog's jaws together. Having completed his demonstration he pushed the paper over the dog's head where it extended around the neck like an Elizabethan collar. The dog began rolling around to get it off. This amused Wolf Head so much that he used up all the paper we had in camp. Then he tied a small piece to the dog's stubby tail and roared with merriment as the dog spun around in vain efforts to catch it. Those who say there is no fun in an Indian would have changed their minds had they heard his hilarious shouts.

August 10th. This morning Wolf Head showed me how to make a fish trap of willows. He sang songs while he worked because in the old days every object made had its ritual. Not to have sung them even in a mere demonstration, might have brought bad luck. The trap is a cone-shaped affair of wicker work. Later I saw the women coming in with large bundles of fire-wood on their backs and caught one of them with the camera, much to her disgust. She said she was not dressed up, etc. In the evening Wolf Head played more tricks upon his dog. This time he tied a condensed milk can to its tail and enjoyed the proceeding more than any one. I showed him some small soft yellow and red stones I had picked up in the gravel along the stream. This was a new idea to him. He said that he would make some new paint of them. All the paints his people now use come from the foothills of certain mountains to which they make regular trips for the purpose of securing them.

August 11th. This morning we went down the river to see an old woman paint some hides for making bags and parfleches. There we met two old widows, one of them blind. They were glad to meet us and enjoyed telling us about a great many things, such as cooking, skin dressing, etc. I bought an old pounder made of stone, covered with rawhide, and a fragment of stone used in scraping hides, all relics of the stone age. These old women live alone in a good frame house but they were resting out under the shade of a tipi cover spread over poles. While we were talking with them there, a mixed-blood man came up with his full-blood wife. The woman was quite fat, her most conspicuous character being a double chin. She wore a red calico dress and a man's hat. The latter had a pointed crown and not much of a brim, looking like a clown's cap. After we came back Wolf Head rode off down the river, but returned in an hour or two saying, "Gun, gun, shoot," and by holding crooked fingers over his head indicated that a steer was to be shot. So I loaned him a rifle. At dark Wolf Head returned with about 100 pounds of meat.

In the afternoon we crossed the river, spending a few hours in archaeological work at the place where I did some digging a few weeks ago. I found a number of stone arrow points and cut bones. When I came back to camp there were two strange Indian women come to visit with Wolf Head's woman. One of them is very old and is able to get about but slowly by means of a cane.

Wolf Head has been anxious to move camp because he fears that the sun may ruin his old rickety wagon. As a matter of fact it is beyond all possible harm from the sun or rain, but I saw him towing it off this morning by a rope tied to the end of the pole and twisted about the horn of his saddle. He says that it is now cached in the shade of some cottonwood trees and that he is satisfied with the present camping arrangement.

In the evening I spent some time in Wolf Head's tent talking to one of the visiting women. She was unusually friendly and tried to joke at my expense. She wore a man's hat trimmed with weasel skins, which she said, in a joking way, was a medicine hat that always kept the wearer on the go. She complained about these modern Indians living in tents where they could not have open fires as in a tipi because of which she found the ground damp and uncomfortable.

August 12th. Nothing much happened today because Wolf Head was called away to doctor a sick child and his old woman went with him to help with the singing. However, they returned hurriedly in the evening, retiring quietly into their tents. Later I heard that the child died while Wolf Head was doctoring. Such a happening is considered the worst luck possible, really a disgrace.

August 13th. Last night we had rain with high wind, it being necessary to use back ropes on our tents to prevent their being blown over. Wolf Head's woman is just now slicing some of the steak brought in yesterday. She has put up a kind of scaffold made of cottonwood poles similar to that of olden times upon which the slices of meat will be hung to dry. Indian dry meat is fair to the taste and seldom strong. It is usual to boil it a little before exposing it on the scaffold. I got ready to photograph the drying frame but the sun went back on me and then a rain with hail came up, driven by a vicious wind. It blew the meat scaffold down, upset our camp stove with the dinner that was cooking, but our tents held fast. In a few minutes the whole affair was over and the sun was out again. However, a little later the wind came up with rain and blew a fierce gale all night. Several times I was awakened by the creaking of tent ropes and the snap of canvas as the wind caught up the slack.

August 14th. The sky is clear this morning but the wind is as strong as ever. Dick's stepmother came in last night bringing the mail. She is a typical Indian woman but very neat in appearance. Her former husband was a white man but now she is married to a young worthless Indian with a mentality too dull for understanding.

In the evening Rock Chief came by with a load of boards for a shed roof and naturally stopped for the night. He and Wolf Head were chums in youth. They make quite a pair, each six feet and weighing about 200 pounds. As they sat opposite me in the tent with a lighted candle between them I was impressed by their physical proportions. Once when Rock Chief was telling of a war experience in which he was shot down in front of the enemy, he leaned over and patted Wolf Head on the shoulder with the remark that it was he who rode in and carried him out by the hair, thus saving his life. Then they sat quietly for a few moments.

August 15th. Early this morning Wolf Head's woman dismantled her tents and loaded everything into their old rickety wagon. I presented them my camp bedding, which according to their tribal custom was the greatest possible manifestation of hospitality. After a brief farewell, we broke camp, drove to the agency, where after dismissing my faithful guides, I left the reservation.

I am moved to add something more about Gertie. She was a woman about six feet tall and of unusual muscular strength. In chopping wood and lifting wagon wheels out of mud holes she could put all of us to shame. Once she and Dick accompanied the writer across the international boundary into Canada. It was open plains country, neither fences nor farm houses in sight. When we made camp in the evening I was startled to see Gertie draw from a bag a heavy belt filled with cartridges. This she buckled around her waist, then drew out a huge silver mounted revolver with a pearl shell handle, which she thrust into the scabbard attached to the belt. Looking around and observing my astonishment, she remarked, "Canadian mens sometimes get funny."

16

Camping with the Indians

WE WERE not long in realizing that the agency was an
outpost of civilization, whereas the nearby Indian
camp was the rear guard of paganism in full retreat.
On a reservation one could shuttle back and forth from
one order of life to the other. Interesting personalities
could be contacted while loitering around the agency,
but there the Indian felt he was in the white man's
country and acted accordingly, whereas if one of these
old personalities invited you to pitch your tent near his
camp or cabin, as the case might be, the tables were
turned, for then you were in the Indian country. Perhaps it was in part imagination, but I felt that once
settled in such surroundings, those cold staring faces,
so familiar at the agency, were seldom seen, having
given way to kindly benign looking countenances. Yet
dignity and calmness remained, even more intensified,
if that were possible. This does not mean that nothing
exciting was to be expected in an Indian camp; quite
the contrary, human nature being what it is, resulting
in a few quarrels now and then, an occasional outburst
of drumming and singing, a wedding, a funeral, etc.,
but in the main, an Indian camp of those days would
have been a fine place for tired nerves.

Of course there were exceptions. One night I was aroused by loud shrill voices. The sounds indicated a family quarrel which rose in intensity, followed by a woman's screams, accompanied by blows. Strange to say, the dogs were silent, perhaps because the sounds were similar to those which preceded their own punishment. Looking out, I saw the Chief leave his tipi and walk rapidly toward the point from which the noise came, then a few crisp words from him, after which quiet reigned. The next day no one mentioned the subject.

In another camp a more serious disturbance brought us out of our beds. In addition to my Indian guide, this camp was of three families, all close relatives. The dominant personality was an old blind man distinguished on many counts, whom we shall designate the Chief. His daughter and her husband, with children, were a part of the camp. The son-in-law, whom my guide called "Bill" when speaking English, was about 27 years old but his wife appeared at least 10 years older, a by no means unusual disparity. Bill spoke excellent English, but seemed unhappy, gambled at every opportunity and got drunk whenever he could. Obviously the routine of the camp bored him, he longed for a life in the white man's town but was never able to find footing therein. Some few days before I joined the camp Bill had gone to the town, gambled, got drunk and into the lock-up. His fine was $20, but the judge suspended sentence on the promise that Bill would return some time with the money. Apparently the hope of the court was that such an arrangement would banish Bill forever.

Shortly after our arrival Bill told me part of the story, viz., that he must pay a fine or go to jail. His proposal was that I buy his feather headdress and certain other objects, easily equal to the amount required. This seemed fair enough, so I was not disposed to question Bill's intentions when he set out for town. Later I learned that instead of seeking out the judge, Bill fell in with old acquaintances, was soon drunk and the money gone, but some of his friends saw to it that he left the bounds of the town and started on the long ride home, reaching camp still drunk, discouraged and sure that he would again fall into the hands of the police.

On entering his tipi he announced to his wife that he was through with this thing and would now kill her, the children and everybody in camp, that a lot of people would go with him to the other world. Fortunately Bill had no firearms and as he hunted for a knife his wife eluded him, dashed from the tipi, shouting the appropriate alarm. The Chief had no gun and the occupant of the other tipi quickly hid his arms in a nearby thicket. Bill secured a knife and pursued his wife into the brush, while the others were hiding their weapons. My guide, awakened by the outcry, called me out to join him in cowing Bill, we having the only guns available. Bill's wife hid in the brush where the darkness of the night was heavy so he returned shortly looking for another victim, but promptly covered by my guide and threatened in terse English, edged away to his horse, mounted and rode away, announcing that he would borrow a gun and come back to shoot it out with us.

My guide sent an able bodied Indian on a fast ride to the agency, while he stood guard against Bill's return. However no one seemed to expect him to come back soon, because when a drunken Indian is foiled, the shock usually sobers him up just enough to weaken his nerve. Anyway by daylight our Indian rider returned with the information that the police were out in force and that Bill would soon be locked up. The final outcome of the case was that Bill was let off with a brief jail sentence, but a year later I heard that he killed his family, was taken alive and given a life sentence.

Indians frequently visited distant reservations, for now they were at peace and like "the grey and the blue" found their greatest pleasure in recounting their exploits, one side in friendly competition with the other, accompanied by oratory and good acting. I recall, among others, an interesting journey with such a visiting party, consisting of four tipis, my tent and that of my guide and interpreter. There were at least 25 Indian ponies and the usual pack of curs. These Indians did not eat dog as did many of the neighboring tribes but they seemed to like to have them around, perhaps an expression of the age-old attachment between dogs and the human race. However, I entertained no such noble feelings for Indian dogs, never trusting them behind my back, for among these incorrigible thieves none of your belongings were safe. I have known them to chew at my tent ropes, seeming to take delight in trying to pull the canvas down over my head. Noting that the dogs in this camp were unusually hostile, I suggested to the Chief that he persuade the leader of the dogs to smoke a peace-pipe with me, but this grim humorist remarked that such a procedure was useless because none of the dogs would trust a white man.

So I took to the war-path, banging with sticks and stones at every dog in sight; a few days of this seemed to so impress my canine enemies that, except for an occasional raid, they ignored me.

As soon as the necessary travel permit was received from the reservation agent our Chief ordered everything made ready to break camp the next morning. Each family had a wagon on which were piled tipi poles, bedding and other necessary equipment, women and children riding on top. The men and boys usually rode horseback and there were a few pack-horses trailing behind, accompanied by two or three colts who got into an occasional panic, alarming their mothers by their loud cries.

By invitation, I rode ahead with the Chief. It was a fine clear summer day, and our trail ahead extended almost the full length of the reservation lands. The Chief was so silent and subdued in mien that I ventured to sound out his hopes or fears as to the journey before us. The import of his reply was that from neither man nor beast had we anything to fear, but that we should not ignore the unseen powers whose acts were for the most part unpredictable. His own feeling was that these powers were now hovering over our trail, whether for good or ill remained to be seen. The Chief then lapsed into silence, as was the Indian custom, assuming that I was silently reflecting upon these utterances.

Glancing at the face of the Chief from time to time, I thought his expression was one of awe rather than apprehension. Presently, looking ahead, I saw lying on the ground a large Indian pipe. The bowl was of redstone, the long stem decorated with feathers, and the mouth-piece pointed toward us. An exclamation from me called the pipe to the attention of the Chief who instantly gave the command to halt. He then harangued the party, explaining that something mysterious was happening; that their white guest was about to receive something from the unseen powers; that as a symbol of this, a pipe was to be given; and that he would now instruct this white man as to the manner in which he was to take up the pipe.

At his request, I dismounted and stood by his side facing the pipe, while the Chief recited a prayer too ritualistic for me to understand. We then advanced a few steps, pausing for another prayer. Once again we did this, after which I was told to advance and take up the pipe.

An old woman now came forward with a piece of calico, took the pipe, and wrapped it up with trembling hands, muttering a prayer that the pipe be not angry with her. The Chief explained to me that the rule was that a woman must care for such objects, so she would carry it. I was impressed by the solemnity of the party. Clearly they were all deeply moved, and the remainder of the day's journey was accompanied by unusual silence.

Early in the afternoon we came to a little stream, where the Chief selected a camping place for the night. To set up a camp is no small task but to the Indian it presents no problems, so the tipis and tents were soon up, firewood gathered, kettles put on the fire and the usual routine of housekeeping taken up. As darkness came down, one by one the Indians rolled up in their blankets, but in the morning, before the sun cleared the horizon, the women were astir; one could hear the breaking of dry sticks to start the fires, the occasional scolding at dogs and presently notice the odor of Indian camp smoke. The white man's camp fire usually has a different odor, probably because he chooses his fuel according to his own ideas; the Indians had a kind of proverb which ran thus: "White man builds a big fire and sits far off from it, Indian makes little fire, sits close."

The next morning we took up the trail, and again I rode ahead with the Chief. Later in the day an exclamation from several Indians caused me to look behind and, guided by the pointing Indians, I saw that a dog was closely following me. It looked sleek and friendly, not like an Indian dog. When we stopped, it sat upon its haunches and waited. No one seemed to have seen this dog arrive and none of the camp dogs paid the least attention to it. All this struck the Indians as queer, but I gave no thought to it at the time.

When we camped at noon to rest the horses and to

lunch, the new dog kept close to me. In fact whenever I moved, he rose to follow. I offered him a handout as I ate, but either he was not hungry or possessed finicky tastes. All that afternoon he followed and kept close to me as camp was pitched. The woman caring for the pipe found on the previous day, brought it to my tent and hung it on the back wall where, according to Indian custom, a medicine bundle should be. The dog watched the woman closely and after she had gone sniffed at the bundle, then lay down in the door of the tent where he stayed during the night. I suspected that the dog was lost and belonged to the people who had dropped the pipe, but eventually I learned that the Indians had a different explanation. They, as all of their kind, had been born into a society which sanctioned a totally different point of view from that entertained by the white man. All happenings in the least out of the ordinary were to them signs of the supernatural.

The next day's journey was uneventful, though the dog was still close at my heels and at night lay on guard at my tent door. However, the following day, the Chief told me of a curious dream he had during the night, in which he saw a strange Indian sitting in my tent door smoking the pipe.

Later as we rode along, heavy clouds appeared to our left, and as we descended into a narrow valley, it appeared that the storm would soon be upon us. So the Chief ordered the tipis to be pitched. Everybody began to work as fast as they could, the storm approaching nearer and nearer, with repeated crashes of thunder. While struggling with my tent, I noticed a bird hopping around at my feet; several times I with difficulty avoided stepping on it. At last the tent was up and I crept under it to rest and await the rain. Then for the first time I noted that though the storm was near and the thunder terrifying, its direction had changed, for instead of heading our way it was now passing over the opposite terrace of the valley. All at once I thought of the dog and the bird, but neither was in sight. After so many strange happenings I began to feel that maybe the Indian did live in a different world, as pipe, dog, dream, bird, escape from the thunderstorm followed one another in a sequence of mystery.

Common sense suggested that the dog had found a familiar trail and was now trotting merrily along toward home, that the bird had some young in the grass, so I dismissed the subject. Since the Chief said nothing about the storm I assumed that he saw nothing unusual in the situation.

In due time we reached the other reserve, joining a camp of friendly Indians who gave us a hearty welcome. There was a grand old medicine man there, called Yellow Spot, now all but blind, yet dignified, intelligent, and credited with unusual powers. One evening he invited me to his tipi where I found a few head men assembled, among them our Chief. I was surprised to be offered the seat of honor next to Yellow Spot. For a time nothing was said, as was the custom, the pipe passing back and forth. Finally the old medicine man began to speak.

In substance his rather long monologue, as interpreted to me, recited first his satisfaction that I had honored him by this visit, that I came as a friend of Indians that he held in high esteem, but especially because the same unseen powers that looked after his people held me in high regard. He had been told that the Indians in our party had seen mysterious happenings, which the wise medicine men of old were able to understand and the wisdom of which had been passed on even unto the present generation. Indians who experience such communications from the unseen do not speak of them for a time and he noted that I had been silent upon the subject. To his mind this was further proof that I understood the importance of the events of the past few days. No doubt these powers had and would again appear to me in my dreams and promise me long life and prosperity. This was why he felt honored by my presence, I who had received great power and would soon receive even greater powers.

I was somewhat mystified by all this but knew enough about Indian thought and belief to recognize the point of view and to appreciate the sincerity and faith of this aboriginal philosopher. So far he seemed to have addressed his remarks to me, but now by his manner indicated that he spoke to the Indians present. In outline he followed the events of our journey, showing that the Chief and other members of our party had lost no time in circulating the news. The rapidity with which Indians could disseminate information always amazed me. The old medicine man told accurately enough about the pipe, which he considered no ordinary pipe though possibly made by human hands; yet the dream of our Chief he interpreted as the truth back of the event, the pipe being but the symbol of the power transmitted to me by this new-found guardian spirit.

The dog was to his mind a manifestation of guardianship, not so much for the pipe as for me who was venturing into a strange country. But the important happening was the demonstration of power over the thunder. Almost every year some of his people were killed by lightning, so the thunder was to be feared—it was a great power. Yet they had it from their ancestors that from time to time the thunder gave the Indians a pipe as a sign that he would hear their prayers, and take pity on them. So the power of the pipe had unquestionably turned away the storm. The bird fluttering at my feet was according to tradition in touch with the unseen powers and so there could be no doubt as to the reason for its presence. Neither the dog nor the bird were to Yellow Spot's mind real animals, but the form in which the unseen chose to be made manifest.

After returning to my tent, I reflected upon these

experiences and the reactions of the Indians, so different from my own. To me, it was merely a matter of chance that an Indian lost a pipe, that my trail crossed that of a lost dog, that I happened to pitch my tent too near a nest or a brood to suit a parent bird and that we misjudged the direction of a thunderstorm. The Chief's dream could be explained by a psychologist as a trick of his nervous system. Yet was there any particular virtue in my explanations other than to say that the customs and habits of my people demanded them so? On the other hand our Indian friends had been born into a society which sanctioned a different point of view, one which committed them unconsciously to an assumption that such happenings were signs of the supernatural. It is not difficult to realize, then, that though a white man and an Indian may walk side by side, they do not see alike, or if they do see the same objects, these may mean one thing to the white but quite a different thing to the red man. Each may justly regard the other as a fool. Possibly here is new light upon the problems of the reservation: white men knowing but one view of life, that of their ancestors, Indians firm in the faith of their ancestors because they knew no other, a supposedly enlightened government expecting these white men to lead the Indians along the road to civilization, a case to which an old saying applies—the blind lead the blind.

It came to me gradually that my Indian friends were entitled to enjoy whatever values they could read into the aforesaid sequence of events, since they felt that a ritual and a few songs belonged therein. I suspected that sooner or later either our Chief or Yellow Spot would dream something of even deeper significance. Anyhow, some days later the Chief hinted that he had in fact learned a song when he first dreamed of the man sitting in my tent. Realizing that I should never acquire a song in this way I decided to put the pipe and all it stood for in the keeping of the Chief. The only injunction laid upon him was to keep it, and take it with him when he died. He seemed deeply moved by this unexpected generosity.

The reader may wish to know what life on a reservation meant to the Indian women. There are good and sufficient reasons why men were the chief actors in my adventures, but when camping with Indians, women were always a part of the picture. I am sure that the Indian man was the real victim of reservation policy. When the soldiers herded a tribe into a reservation the Indian men joined the ranks of the unemployed and went on relief. They would gladly have hunted, followed the war path and engaged in all the other occupations they had been trained for, but there was no chance. So they sat around in idleness. On the other hand, the Indian woman had no time to loaf. As of old, she was the housekeeper, gathered the wood, reared the children, cared for the sick and made most of the clothing. Then it was her job to gather whatever vegetable food was to be used. Any day in camp would reveal the females toiling early and late. To see so many useless males around frequently aroused my resentment but the women never complained about it. True, they were often vociferous in demanding the return of the good old times but not with the idea that they would have less to do. So far as I could see, the morale of the women was far less shattered and it was they who saved tribal life from complete collapse; but let us turn back to the daily routine of camp life.

The women owned the tipis, took them down and put them up. It was always interesting to watch the women choosing spots upon which to erect their tipis. They walked slowly back and forth looking closely at the ground, often hesitating as between two or three choices. Several times I tried to question the old women as to the logic of the procedure but without result, because the question merely excited merriment. The joke lay in the idea of a man asking such a question, one old lady saying, "Is our grandson turning into a woman?" No one believed that I really desired such information, thinking that I was merely making fun, but at last I came to an understanding of the fundamental principle governing the choice of a camp place. It was on a trip with three families, and at every camp we made, the oldest woman in the party selected the spots for each tipi and my tent. The Chief—there must always be a chief in every party—selected the camp ground, a flat beside a swift running stream, but the old woman was unusually deliberate in locating tipi sites. It had begun to rain, so that even the Chief became impatient, but said nothing within hearing of the woman. Obviously it was her prerogative to choose. Finally, she set up a stake and by signs indicated that I was to pitch my tent upon that spot. Then slowly one by one she chose the tipi sites. After dark the rain grew heavy, continuing without intermission through the night. At last when the light of dawn made objects visible, I looked out. A sheet of water covered the flat, the only spots of visible earth being slight elevations upon which the tipis stood. Neither within my tent nor the tipis was there standing water. Later I tried to compliment the old lady, but she waved my words aside, "Grandson, why do you worry about such things; leave them to the women."

We camped at this place for a while, the weather soon clearing. Other families joined us until there were more than twenty tipis, though pitched on the opposite side of the stream, since our women had pre-empted all the safe spots upon our side. One of the party had a permit from the Major to kill a steer. (Perhaps we should explain that in those days cows had been issued to the Indians to encourage stock raising and as a necessary precaution no one could kill or sell an ani-

mal without a permit.) I did not go out to see the
butchering, but several interesting events followed. The
supply of fresh meat sent a wave of happiness over the
camp for, true to custom, everybody would share, even
the dogs. Women were soon putting up scaffolds upon
which to hang steaks for drying, while the odor of
boiling beef was heavy in the air. One old medicine
man decided to hold a ceremony and accordingly was
busy with a companion or two rehearsing the ritual,
drumming and singing. Our Chief sent me an invitation
to call at his tipi, where I found him glowing with
enthusiasm. Ordinarily he would have said nothing for
ten minutes or more, as was the custom of his tribe,
but on this occasion he began at once by reminding me
that I had asked him many questions about war parties, but not how the men cooked their food when in
camp without women. It was a point I had overlooked,
one concerning which I was ready for information to
record in my note book, but had not anticipated a
demonstration of the procedure. Yet this is what he
had in mind and must have planned it in advance since
he had been given the paunch of the steer and a bowl
of blood. It was then explained that when about to
camp, a war party would kill a buffalo, remove the
tongue, take out the paunch, empty it, then fill it with
blood from the lungs and the abdominal cavity, add a
few cuts of meat, then return to the camp fire.

A briskly burning fire was just outside his tipi, near
which the Chief set up several stakes, about 18 inches
high, in a circle, and hung the paunch upon them in
such manner as to form a container, the bottom all but
touching the ground. To the thick blood he added
some water, then threw in a few fragments of fat and
meat. He then turned to the fire in which were a number of small stones, obviously now very hot. Using two
sticks as tongs, he transferred a few of these stones to
the paunch and quite to my surprise the water and

blood began to boil. By returning a stone to the fire now and then and throwing in a hot one, he kept the mixture boiling merrily. From time to time he stirred it with a stick. Finally after tasting it from a buffalo horn spoon he announced that we had a good quality of blood-soup. By this time several old men had gathered around, commenting upon the old time aroma and clearly eager to join in the feast. Though to our mind a discordant note, tin cups were produced and each guest in turn dipped into the paunch. On my part the soup had a queer strange taste—salt was one thing missing —but it promised to be nourishing.

"There," said the Chief, "you have been with us on the war path. This soup makes me feel like a young man."

One by one those present spoke of war adventures and tales of heroic deeds. An old man became so animated that he tried to enact an adventure of his own in which he rushed upon an enemy bare handed, jerking a gun from his hands. He asked the Chief to hold a stick in his hands as if it were a gun, then backing off some distance, he rushed forward but became so short of breath that he could do no more than take the stick, when held out by the Chief, and then drop into his seat.

As I turned to go I saw the Chief's wife sitting on the ground beside the pegged out hide of a steer with a number of curious implements scattered about. She was scratching designs upon the surface of the hide with the point of a steel butcher knife. On the ground were several fresh-water clam shells containing pigments—blue, red, green, yellow and black. Adding a little water to each, she soon had as many water colors. Then she took up curious wedges cut from the porous heads of the large bones of some animal—afterward she told me they had come down from buffalo days— which she used as brushes or pencils with which to lay on the colors. Thus for the first time I saw an Indian

woman make those interesting attractive raw-hide bags
we see in museum cases. I marveled at her skill in
drawing straight lines and equal angles, free hand, neither ruler, square nor stencil being a part of her
equipment. Even the pigments, except the blue, were
natural pigments gathered by the Indians. Here again
was a hold-over hand-craft from aboriginal days, but
visitors to the reservation now will see nothing like
it.

In pre-reservation days a woman was judged by the
number and quality of skins she had dressed, the bas-
kets she had woven, or the pottery moulded; and her
renown for such accomplishments might travel far.
When by chance you met a woman who had distinguished herself, it was proper to address her in a manner to reveal your knowledge of her reputation, as:

"Grandmother, we are happy to look upon one
whose hands were always busy curing fine skins."

The reply might be: "Grandson, you see me now an
old useless woman. Once these hands were strong and
smooth, able to handle the heaviest skins. Many, many
have they finished. There hangs my work-bag, but the
tools are idle."

An old woman once gave me a skin scraper made of
an elk antler. It was polished by much use and upon
one side was a long row of marks indicating the number
of skin tipis she had made single handed. A gold
medal could scarcely match the significance of this
relic of a heroic life.

One day I noticed an old woman sitting on the
ground, striking at a deer skin in an unusual manner,
and drawing closer I saw that her implement was a
rude pebble with a scraping edge. So here we were
transported back to the primitive days when the Indian
woman used so simple a homemade tool to produce a
buckskin as soft and durable as any in the age of
steel.

"Grandmother, why do you use a stone?" I asked.

She replied: "Grandson, in the long ago our people had nothing but stones. Then the white man came with his sharp iron knife. Such knives are better, but they often cut holes in the skin. Now I am old, my eyes are failing and my hand shakes; so I have gone back to stone. The ways of our fathers are still good ways."

I like to think of that courageous old soul as the symbol of the twilight of the Great West.

17

The Mysterious Medicine Men

ONE OF the first reservations visited gave me a chance to see medicine men in action. A great tribal ceremony was under way, so early next morning I set out for the Indian camp with an interpreter for a guide. I learned that a contest was about to be staged between two medicine men, Bull Shield and He-crow. The former was well on in years, long famous for his varied powers; the latter still young, ambitious and rising. The occasion for the contest was a tribal festival at which time, according to custom, a medicine man or two was expected to see to it that good weather was maintained, particularly that there should be no rain and that the sun should shine. For many years this obligation had been assumed by Bull Shield, without failure, but long before the appointed time, in the year of my visit, He-crow had boasted that he was a great rain maker and would use his powers to humble his rival.

I arrived at the ceremonial grounds early. It was cloudy and misty. He-crow was strutting about declaring that his incantations had brought up the clouds and that he would produce rain to prevent the ceremony. Now and then when an audience would assemble, He-crow would dance, jumping high into the air, pointing toward the clouds with the stem of a small pipe and occasionally crying out in tones which he fancied sounded like those of an eagle on the wing. Obviously this was meant as an appeal to the Thunder Birds. Altogether it was not an inspiring scene, partly because He-crow was a small unimpressive person. Anyway he had few sympathizers.

Bull Shield, busy in his tipi, was by far the more picturesque, stripped to his breech cloth, his body painted yellow, with many symbols in blue, so distributed as to emphasize the symmetry of his figure. His ritual for fair weather consisted in songs and prayers to the Sun, whom he regarded as the one great supreme power in the universe. Some of his friends and understudies had gathered in to help with the singing, and to fill the ceremonial pipe.

Every now and then, there would be a rift in the clouds through which the clear blue of the sky could be seen; then He-crow would come forth to dance frantically, crying out to the Thunder Birds and after an interval the clouds would unite and threaten rain. Then He-crow would walk about smiling and boasting about how he offset the power of his rival. Soon the deep tones of Bull Shield's drum would be heard and the low but tense singing of his followers, continuing until another rift in the clouds materialized. In the afternoon, the sun broke through for brief intervals causing He-crow to engage in violent dance contortions and strain his hoarse voice still more. The white people standing about now felt that Bull Shield was winning; it was plain that their sympathies were with him anyway. Finally the western sky cleared, the sun cast a glow over the whole landscape. We saw no more of He-crow, but Bull Shield in his glorious paint came out, offered a pipe to the Sun and prayed for all the people. It was a great triumph for him; he obviously enjoyed it to the full.

My white friends were impressed. They shook their heads mystified, saying they knew not how it was done but that everyone could see that these old Indians had some control over Nature and that a medicine man could do what no white man could do. I offered another explanation, but it fell upon deaf ears. And even the Catholic priest of the reservation, who pronounced it the work of the devil, received not so much as an encouraging look. Perhaps after all civilization has little resistance when faced by first class magic.

Indian medicine men always intrigued me into seeking their acquaintance, because they were so aloof, so reserved, distant, haughty and proud in manner. Other Indians loitered about the agency, but not the medicine man; he was always going somewhere or coming, with the manner of one who had use for every moment of his time. No doubt this behavior alone was sufficient to arouse both respect and hostility, for to the churchman he was the symbol of pagan iniquity, to the reformer he stood as the greatest obstacle, to the official he expressed the determined conservatism of pagan life, the self-appointed leader of the opposition. Even the trader had little use for him because he bought sparingly and set his influence against credit, debt, and changes in the standard of living. About the only person taking a neutral attitude was the agency doctor, perhaps because he understood humanity better and knew more of Indian life than any other white man, not overlooking the recognition that in spite of all that could be said to the contrary, the medicine man was a physician.

Within his domicile, the medicine man relaxed, spent much of his time in thought, meditating upon nature, man and the heavens. Often he was not politically minded, was not the leader the reservation agent supposed him to be, but was still a mighty power in defending the old views of life, and in one brief monologue, he could nullify 50 sermons by the missionary.

The young educated Indians, many of whom had been converted to Christianity, would vie with each other to tell me how foolish and silly they believed the medicine man to be, but not within his hearing, for in reality they respected and feared what he stood for. Should one of them be really ill, this same medicine man would be welcomed. This duplicity was one of the most obvious results of the Indian education of that day; perhaps not conscious duplicity, just a matter of building up a complex of white beliefs in one part of the Indian youth's personality without disturbing or displacing the other complex derived from his elders at home. And that ancient complex was the stronger in the end. Nevertheless, this effort to prove that they were civilized like white men irritated me; it sounded so hollow and unreal.

My efforts to become acquainted with medicine men were often thwarted. Some of them would not grant as much as a single interview. Then they were often so jealous of each other that a call upon one would automatically black list me with another. Naturally, I record here not my failures but the few personalities with whom I did become more or less friendly.

Most medicine men were individualists, some of them very eccentric. Old Spotted Horse was in the latter class. I could make little headway with him, as he was always opposed to anything I wanted to do. There was nothing invidious about this since he treated his fellow tribe members the same way. As to getting information from him, I had little success, his attitude being that it was none of my business anyway. One of his pet hobbies was denouncing photography. At every gathering where white people appeared, he stalked about haranguing the Indians upon the dangers to be incurred in facing a camera. Ill luck, disease, and even death were the penalties. One day, with a camera in hand, I called upon him, hoping that this would lead to an argument. It succeeded admirably. After a long exchange of words, I asked if he understood how photographs were made, and upon his stating that no one had ever explained the thing to him, I offered to demonstrate the process. He became interested and asked keen intelligent questions about every point. I had the feeling that he was grasping the gross mechanical, chemical and optical principles in photography. Finally he wanted to know what really put the picture on the film, to which I answered "It was the sun."

Old Spotted Horse then lapsed into silence. I had hoped that when he discovered there was nothing mysterious about the camera he would cease to oppose its use, but there is where I was wrong. Presently he began to speak. He said he was grateful to me for explaining the process so clearly, that he had always felt there was something wrong in taking pictures, but he did not know what it was. Now he knew, for I had set him right. It was the power of the Sun which did it. The Sun was the supreme power ruling over his people; to be photographed was trifling with that sacred being; in short it was sacrilege! Henceforth, he intended to oppose photography with all his might.

I should have known better than to try it. I have never seen a white person with a firmly fixed idea who could be swerved by facts. He could always interpret them his way. Nor have I found Indians any the less skillful in such manipulations.

Notwithstanding all I have said about Spotted Horse, he was a man of character and ideals, but lest the reader get the idea that all medicine men were noble personalities, I introduce one of the opposite kind. For example, there was an Indian the white people called Jim Crow. On festive occasions he functioned as a self-appointed jester, stalking about trying to say smart things, his chief stunt being to imitate the actions and call of a crow. He was tall and slender, his make-up in a head handkerchief giving him a rakish appearance. Further, he was the only medicine man I ever met wearing a chin beard, even though it was thin and straggling. Many Indians would have a thin beard if they did not pull out the hairs.

As a medicine man he was respected only in the sense that he was feared. His specialty was black magic in its worst forms; he was a racketeer, living by intimidation, black-mail and probably murder.

It was some time before I could get an interpreter willing to make a call upon Jim Crow. They all said that his eyes were so evil looking it would be risking their lives to go there. At last I found a white man willing to interpret for me. The first interview was characterized by various shady proposals, such as gambling with me to see who was the most clever, procuring mistresses, and trials at sleight-of-hand, though he did not call them that. He was celebrated for a trick with fire, which was described as picking up a flame, carrying it around in the hand, then dropping it into a bag. At the first interview, he challenged me to go into a tent with him in complete darkness to see if I was courageous enough to stick it out when ghosts appeared. However, when he found that I was ready to call his bluff, he became evasive as to setting a date. Behind my back he boasted that I refused because afraid. So far as I could see, he was shallow, sensuous and immoral, according to the Indian code.

Aside from the three formal calls at his cabin, I had no direct contact with him, considering it wiser not to be seen in his company. On the other hand, he made no attempt to be friendly and never sent me an invitation to camp with him. Shortly after I left the reservation he was arrested for murdering a woman, convicted and executed.

Bull Shield, who triumphed over his rival in control of the weather, became a real friend of mine, but was reluctant to discuss the lore of his profession. So, though I learned little about him as a medicine man, I was under obligations to him as a considerate host. At times he went out of his way to show his friendly regard. Once when camping with his band, he asked if I would consent to receive an Indian name. He explained that most white personal names could not be translated into Indian, thus making it difficult for Indians to speak of their white friends. I was pleased with the idea and suggested that he confer such a name. He was willing but remarked that the customs of his people required that the recipient of the new name furnish a steer and several boxes of crackers, so that a feast could be served. In other words Bull Shield would give a real party if I paid the charges. After all this seemed fair enough and Bull Shield looked as if he needed a good meal. So a crier was sent out to ride around shouting out invitations to those considered worthy of participation. Imagine what a furor there would be in a white town if Mrs. Jones decided to give a party and sent out a man with a megaphone voice to ride through the streets telling all about it and giving the names of those invited to be present! Well, the Indian way is not the white man's way and, come to think of it, there is considerable merit in the Indian method; all the mystery and suspicion are thereby foregone when one gives a party.

Upon the appointed day everyone was so radiant with happy expectation and so enjoyed the aroma of boiling beef which filled the outdoor air, that I felt amply repaid for the expense involved. The leading men sat in a great circle passing a big pipe back and forth amid dignified silence broken only occasionally by subdued conversation. I remarked the contrast here, for if one brought an equal number of white men together there would have been such a chatter that even the magpies would have retired discouraged. After the feast, Bull Shield made a speech explaining why the Indians had been called together, as if they had not already known it for a long time. Several other old men made long speeches, the tenor of which I dimly understood to be that they approved of the idea. In due time Bull Shield announced that he was ready to give out my name, that of a distinguished chief long dead, meaning in English, "He-who-gets-what-he-goes-after." So far as I could see, it was a good enough name, though just how it applied to me, I could not understand. But since Mr. Black need not be a negro and Mr. Young may have gray hair, one need not consider its real meaning. After all a name is a name and nothing more. We saw nothing about our host to remind us of a bull, nor did he look like a shield. It is a popular illusion of white people that an Indian name describes the person owning it.

As soon as the name was announced, the crier mounted his horse and rode about shouting out my new name. The women cheered and that was the end of it. Many times I visited that reserve always to be greeted by that name. Even the children knew it. Some people fancy that when a name is conferred upon a white man he thereby becomes a member of the tribe, but that is nonsense. I asked old Bull Shield how one became a tribe member; at first he said a white man could not do it, but afterward qualified the pronouncement somewhat by saying that if one would take an Indian woman, settle down there, learn the language, etc., he might finally be tolerated; yet even after all this, he would still be a white man.

I had another interesting experience with a medicine man named Day Star which brought out the peculiar attitude of the old-time Indian toward the white man's machines. It is difficult for a white man to understand what an Indian sees in a machine; such a contrivance does not fit into his scheme of things. To him, if something is accomplished, there must be a living agent. I had come to know this but every now and then would be taken off my guard. Day Star was such a hardheaded and sensible fellow that I thought him a good bet for securing information as to certain rituals and, since songs were an important part of the affair, I persuaded him to sing them into a phonograph. He claimed to have heard such a machine in a trader's store. However, when I brought out the apparatus, to explain its operation, he remained silent and apprehensive. I played a record, sang into the machine, and let him hear the reproduction. He was obviously uneasy. Had a spring broken or something unusual happened, I suspect he would have rushed out in a panic. The only thing he would say was: "Wait, wait!"

For a long time he sat facing the machine, occasionally moving his lips as if in prayer. Then he began a monologue addressed to the machine, telling who he was, reciting his autobiography in some detail, explaining what he had promised to do and why. Finally, he pleaded with this new mysterious presence not to misunderstand him, that since his motives in singing these songs were pure and worthy he hoped it would exercise due care to see that no harm came to him or to his family. It was an impressive scene and I began to have serious doubts that he would so much as speak a word into the machine, especially when he arose to take his leave. However, he promised to return the next day after he had consulted his spiritual guardian about it.

My hopes fell. Past experiences with Indians gave little ground to expect Day Star to face the machine again. But he did. He came next day, ready and anxious to begin. At the outset he expressed doubts that the machine knew Indian well enough but the first trial convinced him that it could speak Indian just as well as he could. He was now more firmly convinced than ever that he was dealing with something far superior to a material contrivance. However, he quickly warmed up to the task and would have continued for hours had I been willing but I suggested that he take a rest and return the next day.

This time Day Star failed me, nor did I see him for a long time, but finally he came in, obviously ill at ease. Without waiting he announced that he would have nothing more to do with that machine. By persistence I got from him the story of what had happened. While Day Star was singing into the machine, his wife was taken with a hemorrhage of the nose, something she had never experienced before. Eventually the family, becoming alarmed, dispatched a rider to recall Day Star, meeting him on the way home. Now, Day Star was a famous medicine man, one of his specialties being to stop bleeding. Always he was sent for in such emergencies. According to his story he labored long and hard, praying, singing, drumming, before the bleeding stopped. This, he said, was a warning. He had offended the spirits that guarded him by tampering with the spirit in that machine. No more would he speak or sing to it.

Naturally, I agreed that logic was on his side and hoped he would take no chances with his wife's health. Incidentally, I remarked that I had some skill in stopping such bleeding and, noting that he was interested, explained the procedure. Taking up some cotton, I showed him how to pack a nostril. He asked many keen questions about it, seeming to grasp the rationality of the various steps. Finally I packed his own nostril to let him know how the patient would feel under the treatment. At the end, he asked where that stuff was to be had; the soft pure cotton impressing him as a remarkable substance. My answer was to present him with a package of surgical cotton. He was surprised and tremendously pleased. His eyes sparkled and he made a long speech, the substance of which was that I had given him a great new power, that his usual fee for a treatment was a horse and that this package of cotton should bring in at least twenty.

Afterward I learned that according to the customs of his people, when one medicine man gives a secret to another, the recipient is thereby obligated to do in return whatever may be requested. So, inadvertently, I had put Day Star into a tight place. He was now duty bound to keep his promise. After some hesitation he requested me to get out the machine, that he was ready to sing. From that time on his interest in the machine grew, though he occasionally made long speeches to it. My chief difficulty was to prevent him from using up all the blank records and to overcome his opposition to letting other Indians use it.

One day I casually remarked that the man who made the first phonograph was still living, that all the white people thought him an unusually brilliant man. Day Star was not especially impressed and looking affectionately at the machine said that the inventor was no better than other men, that he did not invent the machine because he possessed special virtues, but that he was merely a lucky man, not a great man. This was strange philosophy to white ears, so I inquired as to what was meant by luck. Day Star said that Edison was undoubtedly sleeping one time when some of the powers appeared to him, telling him to put wood and iron together, thus and so, and the voice could be reproduced. He did nothing himself, but he was very lucky in being chosen as the person to introduce this machine into the world. So, he said, it is with everything, man himself creates nothing.

I have often pondered upon these words and met other Indians who had much the same view, though I would not claim such a belief common to all members of that race. Maybe there is some truth in it, for after all, why ideas come to some people and not to others has never been adequately explained.

Since the professors have written all that is needed about the place of the medicine man in society, we need not be concerned with that subject, this chapter being a bit of gossip about medicine men we have met. However, I found them, as a class, the wise men of the reservation. Reflective thought, the formation of explanations, was what distinguished medicine men from their fellows. They were relatively speaking not men of action, their attitude being one of detachment rather than participation, though when professionally engaged they could proceed swiftly and continuously. I heard many narratives about the mythical heroes of the profession, to which there was usually a biographical introduction. In most cases, the medicine man as a boy did not play about with other children but sat upon the hills or walked about alone. Often he had some slight deformity or some disgusting habit, which tended to isolate him; in short the idea seemed to be that a medicine man must begin his preparations early in life. Yet no one ever suggested that one must be born with a special talent; those childish peculiarities were worked into these stories as predictive signs that a medicine man was in the making. I supposed these rationalizations were a kind of reading backward, because most medicine men, like our own scholars, seemed more or less queer; and conversely, if not queer, one could not be a medicine man. However, I observed that most of them went through a long period of training. Even as late as my days on the reservation, each medicine man had one or more understudies. Some of these apprentices had entered into such service while still boys and many graduated only upon the death of their teachers. The duties of such a student were various, he took care of the pipe and the ceremonial equipment, helped with the singing, thus gradually learning all that his superior knew. From time to time his teacher delivered long monologues or lectures on the mysteries and the technique of handling the sick. I came to know some of these understudies, their hopes and disappointments. There was one called Willy Bear, a moron if ever there was one. He had learned to speak English in school, was moderately successful in stock-raising, but longed to be a medicine man. Hours and hours he attended his teacher, shook the rattles and beat the drums vigorously, felt that the finest things in the world were to be found in the rituals and teachings of the great medicine men, but with tears of disappointment he would confess to me that though he tried and tried, he could not master the subject. He was then nearing fifty, and went on trying harder and harder, even to the last day of his life.

Having known white men who behaved in similar ways, we suspect that these are basic patterns of expression found in all modes of life. But we were led into these academic speculations by memories of one of the outstanding intellects of the profession,— Spotted Buffalo, sometimes called One-spot. He was unusual because of his versatility, having been at intervals a war leader and a chief, but continuously a medicine man. He systematized his thought and his explanations were filled with surprises in illustration and figures of speech. Naturally to such a mind the ways of the white man often seemed contradictory. One day he remarked that the white people were hopelessly inconsistent and when I asked that he elaborate, presented the following:

"If I should have a quarrel with my old woman and find it necessary, I would give her a good beating. Then, if the old woman complained to the agent, he would have me arrested. He would tell me that was not the way to treat a woman, that the law protected all persons regardless of age or sex; he would then put me in jail.

"If again the old woman and I should quarrel, and I refrain from striking her, she might cease to fear me and knock me down with a stick of fire-wood. Then, recalling what the white man's law said, I complain to the agent. But, he laughs at me, calls me an old loafer, says he is glad I got it once, that he hopes the old woman will do it again.

"Now, what is the sense of it? What kind of thing is white man's justice!"

Can the reader adequately explain this situation! If he can, he is far on the road to an understanding of the Indian problem. As One-spot talked, I saw in imagination, the shadowy forms of knights and ladies, the flower of Chivalry, an historical vista, giving shape to customs and ideals, none of them truly rational, but still very real to us. I tried to explain all this to One-spot but in the end he again shook his head saying, "it did not make sense."

I spoke of One-spot's superior intellect; he knew little English and of course could not read, but he carefully kept a few copies of an illustrated magazine, much worn, at the pictures in which he gazed for hours. I suspected that he longed to read the printed page but somehow failed to get a start at it. At times he spoke enviously of the white man's way with books, and the great store of wisdom he thought must be recorded there. My taking notes of his monologues pleased him because he felt that, once his words were written, they became imperishable and little short of sacred. Finally I made him supremely happy with several illustrated magazines and a mail-order catalogue. In passing, I realize how stupid the white people were not to plan and execute a system of pictorial education for the more intellectual Indians.

One day I found One-spot seated with a number of

fossil bi-valves spread out before him. Each was brilliant in a coat of fresh red earth paint. I knew that such objects were often wrapped carefully in buffalo wool and kept in leather bags as sacred objects, but was still ignorant of their significance. From his manner it was clear that he regarded these homely fossils as gods. He explained to me that no one found them but that they gave birth to young ones, which in turn grew to maturity. In rebuttal of my skepticism he pointed to a few small ones and then to one of the large ones to the side of which adhered a tiny fossil bi-valve. This he considered sufficient proof for any one in his right mind. To him they were living supernatural beings, not inanimate objects. It seemed to me rather naive, but I saw that One-spot was in earnest and firmly believed what he said. Reverently these sacred fossils were tucked away into the medicine bag.

Not many days after this One-spot was standing with us looking down the valley of the little creek near his cabin. It was a simple but a pretty scene. Casually he remarked that once all the hills round about were under water. Now, most Indian tribes have a myth about a great flood, or a time when the whole earth was covered with water. The good solid earth was then created anew from some mud brought up by a muskrat —all of which quickly flashed through my brain, causing me to say that I knew that old, old story. But One-spot had something else in mind, for he said that this had nothing to do with the sacred myth. He declined further comment, suggesting that we first walk to the top of an adjacent hill. When we arrived at the summit, we faced a low outcrop of sedimentary rock in which were to be seen fossil shells. Pointing to these One-spot asked if such creatures did not live in the water and upon my assenting, dryly remarked that this proved that the hill was once under water.

This set me thinking. By the way, the same kind of

fossils were sticking out of this rock as were in the medicine bag. One time One-spot used cold logic and a sense of reality when looking at fossils, another time some of them, at least, were gods, alive and producing their kind; one time he reveled in magic and the unreal, next he applied common sense and what might well pass for scientific acumen. Yet why be surprised, even we have water-tight compartments in our personalities just as inconsistent, the one with the other, as were these attitudes of One-spot. One of my neighbors believes that objects can be lifted by a medium in a trance, but once when I suggested that such a medium could be used to dig a trench for a drain in my yard he laughed me down. Lifting something in a seance had, to his mind, no relation to the realities of every-day life.

Medicine men found wisdom in a wide acquaintance with the passions, hopes and fears of men and women. As in the case of the old time family doctors, the aid and advice of these medicine men were sought concerning all the tensions of life. Conversation opened the way to frankness and privacy. They were the sources of powers for good and evil. An amorous male or female came for advice as to how the object of their desires might be forced to yield. If going to war, it was to the medicine men that one went for charms and formula to render the arrows and blows of the enemy harmless. Murderers sought their aid in enabling them to escape detection. In brief, no matter what was desired the medicine man was visited. Thus there passed before them an unending array of situations, the whole gamut of human behavior, good, bad and indifferent. So when one of these wise men wished to be generous he dispensed charms and recipes. It was probably because of such generous impulses that old Lone Pine surprised me one day by the present of a war-charm—the stuffed skin of a blue-bird. He said in general that since he no longer expected to go to wars and since Indians had given up war forever, there was no need of such protection, but that I being white might some day find myself in war, in which case I was to carry with me this charm. It so happened that the white people did have a war, not many years later and contrary to Lone Pine's expectation many Indians took an active part therein.

We exploited One-spot's superior intellect by submitting all the questions about Indian life we found provocative. Almost without exception we were well rewarded, the prize answer in our collection will be a fit conclusion to this chapter. When we asked him to define a medicine man, his answer was in substance that a medicine man was just a man, like any other man, except that he might be able to do one or two things no one else could do. The answer astonished us, it was not what we expected, but in time we came to the same view,—a medicine man was nothing more or less than a superior Indian.

18

Coming Sun

WHEN IN the Major's office one day, it was suggested
that I seek the acquaintance of an Indian known as
Coming Sun. Upon inquiring I learned that he was
employed by a bank in the near-by railroad town. This
was news, of all things, an Indian in a bank! However,
it turned out that Coming Sun was not really in the
bank but employed as an Indian adviser. He was provided with a small office in the bank building where
Indians could advise with him upon financial matters,
all of which may sound like a joke. As best I could
interpret the situation, the owner of this bank was
philanthropically minded, believing that the allotment
system then going into effect would soon make prosperous farmers of these Indians, but that what they
needed most at the outset was elementary guidance in
finance. So he selected an Indian of good judgment,
who could speak English and was familiar with the
ways of the white man, whose primary job would be to
explain the bank to the Indians and act as interpreter
in case an Indian had business with the bank. The idea
was sound, for Coming Sun was a wise counselor. It
was an ideal job for an Indian, since it would give

unusual prestige, widen white contacts and above all offer a chance to learn a great deal more about white culture. The pay was $15.00 a month. Remembering that a kind government paid for most of Coming Sun's family up-keep, this was a handsome salary. Then he was not expected to stay in his office but rather free to roam about, thus able to care for his live stock, do a little farming, etc. Thus it happened that my first call upon him was at his home.

I soon learned that Coming Sun had acquired the white man's technique for dealing with callers, he explaining to me that he was now occupied but that later in the day he could meet me at his office in the bank. As contact with this unusual person progressed, I found that he could play the white man's game well, but was thoroughly Indian; finally when convinced that I preferred him to be Indian, while following the speech and conventions of the white man, he became one of the most willing and efficient of informants.

Some months after I returned from the Indian country, a carefully worded letter came from Coming Sun, revealing what was suspected, that he dreamed of writing a book in English, setting forth the cultural history of his people. However, he had found the task baffling, he not being able to work out a logical plan of presentation and so would I be willing to spend some time with him, helping formulate such a plan. After an exchange of letters I suggested that he meet me at some convenient point for a brief summer vacation. We could then discuss the plan for his book in detail. Accordingly we arranged for him to meet me at Mackinac Island.

Arriving a few days in advance, I selected a suitable hotel. When I explained to the manager of this hotel that I wished a room for an Indian, he was curious. Learning the name and address of Coming Sun, the hotel keeper surprised me by remarking that he knew this Indian, having once worked in a hotel in the vicinity of the reservation, that he had always admired him and so was glad to have him as a guest. A telegram from Coming Sun gave the time of his arrival so I was at the pier to meet the boat. His big Indian hat and dark face enabled me to identify him among the crowd on deck before the boat docked and a wave of my hand brought me to his attention. He was obviously relieved to find me there. The manager was at the desk in the hotel to receive him. Coming Sun was so moved that he embraced his white friend; then turning to me said, "Now I shall not be homesick."

Later in the large dining room he was ill at ease, not because he was unfamiliar with hotels, but because he was stared at curiously by the assembled tourists. Further, most of the guests were women and it had been my experience that Indian men were uncomfortable when a number of white women were around.

The next morning I found his room empty, but after a brief search saw him on the pier watching some sailors scrubbing the decks of a steamer. I learned that he was up before dawn, had breakfast and explored a large part of the Island. When lunch time came, he inquired with some hesitation if I would approve of his eating out alone. Little by little I sensed that he was far from comfortable in the hotel dining room and that he had found a place in the village more to his liking; that he would prefer to eat with me, but not at the hotel. So I accompanied him to this new-found place, a small shack on the edge of the lake, in which was a lunch counter. The counter was covered with table oilcloth like, even in pattern, to the covers on tables in Indian houses and on agency lunch counters.

Coming Sun ordered soup, which came in a huge white bowl. Into this he put several handfuls of crackers, and with his great black hat tilted backward, ate heartily. I made him happy by announcing that I liked the place and that we should eat here regularly. Soon he was on friendly terms with the manager, who, as it turned out, was a hotel chef on a vacation. Most of the men—we never saw a woman there—who came to this lunch counter were sailors and workmen, who, at first, gave Coming Sun a once over, but after that ignored him. This was not the way of the tourists at the hotel; but it pleased Coming Sun.

We did not measure Coming Sun but guessed he stood six-feet-two and weighed 200 pounds. His posture was erect, his bearing fearless but dignified. His hair was cut short, and his dress that of a conventional white business man, except that the color of his suit was black and that he wore the large black hat peculiar to reservation Indians. Every tourist assumed an Indian when he saw such a hat. The reader might suspect that Coming Sun would have preferred to pass as a white man, but not he. A few Indian families were on the Island; for several generations they had lived among whites and were for the most part mixed-bloods. One day I asked Coming Sun if he had called upon any of these Indians. His answer was that he had not, and further that he had no such intention. In time I learned that he had made approaches to some of these Indians, but formed the impression that they were anxious to conceal their Indian ancestry. He said with feeling, "I am an Indian and proud of it. I hate to see anyone with Indian blood and ashamed to admit it."

On the other hand, Coming Sun thoroughly disliked the cheap patronage of the tourists around the hotel. At first a man might slap him upon the back and say, "Big Chief, how are you today?" Coming Sun's reaction would be a fierce penetrating look, then turn his back and walk away. When a woman attempted to open conversation in a somewhat similar style, he merely turned away. On the other hand, if a man approached him as he would another white man, he was welcomed cautiously, and Coming Sun would carry his part of the conversation satisfactorily. In this way he made a few friends but always declined invitations to walk, play games or drink. He harbored a deep distrust of all strange white men, though skillfully concealing it when politely treated. The one man he warmed up to was the Chef who operated the lunch counter, but who always treated him as if he were a white man of character. Once Coming Sun spontaneously took a hand in helping the Chef evict two drunken sailors who seemed to have the Chef at a disadvantage.

The life history of this Indian seems worth recording. He neither knew his exact age nor the date of his birth, his parents having died early; but had they lived he may have been none the wiser. When he entered school his age was estimated at six years, which he later accepted. As an adult, finding that white people expected everyone to have a birthday, he adopted one, March 25th. In response to my curiosity he said that having decided to choose a birthday there gradually came the feeling that the month was March and eventually that the day was the 25th. He attended a government boarding school, graduated with honors, sought and obtained a position as disciplinarian, athletics director and drill master. After a few years he saw no future in such a job, so resigned and returned to his reservation, married and set up a home. Shortly thereafter he became a policeman. The job was not to his taste but he served ably and fearlessly. His one great adventure was during the Ghost Dance excitement.

In an earlier chapter we remarked upon the rebellious attitude of the former buffalo hunting tribes, culminating in bloodshed in South Dakota. Coming Sun's people were tense with excitement, the younger hot heads eager to get into action. The agent had forbidden them to leave the reservation and though the older heads were in favor of neutrality, they were moved by the exaggerated reports of successful resistance by other tribes and far from deaf to the urgent appeals for help reaching them by underground channels. Naturally the Indian police were busy, watching, admonishing and occasionally arresting an agitator. Several times the agent had argued and threatened, while irate Indians swirled about with knives in their hands. His coolness saved him.

One day Coming Sun, upon patrol duty, came to a camp of the most radical Indians, debating a break out into the open, to raid, burn and fight their way to South Dakota. His appearance automatically turned their attention to himself as the lone representative of Government authority. Coming Sun had no illusions as to the danger confronting him, but entertained one idea only, to do his duty. As a precaution he placed his back to a cabin and said he was ready to hear their words. When they declared their intention to leave the reservation, Coming Sun firmly demanded that they remain. His life was threatened time and again, but he calmly insisted. When permitted to speak, he would call their attention to the futility of such a break; that thousands of soldiers, with gatlin guns and cannon, were within a day's ride by train, that a large body of cavalry was being held within a day's march of the spot upon which they now stood. Time and again he would say, "You can kill me, I am alone, you are many, but think how it will be. The soldiers will overtake you, men, women and children will be shot down. You cannot win. It will be easier for the soldiers to kill you, than for you to overcome me, etc."

Eventually Coming Sun won. I suspect it was the old unflinching stamina of the bravest of his race, that he exemplified. Even the rash realized that after all here was a man, here was the power of a man which even death could not overthrow.

I asked Coming Sun what he would have done had an Indian struck. His reply was to the effect that when anyone came dangerously near, his hand went to his six-shooter, that in case a real attack was launched he hoped to kill at least six before he fell. Then the spirit of his ancestors flashed from his eyes as he said, "It would have been a glorious death. It had been better so, than to die slowly of old age and dishonor!"

Shortly after the subsidence of the Ghost Dance excitement, Coming Sun retired from the force, taking the position at the bank, developing his farm, and acting as interpreter. He accompanied committees of the Chiefs to Washington for conference with the Commissioner of Indian Affairs and, of course, to call upon the Great Father. Going to Washington was then the favorite pastime of Indian Chiefs. Upon such visits Coming Sun was the spokesman and pleader; no doubt he acquitted himself creditably. However, when he gave up his position in the government school and returned to the reservation, he volunteered to interpret for a missionary lately arrived and totally ignorant of the native language. This preacher was a Baptist; the sermon was conducted in the following manner: the preacher would hand the Bible to Coming Sun, designating the text, which would be rendered into Indian and explained. Then came the sermon, the preacher delivering a few sentences, Coming Sun repeating their substance in Indian. Apparently the Indians were pleased with his dignified bearing and so was the preacher. Soon the Methodist preacher sought his services also, and Coming Sun liking the prestige and intellectual stimulation inherent in the situation accommodated him. Thus he divided his time between these two somewhat hostile churches. Finally he interpreted for the Methodists only, a function he fulfilled at intervals for many years.

Knowing something of Coming Sun's intellectual

keenness and linguistic skill, I frequently encouraged him to tell of these church experiences. Naturally he had acquired an extensive reading knowledge of the Bible and could, if the occasion required, preach a sermon. I learned, further, that he did not hesitate to polish up the preacher's words and do what he could to improve the discourse. He claimed he was honest in first giving a close translation of the pastor's words and then offering what he considered the significance of the statement. I suspect that more than one of these preachers felt greatly pleased with the apparent impression his sermons made upon the Indians, not suspecting that Coming Sun was the real preacher.

We turn now to another section of this interesting biography. Coming Sun was an industrious student of his own culture. He was familiar with the ways of the medicine men, knew the complicated rituals for tribal ceremonies, etc. Now and then he would conduct such a ceremony. Many times after such a ceremony he would hastily wash the paint from his face and body, put on the Sunday clothes of a white man, and hurry to the church where he would improve upon the admonitions of the pastor. Possibly even the reader who has followed through the disconnected narratives in the preceding pages will be surprised or shocked by such dastardly conduct. To many it may seem the height of iniquity. On the other hand, Coming Sun saw nothing amiss; he found intellectual and emotional satisfaction in the white man's church far above that of the average devout church member; yet stripped to a breechclout and liberally daubed with paint, he was an enthusiastic pagan. Like many other members of his race, he saw no difficulty in being a sincere devotee, as Catholic, Protestant and pagan; to him all were but manifestations of the same galaxy of superhuman power.

On Mackinac Island one of Coming Sun's diversions

was to wander in the woods—those surviving little patches of the aboriginal forests which once covered a large part of North America. The trees and plants were new to him, which may have been the chief intensifier of his enjoyment. I often watched how he surveyed the flora; each strange plant catching his eye was carefully scrutinized; most of them were passed by but every now and then he would go down upon his knees to dig up the roots. These he would examine critically, feeling them, sniffing and eventually tasting a tiny bit. Then a final judgment would be formulated, thus: "This is no good," or "This is medicine; it has some kind of power. I do not know what, but some of our medicine men may know." He returned from every trip to the woods with a small bundle of such roots. I sought an explanation of the criteria used by him in selecting these roots, but this was one of the very few subjects upon which he was uncommunicative.

One time I invited Coming Sun to join me at my country home, bringing his papers to make a start on his book. Here he seemed quite contented, adapted himself readily to all situations and was, naturally, something of a sensation to the neighbors. Every now and then he would surprise us all by his learning. Thus, one morning he was late to breakfast, but when seated apologized, giving as an excuse that he had been looking at a picture upon the wall of his room. He said it represented the burning of Moscow and the retreat of Napoleon. Most of the family had forgotten this little lithograph in its tiny frame. Then he began a monologue, in Indian fashion, upon Napoleon, his career, grandeur and weaknesses. At the end we expressed astonishment, which brought from him the statement that he had read many books about this great personage. A neighbor, calling one day, was commenting upon the best fiction seller of the previous year; presently Coming Sun joined in, it soon becoming apparent that he had gone deeper into the book than anyone present. Several hours each day he worked at a table in my study, where he was constantly under observation. At times he consulted the books around the room, as if he knew just what he wanted. One day he asked if a copy of Longfellow's poems was to be had; upon our suggesting that he look upon the top shelf, he soon located the book, scanned the index, then turned directly to the appropriate page in the text, read for a few minutes, then replacing the volume returned to his writing.

Yet with all his knowledge and skill there were occasional situations to which he found adjustment difficult. One morning he was in distress, complaining of a restless night, which he attributed to lemon pie, eaten the preceding evening. Such a pie always made him ill, he said. We expressed surprise that he did eat it, knowing as much. His reply was, in substance, that the customs of his people not only required that a guest eat of every kind of food offered him by the host, but that no matter how often presented, must not be refused. So the story was out, as host following the customs of white people, we inadvertently forced Coming Sun not only to eat what did not agree with him, but gorging him as well! After a detailed explanation of the white point of view, he grasped the idea that the guest was at liberty to refuse. From that time on, he seemed much more at ease at the table and his health improved.

The local minister took a fancy to Coming Sun, finally inviting him to speak at the Church on Wednesday evening. A large audience was on hand to hear, as they supposed, something about Indian life and history, but were surprised when Coming Sun opened the Bible, read a chapter, and then delivered a sermon. It was not a conventional sermon, to be sure, and so novel in that respect. The next day I asked him why he preached that sermon.

His startled reply was, "Was not that a Church?"

When I said that it was, he answered, "What else could one do in a Church?"

The writer's father was living in the house. Coming Sun seemed friendly to him, but made no demonstrations of personal interest, looking upon me as his host. One day a maternal uncle called in order that he might be presented to the Indian. Coming Sun surprised us by showing the greatest possible regard for Uncle. He put his hand upon Uncle's shoulder, saying to me, "Now you have done me a great honor. You have introduced me to the one person in the world who means something in your life. He will make many sacrifices for your welfare and to him you will show the highest regard." Gradually an understanding of the situation came to us. Coming Sun's people followed a different system in that a child inherited through its mother and consistently enough, her oldest brother looked upon his sister's child as his successor and dependent upon him for his right bringing up in the world. The biological father had an economic responsibility to his wife's children but his sister's children, especially her son, was not only the hope of his old age but his successor in practical life. Here, once again, Coming Sun fumbled the ball in playing on the white man's field.

From time to time we observed how, under stress, the Indian background of our guest's experience broke through his acquired white habits. As when we caught him unawares in a secluded part of the orchard, burning incense and singing songs. Later we learned the reason for this unexpected procedure. We had announced that on the following day we would take him on a trip to an interesting series of earthworks, supposed to have been the work of mound builders. He had read of such, but never saw a good example. However, we had remarked that our going depended upon the weather; should it rain or a storm threaten, we would stay at home. So Coming Sun reverted to a medicine man, performing the ritual believed to give good weather.

On another occasion his courage was put to a test. A tornado broke over the place, there was a terrific wind, shaking the house and breaking down some of the trees. For a time Coming Sun gazed quietly out upon the storm, then we heard him singing, barely audible, but in deadly earnest. Afterward he confided to us that he was in great fear, that he thought death was near, and so sang his death song. Thus he played his last card, a pagan charm.

During the storm we noticed some flickers clinging to the trunk of a tree—wood knockers, he called them. The incident so impressed him that he referred to it many times. Finally he announced that he had learned a song from one of these birds which he believed would give protection in storms. Of course, here was the Indian medicine man running true to form.

There seems no point in writing more about this interesting person. Not long after his last visit to us, he died; the great book he hoped to write was still in his head, a glorious vision never to be realized. We feel sure that in his last conscious moments, he whispered his death song, but his funeral was in the Methodist Church according to the white man's ritual, all of which was fitting, and as he had lived.

19

Wolf Chief and
Sun-Lights-Her-Pipe

MY MOST vivid impressions of the Indian country have
to do with personalities, so it seems fitting that I should
single out a few for special mention. That they are
outstanding renders them none the less characteristic
of reservation life. Above all I place Wolf Chief. Just
to see him walking briskly about the agency was sufficient to inform one that here was somebody. When yet
a stranger to his reservation I asked the Major to name
some of the most interesting Indians under his jurisdiction. Without hesitation he put Wolf Chief at the head
of the list, though he confessed that upon the one or
two occasions when he had offered his hand to Wolf
Chief that haughty soul had turned his back and strode
away. Not so long before, it was said, a Congressional
Commission had visited the reservation to hear complaints and to promise great things, as all such delegations did. Yet Wolf Chief not only refused to come to
the agency at their request, but turned away from the
one member of the Commission who called at his
home. All this intrigued me to such a degree that I
decided to call upon this proud aboriginal without
delay, thus placing him on my preferred list of Indian

acquaintances, feeling that though he would certainly
turn his back upon me, he should at least know that of
all Indians I paid my respects to him first.

I secured the services of an English speaking Indian
to guide me to the home of Wolf Chief. We found his
log cabin locked, but from signs intelligible to Indians
only, my guide said we should find him in an adjoining
valley at a hay-maker's camp. Whether this was a mere
guess or a correct reading of the signs I do not know,
but we did find the hay-camp and a strange Indian
pointed out the tipi of Wolf Chief. As a matter of
strategy I sent my guide to open a way for me, charging him to explain that I knew Wolf Chief to be the
outstanding medicine man of his people and so my first
act upon the reservation was to pay my respects to his
genius, that all I asked was the privilege of taking him
by the hand, that I would be duly honored thereby. In
due time my guide returned with the encouraging news
that Wolf Chief was ready to receive me.

He allowed me to take his hand and apparently listened unmoved to my laudatory speech. After a time
he replied laconically in substance that he appreciated
the respect shown him, that as a rule he did not welcome white men or even hold conversation with them,
because they looked upon Indians with contempt and
had reduced his people to poverty. The only white man
he had received for years was a traveling bishop and
that he had made this concession only because he understood that all the white men round about regarded
this bishop as the wisest and most learned of men.
There was no doubt that Wolf Chief regarded himself
as a superior person and I suspected that here lay the
secret of his eccentricity. I made haste to disclaim quali-
fications to be ranked with the bishop, but he waved
these protests aside as if to imply that he did not rate
the bishop so high at that.

At this point Wolf Chief took active lead in the

conversation, inquiring rather bluntly my purpose in coming to this reservation since he had learned from my guide that I was in no way connected with the Government, was not a "Big Cat," not promoting missions, and had nothing to sell. Obviously I did not appear normal in his eyes. I guessed that to get on with this dynamic personality one must be frank, so told him what reservations I had visited and how my time had been occupied, that above all I was interested in making the acquaintance of great men, to learn something about Indian life. Apparently this made an impression upon him for he launched into a long monologue the import of which was that he also had visited many Indian tribes but that he was now too old to go so far away; that all his life he had listened to the words of the great medicine men and pondered over what they said.

Wolf Chief had a methodical mind for when he confirmed his surmise that I expected him to answer some questions he immediately announced a program. I was to spend the remainder of the day with him and he would ask me questions, but the next day he would visit our camp at which time I could ask questions of him. Apparently he gloried in doing things the unexpected way, for example he soon called me down for speaking of the future as before us; he said that past time was before and future time behind, in that respect he claimed to differ from all his fellow tribesmen. I forgot the program at this point asking if this was because he saw nothing for him in the white man's world, but he preserved a haughty silence.

He was a keen questioner and it soon dawned upon me that I was being tested, since he occasionally slyly re-formed a question as if to check upon my answers. I realized that every question must have an answer consistent with other answers. For example, he asked if I had ever killed a man. Then he inquired if I had ever been a thief and when I pleaded guilty wanted to know the details. So I told of how in company with several boy friends we raided a farmer's melon patch, scouted around to see if the coast was clear, carried the melons into a cornfield, concealing our trail by walking the fence, etc. He questioned me as to the details of the procedure, pointed out that some of our efforts at concealment were crude and ineffective. Finally he wanted to know what our parents did when we told them about it. I said that we told them nothing. This he considered a foolish mistake because boys should announce their deeds, so their parents could make a feast and praise them to the neighbors. However, he remarked dryly that if we had killed the farmer and brought home his scalp there would have been something to brag about.

Later my host turned to family matters, seeking information as to my parentage and marriage relations, as to whether I had more than one wife. He said he found it hard to understand a people so resourceful and bold as the whites, who were so timid about taking an extra wife. However, I remarked upon the fact that he seemed to have but one, his only comment was that he was no longer a fighting man. Finally he inquired as to how the white people came by the many wonderful things they possessed, as potatoes, corn, etc. This gave a chance to lecture him upon the contributions of the Indian race to the world's economics. For the first time he was really interested, having up to this point been merely playing a game which even he began to find dull, but now his keen mind found something worthy of its powers, and as I explained to him how by patience and good sense some Indians long ago developed the maize plant which was now one of the world's choice possessions, his countenance began to glow. He confessed that since his people were not agricultural he had taken it for granted that it was a white man who devised that wonderful plant, along with tobacco, potatoes, etc. Finally when it dawned upon him that millions of Indians had toiled to the end that great contributions were made to the world, he was inspired; he had found a new reason for being proud that he was an Indian.

At last he launched into a spirited monologue the point of which was that he had known at least one important white person (obviously the venerable bishop), whom the local white people held in high regard; that he had known this white man for twenty years but that in all that time had heard nothing from him worth remembering, whereas he had known me but for a day, during which time I had told him more important things than he could remember. Over and over he said: "Wait until I see the Bishop. Wait until I see the Bishop."

True to his promise, Wolf Chief called at our camp next day answering the many questions I showered upon him. He was an unusual informant because possessed of a superior mind, and I came more and more to admire this rare personality, ultimately looking upon him as a friend. In time I was convinced that to such rare souls life upon a reservation might be a tragedy.

It would be unfair not to complete the picture by remarking upon the matron who presided over Wolf Chief's fireside. It must have been a kind fate that joined them in wedlock, for in the same measure that Wolf Chief was one of the greatest Indians I ever met, so also was his wife the finest of women. Her countenance was feminine, but with the stamp of leadership. Her carriage was graceful but always expressing dignity. It was an inspiration to see her. During the whole of my first visit she sat at her proper place in the tipi, not venturing to join in the conversation, since the custom of her tribe forbade, but now and then she turned to look at me. She was busily beading a moccasin obviously intended for her husband.

"Mother-of-all" was her real name and appropriate, it

seemed to me, expressing in a measure the veneration in which she was held by her neighbors. Yet the usual name used to designate her meant "sun-lights-her-pipe," since she had for many years possessed a small lens, easily concealed between her thumb and finger, by means of which she could light her pipe by the rays of the sun. Perhaps the mystery of this procedure added something to her prestige, but I doubt it, for such a personality as was hers would receive its due anywhere.

In time I learned to know this woman and held many interesting conversations with her. Having observed her trying to cut a bit of cloth with a knife I bought her a pair of scissors, large efficient ones, a gift which almost moved her to tears. She said that for many years she had not been so greatly honored. In this Mother-of-all was not exceptional, for every genuine old Indian I knew was quick to catch the spirit in which a gift was made, it might be the meanest trifle, but if given as a token of good will, would be appreciated without end. So in this case Mother-of-all expressed her feelings in a monologue, the import of which was that many winters had she seen, many honors had she received and that now even a white person had shown her great regard. When she had finished I conveyed to her as best I could that to me she was by far the most deserving of Indian grandmothers.

Mother-of-all, like her husband, was apt to surprise one with bursts of folk-wisdom and though always dignified and high-minded had a sense of humor. She encouraged me to describe the lives of white women, especially in the great towns. One day I told her of women who had nothing to do but lead a dog around by a string. This seemed to her such an absurdity that she indulged in peals of laughter, supported by a chorus of other women present. According to what she knew of dog behavior and human nature nothing she had ever heard was so silly. Every now and then as the memory of our narrative flashed up before her she would ripple with merriment. "Foolish, foolish," she would say, "dogs know best when and where they should walk." Upon one such occasion she asked if I knew why dogs did not talk like people though they seemed to understand speech, and when I professed ignorance on the subject, told me that as a little girl she heard the old people tell a story to account for this peculiarity. I wish a translation could carry the fine style of narration employed by this old lady but since it cannot we must be content with a mere abstract.

Why Dogs Do Not Talk

It seems that once in that long ago when the earth was a much more interesting place than in these days fraught with disappointments, dogs talked like people and lived in the camps with them as they do now. However, they had chiefs of their own. Since they lived with people they used the speech of the Indians they camped with, having no language of their own because none had been given them by the "powers above." Many times the dogs gave good advice to the people for there were medicine dogs among them.

A certain Indian medicine man, Blue Bird, received power from a female dog and they came to be very fond of each other. Many times this dog expressed a desire to be changed into a human being and at last this longing became so intense that she sat upon a hill fasting and howling. Blue Bird pitied her, so he began to pray to the "powers above." At last he had a vision in which he was given instruction what to do, but everything must be kept secret. He and the dog were to go upon a long journey alone. Each night they dreamed as they slept by the camp fire as to where they should go

the next day. Finally they were told to separate, the
man to return home and forget about the dog.

A year or two passed by, then some medicine men
from a distant tribe came to camp. They inquired for
Blue Bird and arriving at his tipi said that in a dream
they had been directed to call upon him, that he was a
great medicine man who would give them new powers.
Blue Bird was pleased at the honor bestowed upon him
and invited his guests to pitch camp with him. There
was much feasting and singing. Finally the leader of
the visiting delegation announced that he had brought
a present for Blue Bird—a new wife. This, he explained, was a mystery woman of great power. No one
knew her history for she staggered into their camp one
day, naked and crying for food. She had forgotten how
to talk. His people had taken pity on this poor woman,
fed her and clothed her. One morning when she awoke
she could speak, explaining that though she knew nothing of her past, in a dream she had been given the
power of speech. So she lived in their camp for a long
time.

Many men offered to take her as a wife but she
refused all offers, saying that the "powers above" had
told her to wait for instructions from them. At last she
announced that she had a dream in which she was told
to marry a man by the name of Blue Bird, that he was
a great medicine man and lived far to the east. Also
several medicine men in the tribe dreamed that they
were to seek out this Blue Bird and present him with
the woman.

Blue Bird was pleased with his new wife. Everybody
paid her great respect. She had one noticeable peculiarity, she hated dogs. She refused to listen to their
speech and when any of them came around threw
stones and sticks at them. Finally the chief of the dogs
called a council to discuss these insults. One very old
dog said that he believed this new woman was the dog

that ran away because she wanted to be changed into a human. He was laughed at, but the chief suggested that the old dog have a talk with Blue Bird. So he waited until Blue Bird was alone to tell him of his suspicions. Blue Bird loved this new woman dearly, the insinuation made him so angry that he sent an arrow through the heart of the old dog.

This so outraged the dogs that they decided not to use human speech again and so they had never talked since.

The narrator sat upon a blanket beside the tipi fire which cast occasional lights and shadows over her face. It was a picture I often recall. Her soft deep voice added grace to the narrative. She had probably never sat in a chair, would have found a white man's bed too uncomfortable for sleep, would have looked upon a fork as an impediment, yet she had grace and fine manners after the way of her people, and as a narrator few white women I have known were in her class.

Old Wolf Chief also had a sense of humor and after a discreet silence remarked, as Mother-of-all was stirring up the fire, that he supposed the reason why dogs went about smelling of people was that they were still trying to find the descendants of the dog who became a woman. As his wife took no notice of this wise-crack I inferred that he was in the habit of saying something like that when he heard the story.

Wolf Chief was obviously proud of his wife, but like many a man married to a genius, was not always comfortable when she held the center of the stage, and now it was clearly apparent from shifts of posture and gesture that he was about to try his hand at a narrative. He began by remarking that the tale I had just heard belonged to the class of narratives told by grandmothers to amuse children, but that since I seemed to enjoy it he would tell me a grandfather's tale.

Turtle Goes to War

Once there was a great camp in which many animals and insects lived. Among others a turtle lived with his sister. One day he said to her, "Now, I shall go on the war-path. I shall pick out my party."

So he went out and invited a coal of fire, a grasshopper, some tallow, a yellow butterfly, and a tipi pin. The turtle called this strange party together and led them out to war. They soon came to the top of a hill as a whirlwind came by. The butterfly said, "Now I shall show you what I can do." So he spread out his wings to make a great flight. The whirlwind, however, began to carry him away and as he was whirled about he cried, "Stop, my brother! Stop, hey!" The whirlwind paid no attention and the butterfly was soon out of sight. Turtle and his party waited a long time, but as the butterfly did not return they went on their way. They soon came to a lot of rose-bushes that were thick and thorny. While Turtle was leading the way through the thicket, he heard some one call for help from the rear. They turned back and found the tipi stick stuck fast in the bushes. They all took hold of it to pull it out. They pulled and pulled until the stick broke. "Now," they said, "the stick will die." So they all stood around it until it was dead. Then they went on their way.

Tallow was overheated and fell down dead before they had gone far. The others came to a large stream with a muddy edge. They held a council and decided that they must jump across. The fire and Turtle got across safely, but the grasshopper, who was too confident of his ability, just reached the edge of the stream and, falling into the mud, stuck fast. In trying to pull himself out he lost one of his legs. His cries brought

Turtle and the fire back, but when they tried to pull him out he lost his other leg. "Now," said Turtle, "you cannot go with us. We must leave you."

Then Turtle and the fire went along and came to a large river. As the river was too wide to jump, Turtle decided to swim across and carry the fire on his back. When they were in the middle of the river the fire began to die, and called out to Turtle to hurry. Turtle swam as fast as he could, but when he reached the other shore the fire was dead. Now Turtle was the only one left of the war party.

As Turtle went along he saw a camp of Indians. He concealed himself at the edge of the creek, where the people came for water. In a short time, a little girl came down. Turtle rose from the water, caught her, and pulled her under. When she was drowned, he cut off her head and stuck it into his shell. Then he walked boldly toward the camp. As he was going along, he heard a man coming behind. The man called in a loud voice, "Here is a turtle!" Many men came out and took Turtle to the camp.

Then Turtle spoke to the men in his own language, saying, "I have come to look for an enemy." As the men did not understand this, they said, "Let us call the spider. He is clever and perhaps he can understand what the turtle says." When the spider came, Turtle said to him, "I have come to look for an enemy."

"Oh! he came to look for an enemy," said the spider to the men.

As soon as the men heard this, they began to make a large fire in the centre of the camp, and said that they were going to throw the turtle into it. When Turtle saw what they were going to do, he said to the spider, "Why, the fire is mine." Then he walked through the fire, which did not burn him much, and came back to the people. The people said, "Why, of course, the fire belongs to him." So they would not let him go into the fire again, because they thought he enjoyed going into it.

Then they consulted the spider as to how to kill the turtle, and the spider advised them to throw him into a deep hole filled with water.

When Turtle saw what they intended to do, he pretended to be very much afraid and began to lament his fate. He told the spider that he would surely die if thrown into the water. So, while Turtle was crying, he was picked up and thrown into the deep place. He sank down into the water, and when the bubbles arose to the surface the people said, "Now, he is dead."

In a few moments Turtle arose in the center of the water, gave a war-whoop, and waved in the air the head of the child he had killed. Then he dived. All the people cried out in rage, "Now, how shall we kill the turtle?" said they. The spider advised them to bring all of their horses, their pails, and their women and, dipping all the water out of the hole, give it to the horses to drink. They worked very fast but the water was not all out when the sun went down. The spider said, "Now, we must rest until morning. But for fear the turtle may escape we shall all sleep around the edge of the water."

While they were all lying there, some asleep and some watching, Turtle succeeded in passing them unnoticed.

Finally, he reached his own camp and related his adventures to the people. He told them that he had killed one of the enemy, and produced the scalp as evidence. His sister held a victory dance over it.

Versions of this myth were heard up and down the Indian country and when well told it is a classic. The Indians see a goodly measure of humor in it, but since most humor depends upon subtle twists to words, the best part of it is lost in translation. In commenting later Wolf Chief said the tale was both humorous and sad; sad because so many of the party never returned, humorous because parts of the narrative were so unexpected.

One day there was an imposing ceremony in camp, two girls having reached that important turning point in life which a poet speaks of as "standing with reluctant feet." It was the custom of the tribe to formalize the coming out of such ladies-to-be by a solemn ceremony in which a medicine man officiated, while there was a great deal of feasting and a good time generally on the side. In this case the girls belonged to prominent families and so quite a show was made of the occasion. Everybody seemed happy and at ease except the two unfortunate girls who waited about with downcast eyes and trembling hands. For weeks they had been trained and coached but now they faced the reality and were duly fearful of making a mistake. I felt sorry for those serious little countenances soon to face the toil, pain and perhaps the sorrows of life, but so it always was and will be.

When the food was passed I looked around for Mother-of-all whose presence had been conspicuous during the proceedings of the morning. Finally I saw her standing to one side upon a little eminence, leaning upon a long staff. She wore an elk-skin dress, decorated with elk teeth, the prized jewelry of her culture, a costume peculiarly becoming to her. Apparently she was wrapped in meditation and about to begin a harangue. There was nothing unusual in this, for it was expected that some one, preferably an old woman, address the assembly at this time. Usually no one paid much attention to such discourses though there was no loud talking. It was about the same as when at a public gathering composed of an equal number of white people, a clergyman is asked to say grace; it is regarded as appropriate that a reasonable silence be preserved, but no one remembers what was said. However, on this occasion I had an intuition that Mother-of-all expected us not only to listen but to reflect upon her discourse; in other words, she was about to make an unusual effort, possibly spreading a masterpiece upon the indifferent air. Too bad that I could not have recorded it verbatim.

She began, speaking slowly and in well-formed sentences, saying that it made her old eyes glad to see many people here, so many happy faces, so many fine horses and wagons, people so well dressed, such an abundance of food for the feast, also the many quilts, moccasins, robes, etc., piled up ready for distribution at the "give-away" to accompany this ceremony. Then she drifted on to remark upon the presence of many children and to dwell upon the significance of this fact in the well being of the people. The greatest calamity to her way of thinking would be to see a powerful proud people with a glorious past grow less and less in numbers.

Next she addressed the young people about to be married. She disapproved of gambling, drinking, sex laxity, and laziness as the cardinal sins of the time but was especially bitter in denouncing the lack of appreciation in and reverence for the ways of their ancestors.

She admitted that times had changed, that her people no longer lived as in the past, that more and more they must adapt themselves to the white man's world, but that there was such a thing as virtue, sterling worth, that must be cultivated by the youth of today, otherwise the whole people must sink into oblivion. "Show me," said she, "where to look for youth of quality to lead the people of the future. Long have I looked about, but still see them not."

In the end, however, she expressed her faith that in spite of the wickedness on every hand, leaders would yet arise. She prayed that this might be so. (She was thoroughly pagan, regarding the sun as the chief power and that an appeal to him was the main hope.) So she prayed to the sun for the two girls to be initiated, for all the people assembled, making special mention of the white guests attending this ceremonial.

It was a creditable performance but Mother-of-all was no doubt repeating what she had said upon many similar occasions. We heard the same ideas presented by other old women at gatherings on other reservations, so there was nothing unusual in them, but other speakers used a sing-song shrill style of delivery, whereas Mother-of-all was the only Indian woman I ever heard speak on the level of oratory.

As always, there came the time for parting. The day before breaking camp, I made a farewell call. Both Wolf Chief and his wife were obviously sorry; my visits seemed to have been one of the happy intervals in their declining years. They prayed that I come again next year to cheer their fire-side as I was fully resolved to do. The next morning I arose with the dawn, but while dismantling my tent was surprised to see Mother-of-all walking swiftly through the wet grass bare-footed. She had come a long way, bearing in her hand two freshly killed prairie chickens as a parting gift. Once more she took my hand in her own and blessed me in a pagan prayer. This was the last I saw of her, for upon my return another year both she and Wolf Chief had passed away. I venerate them yet, that grand old Indian couple.

20

The End

DURING THE brief intervals between visits to these several reservations death took heavy toll among my aged friends. It was almost like coming back to attend a funeral. For a few years after these visits ceased, there were occasional letters, then ominous silence. Soon I ceased to dream of a return, realizing that a strange generation of Indians had displaced the old and that new types of officials presided at the agencies. None of the old Indians could write but knew how to get letters written. One Major complained that during the preceding year his office had written 300 letters for Indians to friends on distant reservations, even to points in Canada. The procedure was complicated; the Indian dictated to an interpreter, who dictated in English to a clerk. At the other end someone read the English to an interpreter who dictated to the Indian recipient in his tribal language. Doubtless a good deal was lost in the process.

The letters I received were not written in the Major's office but by young Indians who had some schooling. They were often quaint but informing.

Once Bull Shield gave me a medicine robe to hang

up in the museum, but cautioned that it should neither be allowed to touch the ground nor be thrown around carelessly. The penalty for this would be a storm. It so happened that on the night after the robe was placed in a museum case, a terrific storm of wind, rain and lightning tore through the city. I wrote Bull Shield about it. A few months later came a reply, brief, but Indian-like, "Bull Shield he get letter. Him say tell you maybe now you have believe medicine things powerful."

A few weeks before Bull Shield died he dictated another letter to me. He was skilled in the use of his tribal language so no doubt worked a fine message, but the young Indian who tried to put it into English produced the following:

"Bull Shield want say he have hard time. He sick. Not go to agency long time now. When you here he do like you say so. Now you may be do like he say. He need new wagon tongue. Send $10."

That cantankerous old Spotted Horse, one of the medicine men I never got on with, had a scolding letter sent to me. In it he named all the old Indians dying since my last visit, claiming this was because they were friendly with me, told me medicine secrets and posed before my camera. He was charging me with manslaughter and evidently boasted that his medicine was too strong for me. I suspected that more than once he tried to kill me by black magic.

I replied that he won, that he was the more powerful medicine man, but that I almost had him once.

A woman who was skilled in work with beads, quills and the tanning of skins, sent me an informing letter:

"This is to let you know that if you want any bead-work and quill-work I have time to do it. I can make many nice things for you. I do not live with Joe any more. You know what kind of man he was. My new man fine fellow, have good job, work hard. I have no children, so last year I take a boy to raise. He fine boy. Write soon."

From another reservation a young Indian writes:

"I thought I would drop the few lines here to you to let you know that Tom you friend has now passed away. Which he did and could not be learn what he had done such a thing as he did. He committed suicide. Shoot him self in head. He never said he was going to do it or write any note. I think a little trouble over his wife. I let you know why if any thing more learn of him. His people are all taking it pretty hard."

It will be noticed how completely this youth had mastered certain appropriate local English phrases but yet blundered woefully when fitting separate words together. Still there is no doubt as to what he intended to say.

There was a rising market for Indian relics when my visits began. A few private collectors were active and two or three museums were beginning to do systematic collecting, which gave a few local people the idea that these objects would command fabulous prices as soon as there were no more to be had from the Indians. The Indians were puzzled over this demand for things now useless to them. So I told them about museums, what kind of places they were and why. The Indians had no difficulty with the idea that a museum exhibit would glorify their past and show future generations of white people what Indian life was like before reservation days, but what sold the museum to them was that no admission fee was charged. It was all so contrary to their experience with white men that most of them regarded it as another white man's lie. However, here and there was an Indian who had been to Washington, where he saw the Indian exhibits in the National Museum free of charge. Yet these witnesses to the truth of my statements left them still puzzled, because white people paid them well for these relics without expecting to make money by the transaction. This seemed to contradict all they had been taught about the white man's way of life.

Now once again I turn to the correspondence file:

"I read the N. Y. newspaper weekly. I find that American Museum of Natural History is in N. Y. City.

"Do you like to collect the Indian relic in Museum for showing? If yes, I have 1 Indian relic—large cedar shingle. Indian man made many large shingle from selection best large cedar trees to build a log cabin. More than 50 to 100 yrs., still stand today at wilderness.

"How much if Museum would buy?

"Let me know very soon."

My reply was that there were museums nearer his address than New York, to which he could offer his shingles. Then he wrote:

"You answered me 1 min. quick without delaying. I am disappointment the words. I don't know First Name on other Museums. Perhaps I will find out.

"I may say some words. About 1 million young students from schools and colleges in N. Y. C. would interest to learn some new ways on Indian's hands to make large cedar shingle in early old days.

"If fire will destroy relic, students will lose to learn. Eskimos and Indians were unschool in north and west. They gained education than Eskimo. They used solid snow to build half-earth for home. I never visit N. Y. C. all my life because R. R. rate too high."

This letter revealed a smattering of school book knowledge, even if the style was surprising, so I wrote for information as to how these shingles were made. This brought a more labored reply:

"I was surprised to get your letter again. I just research in some particular.

"Indian had not money to get knife. They were in

graves, not talking me, but I thought they canoed many miles to Fur post at Mackinac Island—American Fur Company—British—French. It is 300 years old. The island was best place for ten thousand small boats and canoes in triple lakes, Mich., Huron and Superior.

"Europe had many wars since Jesus was born. They took weapons to America for a fur trade and stopped Fort Mackinac. Indian traded furs for knives, swords, guns and others.

"They used a skin knife to split and smooth by, hammering with stone for shingles. Not like a factory cedar shingle, the Indian shingle was large about 24 inches long and 12 in. wide. Almost every houses in 5000 are Mill Cedar shingles but 1 Indian's log cabin. I may show you to draw picture.

"If you get one, N. Y. students will gossip now other museum buildings. They will ask you for Indian shingle. I advise you to get about 6 to 12 shingles and can sell 1 or 2 to museum building and Europe museums from your own mind and you keep 1 or 2 yourself for showing. I can't reach Indian's place because snow is deep 4 or 5 ft. Wait next April I will get 6 or 12 Indian's shingles for you if you wish. I have no time to write other museum but you.

"I hope I will hear from you again or not."

This young Indian had acquired an unusual vocabulary and his historical knowledge was surprising. We can be certain that he spoke his own language well and that he was a regular reader of such English as came to hand. We suspect he did a good deal of clear thinking, partly hidden from us by his fumbling with a rich English vocabulary, in the use of which he was yet awkward. But the importance of such letters is the hint they give of rapid changes in the generation long since come of age. They were then making their first efforts to become literate, stumbling, blundering, sweating, but already well on their way to the white man's goal.

Once, only, did I venture to revisit one of these old reservations, and then after an interval of thirty-one years, but there was no joy in it. Not a building of the old regime was standing, even the little agency cemetery had been obliterated to make way for an expanding town. Where the old trading post stood was a modernized department store. None of the old style wagons with their ponies and dogs came rattling along, but in their stead automobiles of every description, from which stepped smartly dressed Indians.

Diligent inquiry revealed that but one of my old friends survived. He was blind and deaf, but after a time he seemed to understand who stood in his presence. Passing his hands over the writer's head he remarked that there was still enough hair to make a first-class scalp. He was at least ninety and without a grey hair. I should have enjoyed recounting the days when he was a welcome visitor at my camp, hearing his impressions of the changing world and the new generation, but sightless eyes and dulled ears isolated him from me and the present. He had experienced much, between hunting the wild bison with bows and arrows and following the war road for scalps, to riding in automobiles, thus spanning the grand pageant of frontier history. To me he was the last lone rider lingering in the rear of the vanished cavalcade.

In closing, let us listen to the speech of an aged Indian translated by one of my white friends who happened to be present when it was delivered:

"My sun is set. My day is done. Darkness is stealing over me. Before I lie down to rise no more I will speak to my people. Hear me, for this is not the time for me to tell a lie. The Great Spirit made us, and gave us this land we live in. He gave us the buffalo, antelope and deer for food and clothing. Our hunting grounds stretched from the Mississippi to the great mountains. We were free as the winds and heard no man's commands. We fought our enemies, and feasted our friends. Our braves drove away all who would take our game. They captured women and horses from our foes. Our children were many and our herds were large. Our old men talked with spirits and made good medicine. Our young men hunted and made love to the girls. Where the tipi was, there we stayed, and no house imprisoned us. No one said, 'To this line is my land, to that is yours.' In this way our fathers lived, and were happy. Then the white man came to our hunting grounds, a stranger. We gave him meat and presents, and told him go in peace. He looked on our women and stayed to live in our tipis. His fellows came to build their roads across our hunting grounds. He brought among us the mysterious iron that shoots. He brought with him the magic water that makes men foolish. With his trinkets and beads he even bought the girl I loved. I said, 'The white man is not a friend, let us kill him.' But their numbers were greater than blades of grass. They took away the buffalo and shot down our best warriors. They took away our lands and surrounded us by fences. Their soldiers camped outside with cannon to shoot us down. They wiped the trails of our people from the face of the prairies. They forced our children to forsake the ways of their fathers. When I turn to the east I see no dawn. When I turn to the west the approaching night hides all."